Ron Zimmer

Richard Buddin

Derrick Chau

Brian Gill

Cassandra Guarino

Laura Hamilton

Cathy Krop

Dan McCaffrey

Melinda Sandler

Dominic Brewer

Charter School Operations and Performance

Evidence from California

Prepared for the

California Legislative Analyst's Office

RAND
EDUCATION

The research described in this report was conducted by RAND Education for the California Legislature Analyst's Office.

Library of Congress Cataloging-in-Publication Data

Charter school operations and performance : evidence from California / Ron Zimmer ... [et al.].
p. cm.
"MR-1700."
Includes bibliographical references (p.).
ISBN 0-8330-3354-9 (pbk.)—ISBN 0-8330-3414-6 (eBook)
1. Charter schools—California—Evaluation. I. Zimmer, Ron W.

LB2806.36.C517 2003
371.01—dc21

2003013086

Cover design by Stephen Bloodsworth

Published 2003 by RAND
1700 Main Street, P.O. Box 2138, Santa Monica, CA 90407-2138
1200 South Hayes Street, Arlington, VA 22202-5050
201 North Craig Street, Suite 202, Pittsburgh, PA 15213-1516
RAND URL: http://www.rand.org/
To order RAND documents or to obtain additional information, contact Distribution Services: Telephone: (310) 451-7002;
Fax: (310) 451-6915; Email: order@rand.org

PREFACE

In 1992, California became the second state to enact legislation that created charter schools. Charter schools are publicly funded schools that have the flexibility to operate outside normal district control. These schools are designed to provide greater educational choice to families, reduce bureaucratic constraints on educators, and provide competitive pressure to induce improvement in conventional public schools while remaining publicly accountable. In total, 38 states plus the District of Columbia and Puerto Rico have charter school laws with over 575,000 students attending nearly 2,700 charter schools.[1] With the popularization of charter schools have come questions of their effectiveness.

In California, an objective evaluation of charter schools was mandated through Chapter 767, Statutes of 1996 (AB 2135, Mazzoni), which required California's "Legislative Analyst's Office (LAO) to contract out for an interim evaluation of effectiveness." In response to this legislative mandate, SRI International, Inc., released its *Evaluation of Charter School Effectiveness* in December 1997. Later, Chapter 34, Statutes of 1998 (AB 544, Lempert), made significant changes to the charter school legislation and required that the LAO contract out for a second evaluation. Finally, Chapter 673, Statutes of 1998 (AB 2471, Mazzoni) modified the directive so that the LAO and objective evaluators will each make a report with recommendations to the legislature and the governor by July 1, 2003.

---

[1]Three states have charter school laws but no charter schools as of 2002–03 (Center for Education Reform, 2003).

In the behest of the LAO, RAND has completed a comprehensive study of California's charter schools. The study uses primary data, including surveys and case studies, as well as secondary data on students and schools to evaluate operational and performance differences between charter and conventional public schools. The findings have important implications not only for California charter and conventional public schools but for charter and conventional public schools nationally and should be of interest to policymakers, educators, and researchers interested in education.

This study fits into a larger body of research conducted by RAND Education on school reform, assessment and accountability, and teachers and teaching.

CONTENTS

Preface iii

Figures xi

Tables xv

Summary xix

Acknowledgments xxix

Acronyms xxxi

Chapter One
INTRODUCTION, *Ron Zimmer, Derrick Chau, and Brian Gill* 1
Background: Charter Schools Nationally and in California 1
What We Know from Prior Research 5
Focus of This Research 6
Data Sources 8
Primary Data 8
Secondary Data 10
How We Categorized Charter Schools 11
Conversion and Start-Up Charter Schools 12
Classroom-Based and Nonclassroom-Based Charter Schools 13
School Size 14
Independent and Dependent Charter Schools 15

Limitations of the Study 16
Data Limitations 16
Budgetary and Time Constraints 17
How the Report Is Organized 17

Chapter Two
STUDENTS SERVED BY CHARTER SCHOOLS,
Derrick Chau, Dan McCaffrey, Ron Zimmer, Glenn Daley, and Brian Gill 19
Introduction 19
Access to Charter Schools 21
Student Admissions Processes 22
Focus of School Services 24
Characteristics of Students in Charter Schools 25
School-by-School Analysis 30
Summary 36

Chapter Three
ACADEMIC OUTCOMES, *Richard Buddin and Ron Zimmer* 37
Introduction 37
School-Level Performance 39
Statewide Nonlongitudinally Linked Student-Level Data 44
Longitudinally Linked Student-Level Data 53
Competitive Effect of Charter Schools 57
Summary 60
School-Level Analysis of API Scores 60
Statewide Nonlongitudinal Student Data 60
Longitudinally Linked Student Data 61
Competitive Effects of Charter Schools 62

Chapter Four
AUTHORIZATION, GOVERNANCE, AND OVERSIGHT OF CHARTER SCHOOLS, *Derrick Chau, Glenn Daley, and Brian Gill* 63
Introduction 63
Authorization of Charter Schools 64
Description of Chartering Authorities 64
Development and Evaluation of Charter Petitions 66
The Outcomes of Charter Petitions 68

Closed or Revoked Charter Schools 70
Denied Charter Petitions 70
Governance of Charter Schools 71
Dependent and Independent Charter Schools 72
Legal Liability in Charter Schools 73
Charter School Autonomy 74
Oversight of Charter Schools 77
Characteristics of Chartering Authority Oversight of Charter Schools 78
Chartering Authority Actions Toward Charter Schools . . 79
Services Provided by Chartering Authorities 82
Summary 82
Authorization 82
Governance 83
Oversight 84
Services 84

Chapter Five
CHARTER SCHOOL FINANCES AND FACILITIES, *Cathy Krop* 85
Introduction 85
Charter School Funding 85
Meeting Legislative Requirements 88
Participation in Categorical Aid Programs 91
Private Donations to Charter Schools 100
Charter School Expenditures 103
Facilities 106
Other Fiscal Challenges 112
Summary 113

Chapter Six
ACADEMIC ENVIRONMENTS OF CHARTER AND CONVENTIONAL PUBLIC SCHOOLS, *Laura Hamilton* . . . 115
Introduction 115
Professional Development 117
Chartering Authorities' Involvement in Professional Development 117
Teacher Participation in Professional Development . . . 118

Curriculum and Instruction 122
Programs and Scheduling Modifications 122
Courses and Academic Program Requirements 125
Computers 128
Student Testing 129
Parent Involvement 133
Student Discipline 137
Summary 140

Chapter Seven
STAFFING IN CHARTER AND CONVENTIONAL PUBLIC SCHOOLS, *Cassandra Guarino* 143
Introduction 143
The Characteristics of Teachers 144
Teaching Credentials 144
Teaching Experience 147
The Characteristics of Principals 148
Credentials and Qualifications of Principals 149
Administrative and Teaching Experience 150
Working Conditions and Compensation of Teachers 152
Working Conditions and Compensation of Principals 153
The Composition of the Instructional Staff 154
Principals' Use and Perceptions of Control 154
Summary 159

Chapter Eight
SPECIAL EDUCATION IN CHARTER AND CONVENTIONAL PUBLIC SCHOOLS, *Cassandra Guarino and Derrick Chau* 161
Introduction 161
Identification of Special Education Students 162
Special Education Service Delivery 164
The Use of Special Education Aides 167
Inclusion of Special Education Students in Assessments . . 168
Funding and Provision of Special Education Resources . . . 169
Summary 172

Chapter Nine
CONCLUSIONS AND IMPLICATIONS, *Ron Zimmer and Cassandra Guarino* 175
Introduction 175
Findings 175

Student Achievement 175
Accessibility 176
Authorization, Governance, and Oversight 177
Operation 178
Challenges 180
Recommendations 181

Appendix
A. Research Methods 185
B. Charter and Conventional Public School Comparison Methods 199
C. Academic Outcomes 201
D. Surveys Administered for the Study 219

Bibliography 273

FIGURES

1.1. Number of Conversion and Start-Up Schools, 1993–2002 12
1.2. Percentage of Charter School Students in Conversion and Start-Up Schools, by Grade Level 13
1.3. Percentage of Charter School Students in Nonclassroom-Based and Classroom-Based Schools, by Grade Level 15
1.4. Differences in School Size, by School Type 16
2.1. Use of Personal Interviews in School Admissions Processes 23
2.2. Use of Admissions Tests in School Admissions Processes 24
2.3. Racial Composition of Students in Start-Up Schools, Conversion Schools, and All Conventional Public Schools 27
2.4. Racial Composition of Students in Start-Up Schools, Conversion Schools, and All Conventional Public Schools Within the Charter Districts 29
2.5. Percentage of Charter Schools That Deviate from the District Mean, by Racial Group and Direction 32
2.6. Percentage of Conversion Schools That Deviate from the District Mean, by Racial Group and Direction 33
2.7. Percentage of Start-Up Schools That Deviate from the District Mean, by Racial Group and Direction 34
2.8. Percentage of Schools That Deviate from the District Mean, by Racial Group and Direction 35
3.1. Unadjusted Average Stanford 9 Test Scores for Conventional Public Schools and Charter Schools . . . 46

3.2. Adjusted Average Stanford 9 Test Scores for Conventional Public Schools and Charter Schools . . . 47
3.3. Distribution of Students, by Type of Charter School and Grade Level 48
3.4. Adjusted Average Stanford 9 Test Scores for Conventional Public Schools, Conversion Schools, and Start-Up Schools, and Whether the Charter Schools Offer Nonclassroom-Based Instruction 50
3.5. Adjusted Average Stanford 9 Test Scores for Pooled District Data 55
4.1. Percentage of Charters Granted by Different Chartering Authorities 65
4.2. Distribution of the Chartering Authorities, by Number of Petitions Received 69
5.1. The Charter School Block Grant Funding Model Satisfies the Legislative Requirement to Be Simple . . . 89
5.2. The Charter School Block Grant Funding Model Provides at Least as Much Operational Funding as Would Be Available to a Similar District Serving a Similar Pupil Population 90
5.3. Percentage of Charter Schools and Matched Conventional Public Schools Currently Receiving Funding from Various Categorical Aid Programs 94
5.4. Percentage of Conversion Schools, Start-Up Schools, and Matched Conventional Public Schools Currently Receiving Funding from Various Categorical Aid Programs 96
5.5. Percentage of Matched Conventional Public Schools, Conversion Schools , and Start-Up Schools "Eligible for Categorical Aid Funding But Not Applying" 97
5.6. Percentage of Conventional Public Schools, Conversion Schools, and Start-Up Schools That "Don't Know Whether Eligible or Not" for Categorical Aid Funding 98
5.7. Private Funding per Pupil in Conventional Public and Charter Schools, 2001–02 101
5.8. Private Donations per Pupil to Charter and Conventional Public Schools, 2001–02 103
5.9. Acquisition of School Facilities, by Type of Charter School 110

6.1. Percentage of Chartering Authorities Offering Professional Development to Charter School and Noncharter School Teachers 118
6.2. Responsibilities for Paying for Professional Development 119
6.3. Percentage of Respondents Reporting That More Than Half of Their Teachers Participated in Professional Development Activities 120
6.4. Methods for Providing Teachers Professional Development Time During Regular Contract Hours . . 121
6.5. Rates of Parent Participation in Charter and Matched Conventional Public School 135
6.6. Percentage of Students Suspended or Expelled over the Past Year 138
6.7. Percentage of Students Experiencing Behavioral or Health Problems 139
7.1. Teacher Experience 148

TABLES

1.1. Response Rate 9
2.1. Focus of Charter and Conventional Public School Services 25
3.1. Average Annual Growth in API for All California Schools, by Grade Level 42
3.2. Profile of School Districts 54
3.3. The Effect of Charter Schools on Matched Conventional Public Schools 59
3.4. The Effect of Charter Schools on Matched Conventional Public Schools or Their Respective Districts 60
4.1. Number of Operating Charter Schools Authorized by Chartering Authorities 66
4.2. Outcome and Number of Petitions Submitted to Chartering Authorities That Have Operating Charter Schools 69
4.3. Number of Times Chartering Authorities with Operating Charter Schools Cited Reasons for Denying Petitions 71
4.4. Placement of Legal Liability Between Charter Schools and Chartering Authorities for a Variety of Areas According to the Charter, Memorandum of Understanding, or Other Written Policies 74
4.5. Levels of Chartering Authority Control over Independent and Dependent Charter Schools Compared to Control over Conventional Public Schools for Different Types of School Operations 75

4.6. Levels of School Control on a Scale of 1 (No Control) to 4 (Full Control) . . . 77
4.7. Types of Information That Chartering Authorities Require from Independent or Undefined and Dependent Charter Schools . . . 80
4.8. Number of Chartering Authorities Taking Actions at Least Once for Different Situations . . . 81
4.9. Chartering Authority Provision of Administrative Services to Charter Schools . . . 83
5.1. Charter School Block Grant Estimated Funding Rates per Student in Average Daily Attendance, 2001–02 . . . 87
5.2. Categorical Block Grant Funding, 2000–01 and 2001–02 . . . 92
5.3. Charter School Expenditures per Pupil, 2001–02 . . . 105
6.1. Curriculum Programs in Charter Schools, by School Type . . . 123
6.2. Scheduling Modifications, by School Type . . . 124
6.3. Hours of Instruction Offered Each Week (4th Grade Only) . . . 125
6.4. Hours of Instruction Offered Each Week (7th Grade Only) . . . 126
6.5. Years of Instruction Required (12th Grade Only) . . . 128
6.6. Percentage of Schools Reporting Various Responses to STAR Data . . . 130
6.7. Percentage of Schools Reporting Various Responses to STAR Data, by Charter School Type . . . 131
6.8. Percentage of Charter and Matched Conventional Public Schools Offering Parent Involvement Opportunities . . . 134
7.1. Percentage of Teachers, by Qualification Type . . . 145
7.2. Percentage of Principals, by Qualification Type . . . 149
7.3. Principal Experience . . . 151
7.4. Level and Importance of Control . . . 155
7.5. Screening Considerations for Hiring Teachers . . . 158
8.1. Percentage of Special Education and Severely Disabled Students . . . 162
8.2. Service of Special Education Students . . . 165
A.1. Data Sources . . . 186
A.2. Matched School Racial Breakdown . . . 193

A.3. Response Rate 194
A.4. Student Characteristics in the Weighted Sample 196
A.5. Sample of Schools 197
A.6. Core Case Study Schools 198
A.7. Wild Card Case Study Schools 198
C.1. API Annual Growth Regressions for Elementary Conventional Public Schools and Charter Schools . . . 203
C.2. API Annual Growth Regressions for Elementary Conventional Public Schools, Conversion Schools, and Start-Up Schools, and Whether the Charter School Offers Nonclassroom-Based Instruction 204
C.3. API Annual Growth Regressions for Secondary Conventional Public Schools and Charter Schools . . . 205
C.4. API Annual Growth Regressions for Secondary Conventional Public Schools, Conversion Schools, and Start-Up Schools, and Whether the Charter School Offers Nonclassroom-Based Instruction 206
C.5. Stanford 9 Test Regressions for Elementary Conventional Public Schools and Charter Schools . . . 209
C.6. Stanford 9 Test Regressions for Secondary Conventional Public Schools and Charter Schools . . . 210
C.7. Stanford 9 Test Regressions for Elementary Conventional Public Schools, Conversion Schools, Start-Up Schools, and Nonclassroom-Based Schools 212
C.8. Stanford 9 Test Regressions for Secondary Conventional Public Schools, Conversion Schools, Start-Up Schools, and Nonclassroom-Based Schools 213
C.9. Charter School Status Regressions for Fixed-Effects Model on Pooled Student Data from Districts 215
C.10. Charter School Status Regressions for Random-Effects Model on Pooled Student Data from Districts 215
C.11. Charter School Status Regressions for Elementary Reading in Fixed-Effects Model, by District 216
C.12. Charter School Status Regressions for Elementary Math in Fixed-Effects Model, by District 216
C.13. Charter School Status Regressions for Elementary Reading in Random-Growth Model, by District 217

C.14. Charter Status Regressions for Elementary Math in Random-Growth Model, by District 217
C.15. Charter School Type Regressions for Fixed-Effects Model in Los Angeles Unified and San Diego City Unified Districts 218

SUMMARY

BACKGROUND AND PURPOSE

California adopted the charter school concept early and now has the largest population of charter school students in the nation. In spite of this popularity and growth, not much is known about the effectiveness of charter schools in terms of accessibility, achievement, governance, and operation. The California legislature asked RAND to analyze an array of issues that can be condensed into the following four research questions:

1. What population of students attend charter schools?
2. Is student achievement higher in charter schools than in conventional public schools?
3. What oversight and support do the chartering authorities provide?
4. How do charter schools differ from conventional public schools in terms of their operation including finances, academic environment, and staffing?

WHERE WE GOT OUR INFORMATION

We drew our data from primary and secondary sources. The primary data consisted of surveys of principals in all charter schools, a demographically matched subset of conventional public schools, and a survey of chartering authorities. We also carried out detailed case studies at nine charter schools and all but one of their chartering authorities. Secondary data came from a number of datasets including the Comprehensive Basic Education Data System (CBEDS), Professional Assignment Information Forms (PAIF), the Academic Performance Index (API), and state- and districtwide student-level data. The CBEDS data provided information on school-level staffing and student characteristics. PAIF data provided teacher qualifications, demographics, and assignments for most teachers in California. The API, state- and districtwide student-level data provided test scores and demographic data on charter and conventional public schools. We measured key features of schools and students, compared these features across different types of schools, and assessed educational progress over the past several years.

Using these data, we address the questions listed above. However, our study has some important limitations. Because of budget and time constraints, we were not able to survey parents or teachers. Therefore, we are unable to draw strong inferences about parental satisfaction or instructional or curriculum practices. Despite these limitations, this study provides a comprehensive research of California charter schools.

WHAT WE FOUND OUT

Charter schools are not homogeneous. They vary along a number of dimensions: Thus, there is no single charter school effect. These differences affect accessibility, achievement, operation, and governance as our outline below suggests.

Accessibility

To examine student representation in charter schools, we compared the characteristics of the student population served by the charter school sector to that served by conventional public schools within districts that have charter schools. In addition, we examined integration in charter schools by assessing the extent to which charter schools enroll student populations that reflect the enrollments of their local school districts.

Relative to conventional schools and controlling for the heterogeneity within school districts, charter school students are more likely to be black and less likely to be Hispanic or Asian but no more or less likely to be white. However, the racial mix of students varies by charter school type. We also compared the integration of charter schools to that in conventional schools. For blacks, conventional schools are somewhat more likely than charter schools to deviate from the district. For whites and Hispanics, conventional public schools are slightly less likely to deviate and for Asians conventional schools are very slightly more likely to deviate. However, the difference between groups tends to be small.

Achievement

One main objective of charter school legislation is to "improve student learning" (Education Code 47601). Although this objective seems straightforward, it can have two alternative interpretations: (1) Charter schools should improve the learning of their pupils over time and (2) charter schools should outperform conventional public schools. In our study, we evaluated the performance of charter school students relative to conventional public school students because this was deemed the question of greater interest to policymakers. We also evaluated the various types of charter schools relative to conventional schools because this too seems a question of interest to policymakers. Thus, our student achievement assessment addresses two questions:

1. How does the academic performance of students in charter schools compare with that of comparable students in conventional public schools?
2. How does academic performance vary across students attending different types of charter schools? Do students in start-up schools perform better or worse than those in conversion schools? Are students in charter schools with nonclassroom-based instruction performing at achievement levels above or below those in schools that offer instruction in a classroom setting?

To answer these questions, we used statewide school-level and state- and districtwide student-level data. Below, we highlight the results from the analysis of each dataset.

California's API is a composite accountability measure of academic performance for each school. We compared the year-to-year changes in API for charter and conventional public schools while accounting for changes in the characteristics of students attending each school. We found no statistically significant difference in test scores between charter and conventional public schools. However, the aggregation of a composite score at the school level masks variations in important characteristics within schools and distorts linkages between student characteristics and student outcomes.

To estimate the charter school effect more precisely (i.e., to provide more precise controls for the variation of student characteristics within a school), we used student-level data provided by the state of California for all students attending both conventional and charter schools for 1997–98 through 2001–02. The data include a student's math and reading test scores, ethnicity, English Learner status, eligibility for free or reduced-price lunches, and parental education. The data link a student's test score with demographic information and allow a more precise assessment of how these factors affect school-level outcomes. The individual-level data, however, do not provide a student-level identifier to track year-to-year changes in a student's test scores, which reduces the ability to control for unobservable differences among individual students.

Using these data, our analysis suggests that charter schools generally have comparable or slightly lower test scores than do conventional public schools. Achievement, however, varies by type of charter school. Conversion schools that deliver their instruction in classrooms had mixed results, with some scoring the same, higher, or lower than conventional public schools. Start-up schools using classroom instruction had slightly higher test scores in everything but elementary math, where the scores are slightly lower. Conversion or start-up schools that deliver at least a portion of their instruction outside the classroom, also referred to as nonclassroom-based schools, had lower test scores across the board. However, it should be noted that students in nonclassroom-based schools may differ in unique ways from students in conventional public schools that are not captured by our control variables. For instance, if students in nonclassroom-based schools have been pulled out of conventional public schools because of problems they have in traditional settings, then conventional public school students who do not have these problems do not make a good comparison group.

Although the above analysis has the advantage of providing more precise controls for student characteristics, it does not allow for an examination of individual gains, nor does it provide the ability to track students as they move from conventional public schools to charter schools and vice versa. Our third approach examined achievement effects by analyzing longitudinally linked student-level data collected at the district level. By tracking students over time, the analysis adjusts for unmeasured student factors that may affect student performance. This analysis assessed the performance of charter students relative to that of conventional public school students. Because we had limited time and budget and because charter schools are spread over hundreds of school districts across the state, we collected data from six districts (Chula Vista Elementary, Fresno Unified, Los Angeles Unified, Napa Valley Unified, San Diego City Unified, and West Covina Unified)[2] with a prominent share of charter students. The data were pooled across these districts to perform our analysis.

As with the first and second approaches, the third controls for student characteristics. However, unlike the first two approaches, the third approach has a mechanism to control for unmeasured student factors that affect student performance. Thus, it provides the best estimate of a collective charter school effect. Our analysis does not allow an examination of the different types of charter schools in each district because not every district has each type of charter school.

Charter school students tended to do slightly worse than comparable students in math in both elementary and secondary conventional public schools. In reading, secondary charter school students scored slightly higher than comparable students in conventional public schools, and charter status had no statistically significant effect on elementary reading scores. Even the statistically significant difference in achievement by charter status was less than 1 percentile point, however, so the main finding of the analysis is that charters are keeping pace with conventional public schools.

---

[2]We approached districts with the largest share of charter school students.

Summarizing across the three methods, we generally found comparable scores for charter schools relative to conventional schools. Only when charter schools were broken down by charter type did significant differences appear. Most strikingly, we found that non-classroom-based charter schools performed significantly lower than conventional public schools, and classroom-based conversion schools and start-up schools performed slightly higher than conventional public schools in elementary reading, and start-up schools performed better than conventional public schools in secondary reading and math. Again, we highlight that our analysis may not capture the uniqueness of these students and may bias our results.

AUTHORIZATION, GOVERNANCE, AND OVERSIGHT

Over the last few years, the governance of charter schools has received increasing public attention. Policymakers are concerned that charter schools are not receiving enough support or scrutiny both before and after they become charter schools. To analyze the relationship with chartering authorities, we used responses from surveys of chartering authorities, charter schools, and a matched sample of conventional public schools, coupled with information gleaned from case studies of charter schools.

Our analysis of chartering authority surveys shows that of the three types of chartering authorities (school districts, county boards of education, and state board of education) most charter schools are authorized by school districts, and most districts have authorized only one school. However, to be chartered, schools must first submit petitions to chartering authorities. Of the petitions submitted, few are formally denied, and once authorized, only a handful of charters have been revoked or schools closed.

From the surveys of charter and matched conventional public schools, our analysis shows that charter schools report greater control than conventional public schools over decisionmaking ; however, within charter schools, differences exist. Those classified as "dependent" reported being governed much more like conventional public schools than did those classified as "independent."

Operation

The charter law is intended to give charter schools greater freedom over school operations. To assess operational freedom, we examined four categories: finances and facilities, academic environment, staffing, and special education services. For each category, we highlight major findings from our survey of chartering authorities, charter schools, and a matched sample of conventional public schools.

Charter schools, particularly start-up schools, reported using fewer resources per student than do conventional schools. In part, this may occur because charter schools have significantly lower participation in categorical aid programs, which bring additional resources into the schools. However, if charter schools are achieving the same results with fewer resources, they may prove to be cost-effective.

Differences between charter and conventional schools also appeared when we examined academic environment. For example, principals of charter schools reported having more instructional hours in noncore subjects such as fine arts and foreign languages at the elementary level. Charter schools were less likely than matched conventional public schools to offer some types of programs (e.g., gifted and talented education or summer school).

Examining staffing, we found that charter school principals were less experienced and less likely than principals in conventional public schools to have teaching credentials. Charter school principals reported that teachers have higher rates of teacher participation in informal professional development such as mentoring and shadowing programs.

Finally, only in start-up schools did we find a smaller proportion of special education students. Start-up schools are more likely to serve special education students via mainstream instruction (i.e., to serve students in general education classrooms).

Together, these results do suggest some operational differences among types of charter and conventional public schools, and it is interesting to note that despite these operational differences, our analysis generally shows similar student outcomes. Most noteworthy, charter schools are achieving comparable test scores despite a lower reported level of revenue.

WHAT WE RECOMMEND

Charter schools face many challenges ranging from locating facilities to paying start-up costs to meeting the needs of special education students, all while receiving fewer resources than conventional schools. At the same time, they must preserve the independence that lies at the heart of the charter school concept while responding to legitimate demands for accountability. Any recommendations on how to improve charter schools must take these realities into account. With that in mind, we recommend the following:

1. The legislative intent should be clearly and concisely outlined within the Education Code to minimize misinterpretations of goals and conflicting objectives. Currently, many of the objectives are vague or create conflicts among the objectives, offering a great deal of interpretive latitude. Defining the objectives more explicitly would give chartering authorities and charter schools a greater understanding of their goals, enabling them to better develop accountability systems that are aligned with the intent of the law.
2. The state should develop a statewide student-level data system that can track the performance of individual students. Such a system would allow the performance of schools to be more precisely evaluated.
3. The state should require that fiscal information from charter schools be collected and monitored by chartering authorities to enhance fiscal oversight. However, this needs to be done in a way that does not generate a substantial amount of additional paperwork and expense for charter schools. If necessary, support should be provided for this activity.
4. The information collected from recommendations (1) and (2), along with information collected through other possible mechanisms, should be used by chartering authorities to identify poor performing charter schools for targeted interventions and support or possible closings.

5. Part of the reason charter schools may not have the same financial resources as conventional schools is that they do not fully participate in categorical aid programs. According to our surveys, some of these schools are "eligible, but not applying"; others "don't know whether they are eligible or not." Eligible schools that do not apply for categorical aid funds may choose not to do so because of certain requirements that accompany the programs, including requirements that conflict with the schools' educational philosophy. Schools that do not know whether they are eligible obviously lack the knowledge necessary to make an informed decision. To provide the best opportunity for the long-term success of charter schools, the state should find mechanisms for providing them with equivalent funding. This may mean putting more funds into block grants as opposed to individual categorical aid programs, providing training and more accessible information to charter school principals so that they know which programs they are eligible for, and possibly providing alternative avenues by which charter schools can join together or with school districts to apply for and maintain individual programs.

6. Given the differences in special education identification rates and service delivery modes between start-up schools and conversion or conventional public schools, it is important that chartering authorities ensure that special education is adequately funded in these schools and that up-to-date resources are available to them.

7. In light of our findings on student achievement, additional research on nonclassroom-based charter schools is needed, including more information regarding the composition of students, the nature of instruction, and the use of resources in these schools. In addition, it is important to collect information regarding the nature of oversight of these schools and to evaluate the implications to nonclassroom-based schools of the funding cuts required by recent legislation (SB 740). At the behest of the LAO, we will extend this current analysis by examining these issues and will provide our results in a forthcoming report.

ACKNOWLEDGMENTS

We are grateful to our technical reviewers Mark Berends, Tom Glennan, and Patrick McEwan, and also to the Legislative Analyst's Office advisory panel consisting of Larry Boese, Sue Burr, Eileen Cabanski, Tom Conroy, Thomas Henry, Jennifer Kuhn, Joe Lucente, Robert Manwaring, Colin Miller, Macke Raymond, and Dan Troy for their thoughtful reviews and comments. We also thank the members of RAND's Survey Research Group, Amy Howlett, Randa Cerdwell, Judy Cash, Cassandra Frankos, and Jennifer Hawes-Dawson, for administering the surveys. We also express our gratitude to research assistant Seema Mishra for arranging case study site visits and for her general research support and to Brian Stecher, Sue Bodilly, and Sheila Kirby for their valuable input at various stages. We also thank communication analyst Jerry Sollinger and the editorial staff of Patricia Bedrosian, Denise Constantine, and Paul Murphy in improving the writing of the document. Finally, we thank the Legislative Analyst's Office for graciously supporting the research.

ACRONYMS

ADA	Average Daily Attendance
AP	Advanced Placement
API	Academic Performance Index
CAT	California Achievement Test
CBEDS	Comprehensive Basic Education Data System
CBEST	California Basic Education Skills Test
CDE	California Department of Education
CDIF	County and District Information Form
CDS	County-district-school
EC	Education Code
FTE	Full-time-equivalent
GATE	Gifted and talented education
IEP	Individualized Education Plan
LAO	Legislative Analyst's Office
LEA	Local Education Agencies
LEP	Low English Proficient
MOU	Memorandum of understanding

NEA	National Education Association
OR	Odds ratio
PAIF	Professional Assignment Information Forms
PSAA	Public Schools Accountability Act (California)
RFP	Request for Proposal
RQ	Research Question
SBE	State Board of Education
SELPA	Special Education Learning Plan Area
SES	Socioeconomic status
SIF	School Information Form
SSAT	Single Subject Assessment for Teaching
STAR	Standardized Testing and Reporting

Chapter One

INTRODUCTION

Ron Zimmer, Derrick Chau, and Brian Gill

BACKGROUND: CHARTER SCHOOLS NATIONALLY AND IN CALIFORNIA

Charter schools represent the fastest-growing segment of the movement to promote parental choice in K–12 schooling. Charter schools are publicly funded schools of choice that operate autonomously, outside the direct control of conventional school districts under the authority of a quasi-contract, or "charter," granted by a public body. Supporters hope that charter schools will give new options to families, will prove educationally effective by virtue of greater accountability to parents, will promote innovation by reducing red tape, and will provide greater autonomy for decisionmaking at the school level (Finn et al., 2000; Nathan, 1996, 1998). Opponents argue that greater choice may exacerbate current racial segregation and create fiscal strains for states and school districts (Wells et al., 1998; Fisk and Ladd, 2000; Lacireno-Paquet et al., 2002). Despite this debate, charter schools have grown rapidly since the first charter school opened its doors in Minnesota in 1992. Currently, over 2,700 charter schools operate in 38 states plus the District of Columbia (Center for Education Reform, 2003).

Nowhere is this growth more apparent than in California, which in 1992 became the second state to pass charter school legislation. California now has more charter school students than any other state and ranks second only to Arizona in the number of charter schools.[1] Shortly after charter school legislation was enacted in Minnesota, lawmakers in California began considering establishing such schools. Initially, two competing bills were proposed within the California legislature, one by state senator Gary Hart and one by assemblywoman Delaine Easton. Hart's provided the greatest flexibility for schools (Wohlstetter et al., 2002). Hart argued that charter schools could foster greater local autonomy (Hart and Burr, 1996). He envisioned schools that would gain greater autonomy and parental choice in exchange for public accountability through measurable outcomes. His bill allowed for the conversion of conventional public schools to charter schools as well as the creation of new charter schools. The bill required that charter school developers have well-defined educational programs and that they specify measurable outcomes. It is important to note that Hart's bill exempted charter schools from many of the requirements of the Education Code and from collective bargaining. Finally, the bill set five-year renewable terms for the charters. Through it all, Hart tried to minimize the influence of interest groups in the bill. In the end, the bill represented a bold new initiative in California (Wohlstetter et al., 2002).

After much debate, Governor Pete Wilson signed an amended version of Hart's bill into law in 1992. The intent of the law is specified in the Education Code (EC) 47601:

(a) Improve pupil learning;

(b) Increase learning opportunities for all pupils, with special emphasis on expanded learning experiences for pupils who are identified as academically low achieving;

(c) Encourage the use of different and innovative teaching methods;

(d) Create new professional opportunities for teachers, including the opportunity to be responsible for the learning program at the school site;

---

[1]According to the California Department of Education, in 2001–02, 349 charter schools enrolled 2.2 percent of the state's public school children. Enrollment figures for the 2002–03 school year were not available at the time of publication (http://data1.cde.ca.gov/dataquest).

(e) Provide parents and pupils with expanded choices in the types of educational opportunities that are available within the public school system;

(f) Hold the schools established under this part accountable for meeting measurable pupil outcomes, and provide the schools with a method to change from rule-based to performance-based accountability systems;

(g) Provide vigorous competition within the public school system to stimulate continual improvements in all public schools.

Initial analysis suggested that relative to other states California had a strong charter law (Bierlein, 1997; Hassel, 1999). However, in recent years, the original legislation has been modified in a variety of ways. In some cases, these adjustments were made to allow greater growth of charter schools; other changes occurred out of concern about the appropriate provision of education and oversight.[2] We describe the more significant areas of legislative activity in California below.

- *Cap on number of charter schools*: The original California charter school legislation limited the number of schools to 100, with a maximum of 10 charter schools per district. However, the state board of education used its authority to waive the cap in 1997 and approved 137 charter schools. The legislation was modified (AB 544) in 1998 to adjust to the demand for these schools, raising the cap to 250 plus an additional 100 new charter schools in each subsequent year. The maximum per district was also removed.
- *Chartering and appeals process*: The original charter school law did not require that chartering authorities justify their denial of charter petitions, and appeals of charter denials were cumbersome, requiring the creation of ad hoc appeals panels of teachers and district board members. Pressure from the charter school community led to amendments to the legislation in 1998 (AB 544) requiring that chartering authorities justify the denial of charter petitions in writing and clarifying the appeals process.

---

[2]For a detailed discussion of the development of California's charter school legislation, see Hart and Burr (1996).

These amendments formalized the appeals process when a local school district denied a charter. Denials could be appealed to either the county or state board of education. Amendments in 2002 (AB 1994) now require that those denied charters appeal to their county board of education before appealing to the state board.

- *Teacher credentialing*: The 1992 legislation did not require that teachers in charter schools hold a state teaching credential. However, political pressure from teacher advocacy groups resulted in the addition of a requirement during the 1998 revisions to the legislation (AB 544) that teachers hold a credential.
- *Nonclassroom-based schools*: Considerable legislative activity has surrounded the oversight and funding of nonclassroom-based charter schools, such as those offering independent study, distance learning, and home study schools. Concern over the administrative oversight of these schools has led policymakers to develop additional mechanisms to ensure that these schools maintain their public accountability. Additions to the legislation in 2001 clarified the criteria for the apportionment of funding to nonclassroom-based charter schools and gave authority over funding these schools to the state board of education.
- *Facilities*: The original legislation required that a school district permit charter schools operating in its boundaries to occupy unused district facilities free of charge. Start-up schools continued to face acute challenges in acquiring sufficient funding for facilities and in identifying adequate facilities. Effective November 2003, amendments now require that school districts provide furnished and equipped facilities for charter schools operating within their boundaries, regardless of whether unused space is available.
- *Geographic boundaries*: The initial legislation permitted a school district to authorize charter schools outside the district's attendance boundaries. Recent state analyses and public scrutiny have criticized the ability of such school districts to monitor these types of charter schools. Legislative amendments enacted in 2002 now restrict charter schools from operating outside the geographical jurisdiction of the district that authorizes them,

unless arrangements are made with the district where the charter school operates.

Currently, little is known about the effectiveness of the original legislation or the above changes. Below, we outline some of the previous research on charter schools, including California charter schools.

WHAT WE KNOW FROM PRIOR RESEARCH

Currently, there are only a handful of national studies of charter schools. Most of them have analyzed the characteristics of charter schools and charter laws across states (U.S. Department of Education, 2000; Anderson et al., 2002). Researchers have also evaluated charter schools in individual states including Arizona, Texas, Michigan, and Pennsylvania. Many of these studies have focused on student achievement and have produced mixed results. Solomon et al. (1999) found that students in charter schools in Arizona outperformed conventional public school students. Gronberg and Jansen (2001), evaluating charter schools in Texas, found that charter schools that focus on at-risk students provided slightly more "value added" than conventional public schools whereas charters focusing on students not at risk provided slightly less value added than conventional public schools. On the other hand, Hanushek et al. (2002) found no significant differences between charter schools and conventional public schools in the long run. Bettinger (2002) generally found no significant differences between charter schools and conventional public schools in Michigan. Finally, Miron et al. (2002) found that charter schools are gaining ground relative to comparable conventional public schools in Pennsylvania. The inconsistency of these results may be partially explained by varying charter laws across states and suggests that analysis pertaining to one state may have only indirect implications for other states.

Some of the first studies of charter schools in California focused on autonomy, innovation, and parental involvement and found some evidence that charter schools were operating as envisioned in the legislation (Dianda and Corwin, 1994; Corwin and Flaherty, 1995).[3]

---

[3]Over 15 studies have examined charters in various states. Some of them have focused exclusively on student achievement; others have focused on other outcomes

Later, the Little Hoover Commission (1996) studied the oversight of approximately a quarter of the state's charter schools and made recommendations (such as eliminating the cap on the number of charter schools and clarifying state funding) that were eventually incorporated into the current charter law.

Subsequent studies addressed other issues. In 1998, Amy Stuart Wells examined charter schools in 10 California school districts and concluded that these schools were not meeting many of the original objectives of the legislation, including the mandate of being racially representative of the district. Also in 1998, the Los Angeles Unified School District evaluated its 15 charter schools (Izu et al., 1998). The evaluation found that they were using their increased autonomy to improve school administrative operations, which were linked to some improvements in instruction and student performance. More recently, a study by the California State Auditor (2002) evaluated the effectiveness of four chartering authorities. Its main finding was that greater monitoring and oversight of charter schools is necessary to improve charter school accountability. The only other state-mandated evaluation was an SRI study of California's 124 charter schools operating at the time (Powell et al., 1997). This research addressed a broad array of questions. Among its important findings: Charter schools enrolled students with similar characteristics to students in the state as a whole; charter schools have a relatively high level of parental involvement; and many charter schools did not know whether they were eligible for Title I funding, which led to lower participation rates.

FOCUS OF THIS RESEARCH

Collectively, these studies provide valuable insights. However, there is much we do not know about the effectiveness of charter schools in terms of accessibility, achievement, operation, and governance, particularly given the changes in legislation. California's Legislative Analyst's Office (LAO) asked RAND to undertake a comprehensive study of California's charter schools, with the aim of providing broad

---

such as the operation and autonomy of charter schools. This quick literature review includes studies that are most relevant for our current research with a special emphasis on California and states with a large number of charter schools.

policy recommendations that would improve their functioning. For the charter school movement to move forward nationally and in California, it is important that questions of effectiveness be answered through comprehensive and objective research. Thus, the California legislature mandated objective research that would analyze whether charter schools are meeting the (a) through (g) objectives of EC 47601 as highlighted above (AB 2471, Mazzoni).[4] The mandated research on charter schools sets out a vast array of research questions that largely fall into four research areas: accessibility, effectiveness, governance, and operation. These areas are the focus of our current research. More specifically, we address the following research questions (RQs):

> *RQ1. What population of students attend charter schools?* We examine the racial mix of students both at charter schools and at conventional public schools to evaluate the relative integration of charter schools.
>
> *RQ2. Is student achievement higher in charter schools than in conventional public schools?* We assess the achievement levels and gains of students in charter schools and conventional public schools while controlling for student characteristics. In addition, because there is no single charter model, we evaluate the performance of the various types of charter schools (e.g., conversion versus start-up, classroom-based versus nonclassroom-based).
>
> *RQ3. What oversight and support do the chartering authorities provide?* Because charter schools are intended to operate independent of many of the bureaucratic constraints of conventional public schools, the effectiveness of their authorization, governance, and regulation are important issues. In this report, we study the chartering process along with the support and oversight provided by chartering authorities by examining the level of control over decisionmaking reported by principals of both charter and conventional public schools.
>
> *RQ4. How do charter schools differ from conventional public schools in terms of their operation including finances, staffing, professional development, curriculum, and student discipline?*

[4]Chapter 673, Statutes of 1998.

> From the outset, advocates hoped that charter schools would lead to innovations in public education. Our report examines the operation of charter schools by comparing survey responses of charter and conventional public school principals.

These four research areas encompass most of the research questions laid out in the legislation. Additional questions mandated by the legislation relate to the use of memoranda of understanding, fiscal liabilities, charter schools' use of exemptions, dropout rates, and parental satisfaction. Although we address each of these questions in our analysis, they are not the primary focus.

DATA SOURCES

To examine accessibility, student achievement, governance, and the operation of charter and conventional public schools, we collected both primary and secondary data. The primary datasets include surveys and case studies, whereas the secondary datasets include school-level and student-level data provided by the California Department of Education (CDE) and individual school districts. The following section describes each source.[5]

Primary Data

Surveys*:* In the spring of 2002, we surveyed all California charter schools, a matched sample of conventional public schools, and all known California chartering authorities. (To match the charter schools, we used a propensity match methodology that matches schools based on racial and socioeconomic characteristics.)[6] The charter school survey also included a one-page supplemental set of fiscal questions. These surveys asked charter schools and chartering authorities about the charter petition process, oversight, governance, finances, staffing, curriculum, and discipline. Survey responses served as the foundation for analyzing the operational differences between charter and conventional public schools and for examining

[5]For a more complete description of data, see Appendix A.

[6]See Appendix A for a detailed description of this approach.

the oversight of charter schools. Table 1.1 displays our response rate for each of the surveys.[7]

For our analysis, the charter school, charter school supplemental, and conventional public school surveys were weighted to adjust for nonresponse. The weighting is described in Appendix A.

Case Studies: To enrich our understanding of our survey results and to gather information that is difficult to capture in paper-and-pencil surveys, we visited nine charter schools and interviewed all but one of their chartering authorities. These visits were conducted in October and November 2002. Selection of charter schools for case studies was designed to ensure that we included schools that differed on three dimensions: conversion versus start-up schools, schools serving high versus low proportions of minority students, and high-achieving versus low-achieving schools.[8] We also decided to focus only on elementary schools so that we could gather similar information across all schools. In selecting schools from within each of these categories, we also considered such secondary factors as geographical diversity and enrollment and such unique features as having a state or county chartering authority, being operated by an Education Management Organization, or having a unique instructional approach.[9]

Table 1.1

Response Rate

Survey	Sample	No. of Respondents	Response Rate (%)
Charter school survey	352	257	73
Charter school supplemental survey	352	200	56
Conventional public school survey	245	184	75
Chartering authority survey	174	115	66

---

[7]See Appendix A for information on the development of the surveys and samples.

[8]High-minority schools are defined as having at least 50 percent black and Hispanic students; low-minority schools are defined as having less than 50 percent black and Hispanic students. High-achieving schools are defined as being in the highest 50th percentile of Academic Performance Index (API) scores; low-achieving schools are defined as being in the lowest 50th percentile of API scores. Establishing the definitions at the 50th percentile allows for binary classification of schools.

[9]For further information about the sample selection, see Appendix A.

Secondary Data

Comprehensive Basic Education Data System (CBEDS): CBEDS contains information that CDE collects each October from school districts, schools, and certified staff. The CBEDS data include staffing information (e.g., certification and salary ranges) and student characteristics (e.g., demographics and English language proficiency). Our analysis includes the CBEDS data from the 1992–93 school year to the 2001–02 school year.

Professional Assignment Information Form (PAIF): PAIF data are collected annually from nearly all teachers in California, starting with the 1992–93 school year. These data contain information on the qualifications, demographics, and teaching assignments for most teachers in California's public and charter schools and enable us to compare charter schools with conventional public schools and with other charter schools.

J-200: Each year, the California Department of Education collects detailed information on revenues and expenditures for each school district and county office of education across a number of categories as defined by the state. School districts record this information on J-200 forms. The J-200 data provide a good base for determining the type and size of revenues school districts receive as well as how school districts spend their money.[10]

Academic Performance Index: As part of the California Public Schools Accountability Act (PSAA), the API has been established to measure the academic performance and growth of schools. Each school receives an API score based on a numeric index (ranging from 200 to 1,000) that reflects the school's performance on standardized tests.[11] The API dataset includes the state rank of the schools, growth

---

[10]Ideally, we would like to have this level of detailed revenue and expenditure data for both conventional public schools and charter schools to be able to compare their finances. Such school-level data do not exist, in part because most of the revenues and expenditures for conventional public schools are handled at the district level. To supplement the data that currently exist, we included questions on revenues and expenditures in our charter school survey that follow some of the breakdowns in the J-200 data. We present this summary data for charter schools. In addition, we present similar summary data from the J-200 data for school districts in California.

[11]For more information on the API, see http://www.cde.ca.gov/psaa/api/fallapi/apiinfo.pdf.

targets, number of students tested in aggregate and by racial/ethnic group, and student demographic characteristics. The API data are available for the school years 1999–00 through 2001–02.

Statewide Student-Level Data: CDE provided data on all California students for the school years 1997–98 through 2001–02. These data include student reading and math test scores as well as the demographic characteristics of each student. However, the data do not have a unique identifier for each student that would allow us to examine individual progress over time. Nevertheless, they do allow an examination of gains of cohorts over time while precisely accounting for differences in student characteristics that might affect test scores.

District Student-Level Data: Because the state database does not allow us to link the longitudinal performance of individual students or track them as they move from school to school (including students who move to/from charter schools or from/to conventional public schools), we contacted 10 major districts with the largest number of charter schools to obtain longitudinally linked student-level data. We received data from six of these districts (Chula Vista Elementary, Fresno Unified, Los Angeles Unified, Napa Valley Unified, San Diego city Unified, and West Covina Unified).[12] These data also include students' reading and math test scores as well as their demographic characteristics and allow an examination of the gains of individual students in both charter and conventional public schools.

HOW WE CATEGORIZED CHARTER SCHOOLS

One challenge in evaluating the performance of charter schools is that there is no single charter school model. This is not surprising because part of the motivation behind creating charter schools is to foster innovation, which leads to different approaches. To carry out our analysis, we tried to capture the diversity of the schools by segmenting them into major observable dimensions (conversion versus start-up, classroom-based versus nonclassroom-based, school size, and independent versus dependent). These four dimensions may affect the way charter schools operate and ultimately perform.

---

[12]West Covina Unified has only one charter school, but because of an established relationship, we were able to get its data and include them in our analysis.

Where possible, we used these dimensions when analyzing the charter schools and presenting the results. Below, we highlight these dimensions.

Conversion and Start-Up Charter Schools

In California, charter schools can be new schools started as charters (start-up schools) or conventional public schools that converted to charter status (conversion schools). Although the 1997 SRI study found that charter schools were equally divided between start-up and conversion schools, our analysis suggests that the majority of recently implemented charter schools are start-up schools. As Figure 1.1 indicates, start-up schools now account for 70 percent of all charter schools. Evidence from other studies of charter schools (Finn et al., 2000) suggests that start-up schools face different, and often greater, challenges than do conversion schools in providing instruction for students. We discuss differences across these types of schools during analyses of such issues as student characteristics and school finances.

Breaking down by percentage of students in different grades, Figure 1.2 shows that 72 percent of all charter elementary school students are in conversion schools with the remaining 28 percent in start-up

RAND *MR1700-1.1*

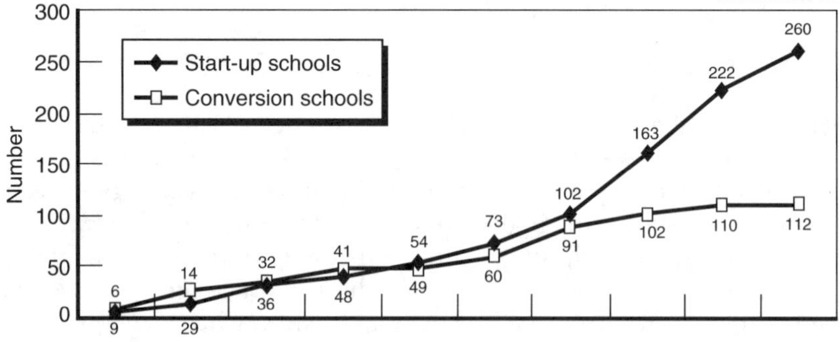

SOURCE: 2001–02 CBEDS data.

Figure 1.1—Number of Conversion and Start-Up Schools, 1993–2002

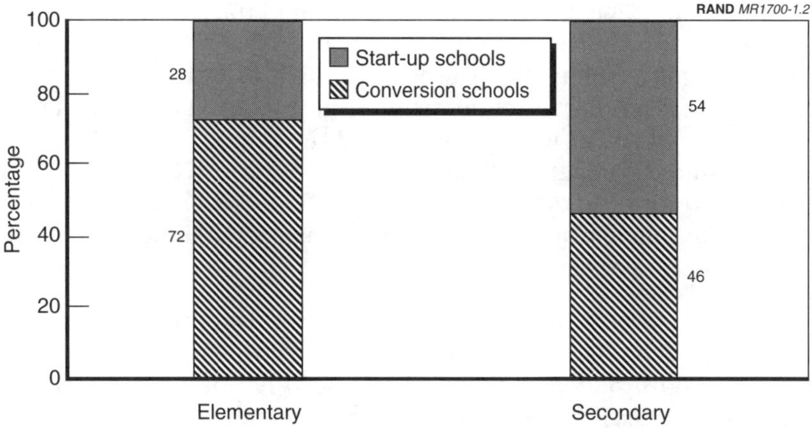

SOURCE: 2002 California Department of Education statewide student-level data.

Figure 1.2—Percentage of Charter School Students in Conversion and Start-Up Schools, by Grade Level

schools. In contrast, 46 percent of all secondary school students are in conversion schools, with the remaining 54 percent in start-up schools.

Classroom-Based and Nonclassroom-Based Charter Schools

CDE defines charter schools as nonclassroom-based "when a school does not require attendance of its pupils be at the school site under the direct supervision and control of a qualified teaching employee of the school for at least 80 percent of the required instructional time."[13] Schools are considered classroom-based when: "1. The charter school's pupils are engaged in education activities required of those pupils, and the pupils are under the immediate supervision and control of an employee of the charter school who is authorized to provide instruction to the pupils within the meaning of Education

---

[13]http://www.cde.ca.gov/charter/regs/sb740covlet0203df.htm. A list of nonclassroom-based charter schools can be found at http://www.cde.ca.gov/charter/whatsnew/SBEfundingdeterminations0102.pdf.

Code Section 47605(l); 2. At least 80 percent of the instructional time offered at the charter school is at the school site; 3. The charter's school site is a facility that is used principally for classroom instruction; and 4. The charter school requires its pupils to be in attendance at the school site at least 80 percent of the minimum instructional time required pursuant to Education Code Section 47612.5(a)(1)." As evident from these definitions, not all students who attend a nonclassroom-based charter school will be instructed in nonclassroom settings and vice versa.

Currently, nonclassroom-based charter schools represent a third of all charter schools.[14] Because of recent controversies surrounding these schools, Senate Bill 740 of the 2000 legislative session was passed to increase the accountability requirements of the schools.[15] Of all charter schools, start-up schools are much more likely to be nonclassroom-based (56.5 percent compared to 11.4 percent for conversion schools). Breaking down the proportion of nonclassroom-based students across different grades, Figure 1.3 shows that students in nonclassroom-based schools make up 17 percent of charter elementary school students and 41 percent of charter secondary school students.[16]

School Size

As Figure 1.4 suggests, enrollments vary by school type. Start-up schools tend to be much smaller than conversion or conventional public schools, whereas conversion schools more closely mimic the size distribution of conventional public schools. Later analyses explore some operational differences across schools of different sizes.

---

[14]Some of these nonclassroom-based charter schools are quite large, with one school having over 4,500 students.

[15]At the heart of this controversy is the schooling of students in private homes. According to the RAND charter school survey, in 13.9 percent of all charter schools, the majority of students are instructed exclusively in private homes.

[16]These numbers represent the percentage of students attending a school that offers some component of nonclassroom-based instruction. Many of these students will also have classroom-based instruction.

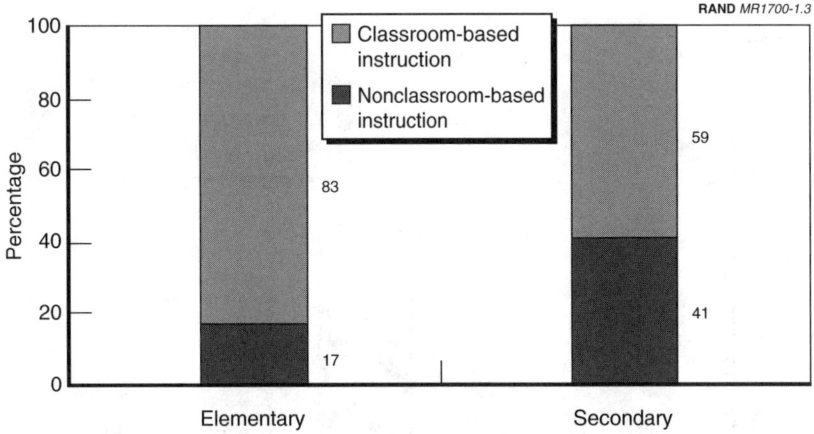

SOURCE: 2002 RAND charter school survey.

Figure 1.3—Percentage of Charter School Students in Nonclassroom-Based and Classroom-Based Schools, by Grade Level

Independent and Dependent Charter Schools

Another distinction among charter schools is the relationship between chartering authorities and schools. In many cases, chartering authorities describe the relationship with charter schools as either "independent" or "dependent." This distinction, however, is not described in the charter law but rather is defined by the individual chartering authorities. In the SRI report referred to above, dependent charter schools are defined as schools subject to district policies and procedures, except when they seek waivers; independent charter schools make their own programmatic, personnel, and financial decisions. In our analysis, we allow chartering authorities to use their own definition of independent and dependent charter schools and then explore the authorization, governance, and oversight of charter schools across the level of dependence.

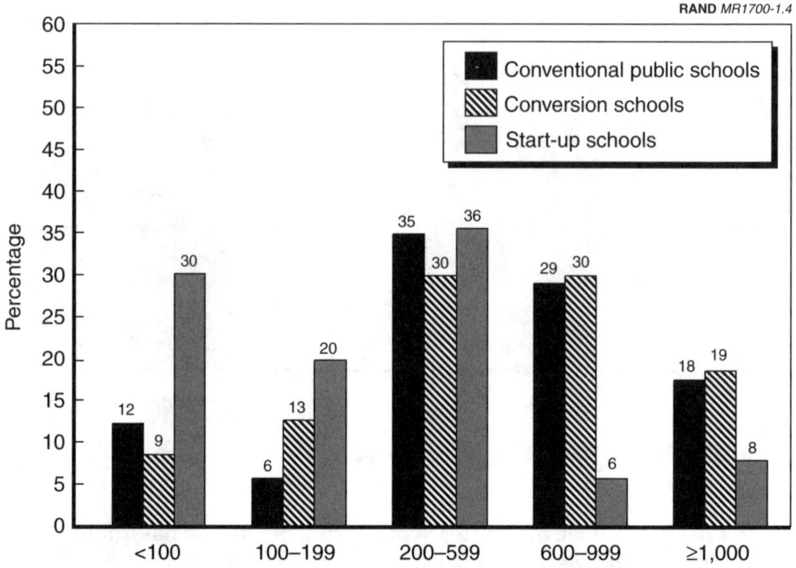

SOURCES: 2002 RAND charter school survey and 2002 CBEDS data.

Figure 1.4—Differences in School Size, by School Type

LIMITATIONS OF THE STUDY

The major limitations of our study stem from data limitations and budgetary and time constraints.

Data Limitations

Currently, the state does not have a mechanism to track individual students over time. Without statewide longitudinally linked student-level data, we are not able to conduct a statewide analysis that tracks students as they move from conventional public schools to charter schools or vice versa. In addition, our measurement of student gains is less precise because we cannot attach a specific baseline test score for each student. Finally, student achievement data are measured consistently only from 1997–98 through 2001–02. Schools that existed before 1997–98 have no test scores to measure their baseline performance.

Budgetary and Time Constraints

Additional surveys would have enhanced our analyses of charter schools. For example, the analysis of school practices, such as classroom instruction, would be more precise if we had been able to survey teachers. In addition, a survey of parents would have provided a much needed perspective on the quantity and quality of parental involvement and the reasons parents choose to enroll their children in charter schools. These surveys are difficult, time-consuming, and expensive to develop and did not fit within the project's budget and timeline.

HOW THE REPORT IS ORGANIZED

Before proceeding with our assessment of student achievement, we first describe students who attend charter schools in Chapter Two. The student achievement analysis follows in Chapter Three. Chapters Four through Eight assess the financing, academic environment, staffing, and special education of charter schools. We end with conclusions and recommendations in Chapter Nine.

Chapter Two

STUDENTS SERVED BY CHARTER SCHOOLS

Derrick Chau, Dan McCaffrey, Ron Zimmer, Glenn Daley, and Brian Gill

INTRODUCTION

One key area of policy interest related to charter schools concerns the student populations they serve. More specifically, policy concerns about charter school students relate to both access and integration. In terms of access, policymakers need to know whether the charter schools are ensuring options for disadvantaged students, including low-achieving ones, racial and ethnic minorities, low-income students, and students with special needs. Although charter school advocates have often touted charters as a means to give choices to disadvantaged students who otherwise lack choice (Nathan, 1998), critics have worried that as schools of choice, charters will "skim the cream," attracting and selecting the high-achieving students and leaving disadvantaged students behind in impoverished conventional public schools (Vergari, 1999; Wells et al., 1998). Even if charter schools do not systematically select advantaged students through their admissions processes, argue the critics, they still may end up serving advantaged populations if they are more likely to be chosen by well-educated, highly informed parents. Prior evidence suggests that the access of disadvantaged students to charter schools has varied (Gill et al., 2001; RPP International, 1999).

The integration of students within charter schools is a different policy concern from that of the access of disadvantaged students. Here the question is not whether the charter sector as a whole serves disadvantaged students but whether students of diverse ethnic groups are taught in integrated settings within individual charter schools. It is theoretically possible, for example, that charter schools across the state serve a student population that mirrors that of the state as a whole, but that the students are served in schools that are highly segregated ethnically. As with access, theoretical arguments can be made on both sides of the integration issue. Charters might reduce integration by offering educational programs (e.g., an Afro-centric curriculum) that appeal to a particular group of students. Or charters might increase integration by breaking the tie between residence and school assignment, permitting students living in segregated neighborhoods to attend integrated charter schools. Currently, few studies have examined integration in charter schools (even though a number of studies have examined access to charter schools) (Gill et al., 2001).

California's charter school law specifically addresses both access and integration. It requires that charter schools admit all students who wish to attend. It also places special emphasis on expanding the learning experiences for students who are identified as academically low-achieving by requiring that chartering authorities give preference to charters that will serve those student populations. The law also requires that charter schools describe in their charters "the means by which the school will achieve a racial and ethnic balance among its pupils that is reflective of the general population residing within the territorial jurisdiction of the school district to which the charter petition is submitted."

These mandates are challenging for charter schools because they may be contradictory. For example, if a district has predominantly high-achieving students of one racial group and has a small population of low-achieving students of that racial group, then the charter school may have a difficult time expanding learning experiences for students who are identified as academically low-achieving while at the same time being representative of their territorial jurisdiction. These contradictions may force the charter schools to comply with only one of these mandates. Therefore, when analyzing racial representativeness, it is difficult to account for these confounding factors. Because of this difficulty, we caution the reader to interpret the results within this chapter with this challenge in mind.

In this chapter we examine four kinds of evidence about access and integration of charter schools. To make judgments about access, we first examine admissions processes in charter schools and our comparison group of conventional public schools, using evidence from our school surveys. Second, we explore additional survey data to examine how charter schools compare to conventional public schools in the extent to which they specifically seek to influence student access by focusing their services on disadvantaged populations. To connect the discussions on access and integration, we present data on charter school students, comparing the characteristics of the student population served by the charter school sector to the characteristics of students in conventional public schools in districts with charter schools. Finally, we examine integration in charter schools by assessing the extent to which charter schools enroll student populations that reflect the enrollments of their local school districts.

ACCESS TO CHARTER SCHOOLS

Two school processes can influence student access to charter and conventional public schools: student admissions processes and school focus.[1] Charter and conventional public schools can develop student admissions processes as a way to introduce the school to prospective students and their parents and to gain a greater understanding of the needs of those students. Schools—especially those operating under school choice policies—can indirectly influence the types of students who apply by focusing their missions or curricula on specific types of students such as gifted and talented or at-risk students. Even though charter schools are required to admit all students, parents who learn of the focus of a school's services may choose not to send their children to that school because they might believe that their children will not be best served in that school. This section first presents the results from our study related to these two influences on student access to charter schools.[2]

---

[1]These are not the only two factors; other factors, such as transportation and the vitality of local schools, can affect access, but these are the two prominent factors under the control of charter schools.

[2]However, it does not examine how parents find out about schools in the area, which is a key way to control who goes to what school.

Student Admissions Processes

According to surveyed principals, the student admissions processes in charter schools do not differ markedly from those used in matched conventional public schools.[3] Survey responses suggest that although most charter and conventional public schools use no special admissions criteria for students, some schools in each group report using academic records, special student qualities, and recommendations to a limited degree. Charter and conventional public schools that use admissions requirements do so in a similar manner. Most use the criteria only for diagnostic purposes. Only small percentages of schools responded that they use these criteria to determine eligibility for admission.

When we examine the results by charter school type, however, some differences appear. Start-up schools clearly differ from conventional public schools in their use of achievement tests and personal interviews. Even so, as Figure 2.1 shows, only about 19 percent of start-up schools use the interview to determine eligibility for admission, according to survey responses, and about 43 percent of these schools reported that they do not use personal interviews in the admissions process.

Likewise, Figure 2.2 shows that only about 3.8 percent of start-up schools use admissions or achievement tests to determine eligibility for admission. Even though these data show that the start-up schools use tests as part of the admissions process, they do not indicate how these tests are used. For instance, tests may be used to determine student ability levels for classroom placement, to confirm whether students are low-achieving, or to identify high-achieving students. Because start-up schools are newly created and are more likely to focus their services on specific student populations, they might need to provide parents with more specific information about how their schools meet the needs of their students. Further research is required to determine how charter schools are using these admissions processes.

These responses suggest that charter schools rarely use academic achievement tests during the admissions process. It should be

---

[3]For each analysis, we highlight the comparison group in the notes to the figures.

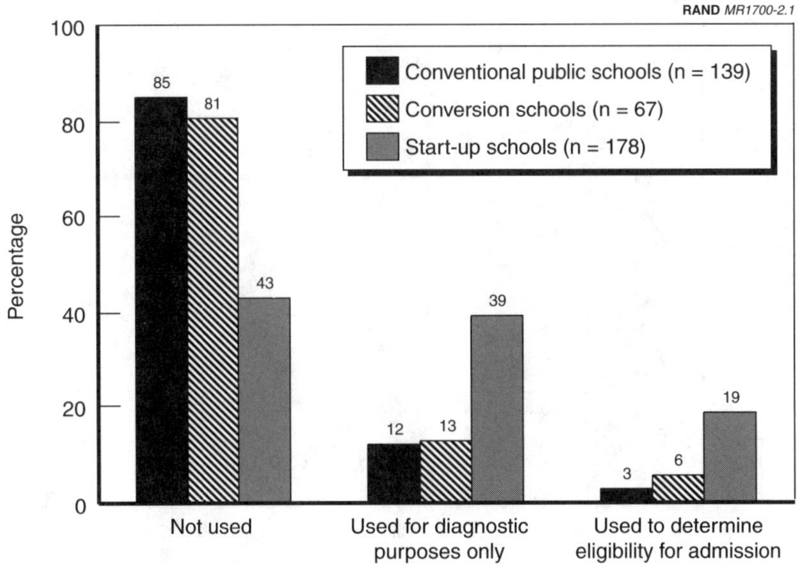

SOURCES: 2002 RAND charter school and matched conventional public school surveys.

NOTE: The differences between start-up school and matched conventional public school percentages using chi-squared tests of difference are statistically significant at the 5 percent level.

Figure 2.1—Use of Personal Interviews in School Admissions Processes

noted, however, that these results are based on principals' survey responses, and they may be reluctant to report practices that could be deemed exclusionary. Moreover, interviews may be used to encourage or discourage enrollment even if they are not formally used to exclude applicants.

In several case studies of charter schools, principals explained that prospective parents and students are offered an orientation to show them the school facilities and curriculum approach. As a part of these orientations, principals interview students and parents to determine whether the charter school will meet their needs. As this example suggests, there may be some ambiguity about the purposes of a personal interview. Additional research is necessary to determine

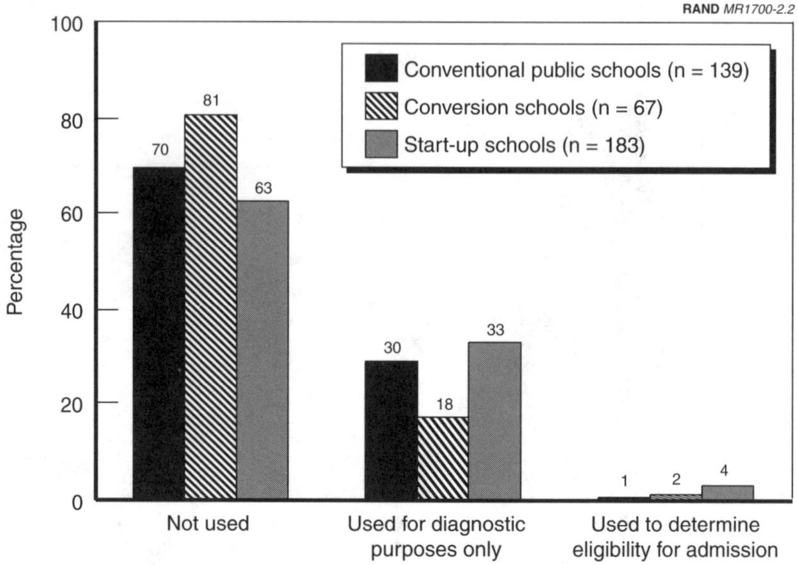

SOURCES: 2002 RAND charter school and matched conventional public school surveys.

NOTE: The differences between start-up school and matched conventional public school percentages using chi-squared tests of difference are statistically significant at the 5 percent level.

Figure 2.2—Use of Admissions Tests in School Admissions Processes

how charter schools are using factors such as admissions tests and personal interviews in admissions processes.

Focus of School Services

The California charter school legislation is designed to increase learning opportunities for all students as well as to encourage the use of innovative teaching methods. To these ends, charter schools can design instructional programs that focus on specific student populations. When asked whether schools seek to focus their services on specific student populations, 33 percent of charter school principals responded that they focus their services compared to only 21 percent of conventional public school principals. Most of this difference is explained by start-up schools: About 36 percent of start-up school principals reported that they sought to focus their services compared to only about 26 percent of conversion school principals. However, our surveys do not indicate how the focus differs among charter and conventional schools. In our survey, we asked conventional and charter school principals if they focus their services across seven different services listed in Table 2.1. As the table indicates, charter and conventional school principals reported that they focus their services on similar categories of student populations. The only significant difference between charter and conventional schools is the percentage of schools focusing on students with disabilities.

Table 2.1

Focus of Charter and Conventional Public School Services

Focus	Charter School (n = 257)	Conventional Public School (n = 184)
Low-income students	21.8	20.0
Students with academic problems	19.2	18.8
Students with discipline problems	14.2	15.4
English Learners	11.5	13.8
Students of specific racial/ethnic minority group	11.2	13.6
Students with special aptitudes, skills, or talents	10.9	16.3
Students with disabilities	7.6*	16.5

SOURCES: 2002 RAND charter school and matched conventional public school surveys.

NOTES: Schools could select more than one area of focus. Percentages were not required to sum to 100.

*Indicates charter school percentage that is statistically different from conventional public school percentage at the 5 percent level.

CHARACTERISTICS OF STUDENTS IN CHARTER SCHOOLS

We have thus far examined information derived from principal self-reports about admissions processes and the espoused intentions of charter schools to serve disadvantaged populations. Now we switch our focus to the students served by charter schools. An important dimension of this discussion is whether charter schools "skim the cream" by focusing on only high-achieving students. To answer this question directly requires statewide data on the prior academic achievement of students entering charter schools. Unfortunately, no such data exist. Nevertheless, as Chapter Three describes in detail, the average achievement levels of students currently enrolled in some type of charter schools are lower than average achievement levels in conventional public schools, which strongly suggests that these charter schools are not "skimming the cream" academically.

Another important dimension is the representativeness of the student population. One major concern surrounding the growth of charter schools across the nation is that these schools might cater to more homogeneous student populations than do conventional public schools. In other words, charter schools might provide a mechanism for creating schools that attract students from primarily one racial/ethnic group.[4] In the state of California, as mentioned above, charter schools are required to describe in their charters "the means by which the school will achieve a racial and ethnic balance among its pupils that is reflective of the general population residing within the territorial jurisdiction of the school district to which the charter petition is submitted."[5]

To evaluate representativeness, we examine the racial composition of charter schools and conventional public schools through a multistep process. The process starts with a straightforward statewide comparison of charter and conventional public school populations and works toward a more specific analysis comparing these populations to the populations of districts. In all cases, the analysis uses counts of students by racial groups (white, Hispanic, black, Asian, American Indian, Filipino, Pacific Islander, and mixed) as reported in the CBEDS data. Our analysis focuses on the four largest racial groups: white, Hispanic, black, and Asian.

Our first analysis compares the racial makeup of all students attending charter schools relative to all those attending conventional public schools in the entire state. We find, as shown in Figure 2.3, that the

[4]For simplicity, we will use the terms "race" or "racial" instead of "race/ethnicity" or "racial-ethnic."

[5]Although the state mandate calls for equal representation of race, equal representation of other demographic characteristics may also be of interest to policymakers. One such characteristic is the representation of impoverished students as measured by the percentage of students entitled to free or reduced-price lunches. However, when examining the data, over a third of charter schools do not participate in this lunch program and data on these schools will underestimate the proportion of impoverished students.

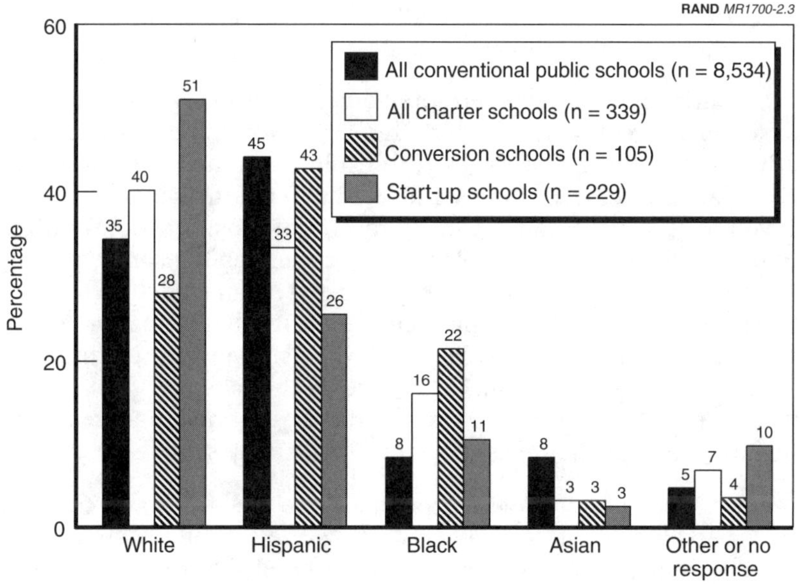

SOURCE: 2001–02 CBEDS data.

NOTE: Figure numbers have been rounded to the nearest whole number.

Figure 2.3—Racial Composition of Students in Start-Up Schools, Conversion Schools, and All Conventional Public Schools

racial composition of students in charter schools differs from that in conventional public schools.[6] On average, charter schools have a higher percentage of white and black students and a lower percentage of Hispanic and Asian students than conventional public schools.

The figure also shows that the racial makeup of students in start-up and conversion schools differs from that in conventional public schools. For example, start-up schools have a higher percentage of white students and a lower percentage of Hispanic and Asian students whereas conversion schools enroll fewer white and Asian students than do conventional public schools. Conversion schools

---

[6]This approach was used by the SRI California charter school evaluation (Powell et al., 1997).

also enroll much higher percentages of black students than do conventional public schools.

A comparison of our data with previous studies of California's charter schools suggests that charter schools are becoming less representative of students across the state. Results from the 1997 evaluation of California's charter schools indicated that charter school students served at that time had a similar racial composition to all public school students in the state. However, as early as 1998 and continuing in 1999, studies found that Hispanic and Asian students were underrepresented in California's charter schools compared to the statewide average, whereas black and white students were overrepresented (RPP International, 1999, 2000). This change in the racial composition of charter school students corresponds to increases in the proportion of charter schools that are start-up schools.

Although the analysis above provides some insights about the students served by charter schools, we must be careful not to assume that differences in the aggregate imply that charter schools are not representative of their local populations. Charter schools do not operate in all districts and there is considerable geographic concentration in student racial populations that might explain the differences between charter and conventional public schools.

Thus, to disentangle the effects of location from differential enrollment rates for racial groups, we compared the racial composition of charter schools to the racial composition of the districts where the charter schools are located. For most charter schools, the chartering authority district provides a comparison district. However, some of these chartering authorities are not traditional school districts but, rather, are the state or the county education offices. In addition, some charter schools are chartered by school districts other than the district in which they are located. For these charter schools, the chartering authority is not a reasonable comparison. Thus, we restricted our comparison to conventional public schools in traditional school districts that chartered the charter school if the charter school is in or adjacent to this district.[7] This restriction created a sample

---

[7]The sample excludes three schools chartered by the state and 20 schools chartered by county education offices. Schools that were geographically distinct from the chartering district were identified through survey responses (14 were so identified) or by

that includes 282 charter schools in 139 chartering districts and 3,077 conventional public schools in these same districts.

Figure 2.4 compares the racial makeup of schools from this sample. The figure shows a similar pattern to that in the above statewide analysis. Charter schools overall have a higher percentage of white and black students and a lower percentage of Asian and Hispanic students than conventional public schools within their chartering districts. Differences also appear by type of charter school.

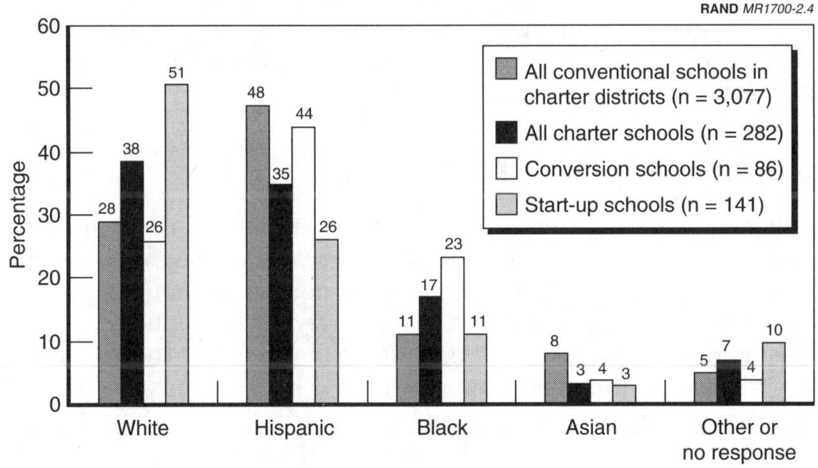

SOURCE: 2001–02 CBEDS data.

Figure 2.4—Racial Composition of Students in Start-Up Schools, Conversion Schools, and All Conventional Public Schools Within the Charter Districts

---

mapping (69 schools without survey responses). For each school without survey data, we mapped the location of the charter school and the chartering school district. Eleven schools were outside the district boundaries. Four of these 11 schools were very far from the chartering district and were excluded from the analysis. However, six of these 11 schools were less than five miles from the district and were included in the analysis. One district was about seven miles away and after careful investigation including street address and school name, we determined that the school should be linked to the chartering district. Thus, we excluded a total of 18 schools because they were not serving the students of the chartering district.

Figure 2.4 does not completely remove the effects of geographic heterogeneity in the student population among districts where charter schools are located. To account for this, we fit models for each racial group that compared conventional and charter schools within districts and tested for the overall effects for charter schools.[8] After controlling for the district effect, charter school students are more likely to be black and less likely to be Hispanic or Asian (all differences are statistically significant at the 0.05 level).[9] Somewhat surprisingly, charter school students, judging by the more rigorous analysis, are not more or less likely to be white. Thus, when we remove district heterogeneity, we find that charter schools serve disproportionate numbers of Hispanic, black, and Asian students but not white students.

SCHOOL-BY-SCHOOL ANALYSIS

Our analysis in the previous section examines racial differences among charter and conventional public schools at the aggregate level. However, the state mandate does not require equal representation in charter schools relative to conventional public schools in the aggregate. Rather, charter schools are required to describe in their charters "the means by which the school will achieve a racial and ethnic balance among its pupils that is reflective of the general population residing within the territorial jurisdiction of the school district to which the charter petition is submitted." Statewide aggregate differences result in part because charter schools are located in districts that do not mirror the statewide population, creating a poor comparison.

In addition, an aggregate analysis can be misleading because averages of student racial composition may mask variations among

---

[8]We use a logarithm of the odds approach to model the proportions as an additive function of a district mean and a charter school deviation. We used quasi-likelihood (McCullugh and Nelder, 1986) to estimate the parameters of the binomial regression model. Quasi-likelihood estimates the parameters using traditional generalized linear modeling techniques and then uses a methods of moments estimate to estimate an overdispersion parameter to account for school-to-school heterogeneity in the proportion of, say, black students that exceeds the variability of the binomial distribution. Models were restricted to elementary schools.

[9]Full results are available upon request from the authors.

charter schools. Many charter schools, including several of our case study schools, have student enrollments that are primarily Hispanic or black.[10] In this section, our research focuses on the question of whether individual charter schools represent the racial distribution of students within the district.

To carry out this analysis, we use two approaches. The first approach describes how student populations at individual charter schools tend to differ from the district populations, and the second approach compares charter schools to conventional public schools to determine if charter schools are more or less likely than conventional public schools to have different populations than the district. For the second approach, we restricted the sample to elementary schools because the distribution of school types, such as elementary, middle, high school, alternative, etc., differs across charters and conventional public schools, with conventional public schools having proportionately more traditionally configured secondary schools and proportionately fewer K–12 schools. These differences are likely to correspond to very different school-to-school heterogeneity for secondary school students. Thus, our comparisons include 137 charter elementary schools and 1,434 conventional public elementary schools. Below, we describe each approach in more detail.

The first approach compares the proportions of black, white, Hispanic, and Asian students separately. The analysis uses the odds, where the odds of being, say, black, equals the ratio of the proportion of black students to the proportion of students of other racial groups. First the analysis estimates the odds that a student in a charter school belongs to a racial group and compares that to the odds for the district to produce an odds ratio (OR). The analysis then estimates a 95 percent confidence interval for the OR.[11] A school is

---

[10]Students in those case study schools represented the demographics of their immediate neighborhoods.

[11]Standard methods provided an estimate of the standard errors of the OR when all proportions are greater than zero and less than one. If the proportion equaled zero or one for the school and the district had fewer than 9,000 students, then exact logistic regression methods provided a 95 percent confidence interval for the OR. If the proportion equaled zero or one for the school and the district had more than 9,000 students, exact methods provided a 95 percent confidence interval for the proportion in the school. Suppose the proportion is zero and let p_U denote the upper limit to the confidence interval and let o_U denote the corresponding odds. If o_D equals the odds

classified as having greater odds than the district if the lower limit of the 95 percent confidence interval exceeds 3/2. A school is classified as having lower odds than the district if the upper limit of the confidence interval is less than 2/3.[12]

The results are shown in Figure 2.5. The odds that a student is black at the charter school deviated from the odds for the district for about 31 percent of charter schools (11 percent lower and 20 percent

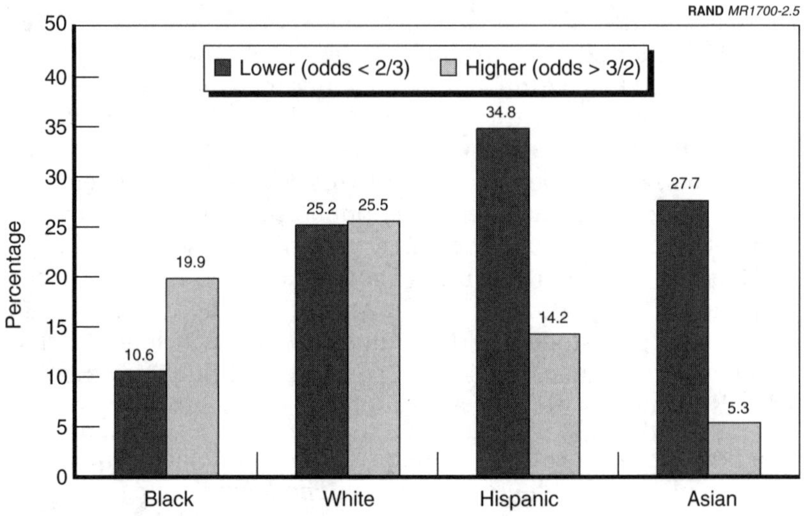

SOURCE: 2001–02 CBEDS data.

Figure 2.5—Percentage of Charter Schools That Deviate from the District Mean, by Racial Group and Direction

for the district, then the upper bound for the confidence interval for OR is o_U / o_D. We did not use exact methods in this situation because those methods become computationally infeasible with large samples, and with over 9,000 students the error in the district odds was sufficiently small to contribute little to the error in OR. The lower bound for the confidence interval is zero. An analogous procedure provided confidence intervals for schools where the proportion was one.

[12]Values of 3/2 or 2/3 represent a moderately large disagreement between school and district. However, other values could have been used for the OR classification (e.g., 1.2 or 2). When using these classifications, the results do not qualitatively change.

greater than the district). The odds that a student is white at the charter school deviated from the district for 51 percent of charter schools with roughly equal numbers lower than and greater than the district. In nearly 35 percent of charter schools the odds that a student is Hispanic were significantly lower than the odds for the district, whereas the odds for the charter school exceed those of the district in only 14 percent of schools. Similarly, the vast majority of the 33 percent of charter schools that deviate from the district in the odds that a student is Asian have lower odds (28 percent of charter schools).

We also estimate the proportions separately for conversion and start-up schools. The results are shown in Figures 2.6 and 2.7. The patterns for blacks, Hispanics, and Asians are similar for both conversion and start-up schools. However, conversion schools that deviate from district averages are likely to have fewer white students than the district, whereas start-up schools are likely to have more.

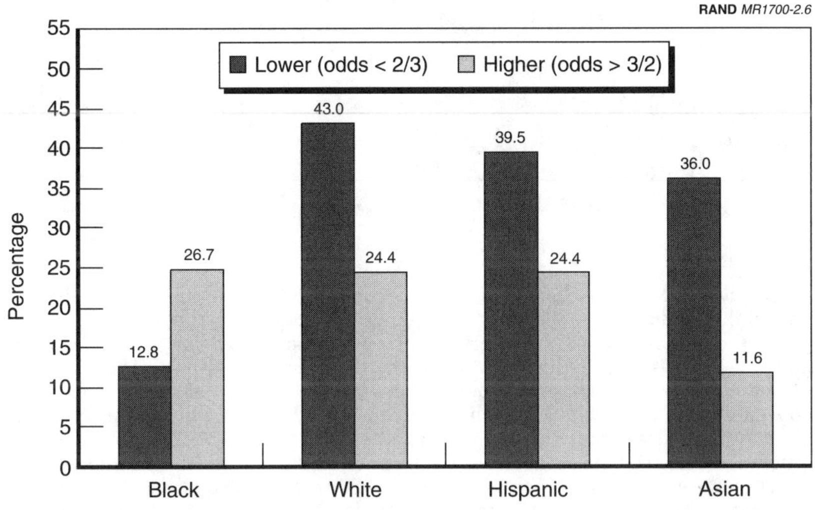

SOURCE: 2001–02 CBEDS data.

Figure 2.6—Percentage of Conversion Schools That Deviate from the District Mean, by Racial Group and Direction

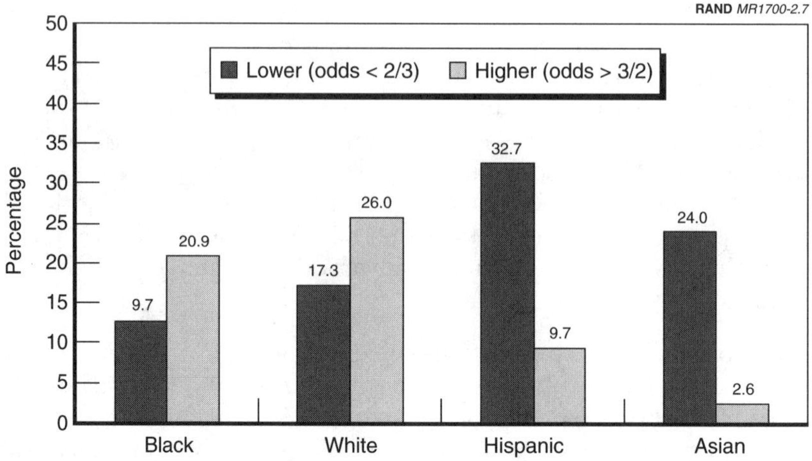

SOURCE: 2001–02 CBEDS data.

Figure 2.7—Percentage of Start-Up Schools That Deviate from the District Mean, by Racial Group and Direction

The second analysis uses the same methods to classify both charter and conventional public schools' racial populations as either greater than, less than, or similar to that of the district. We also calculate the proportion of schools that deviate from the district in both groups.[13]

---

[13]Conventional public schools tend to be much larger than charter schools. For example, the median size of conventional public schools is 607 students and the 25th percentile is 433 students. The corresponding numbers for charter schools are 261 and 141 students. The 75th percentile for charter schools is only 534. The width of a confidence interval is inversely proportional to the square root of school size. Thus, conventional public schools are more likely to deviate from the district according to our definition just because of larger school sizes. To account for this potential confounding effect, we both restricted the sample only to schools with between 126 and 550 students and weighted the conventional public schools so that the distribution of school sizes matched that of the charters. We decreased the weight of large conventional public schools and increased the weight of small conventional public schools. Schools were grouped by enrollment size by groups of 50 students. Within each group, the weight for charter schools is one and the weight for conventional public schools is

$$w = \frac{\text{number of charter schools in group i} \times \text{total number of conventional public schools}}{\text{total number of charter schools} \times \text{number of conventional public schools in group i}}$$

This analysis allows us to compare the relative representativeness of charter schools to conventional schools.

Figure 2.8 shows that conventional public schools are somewhat more likely than charter schools to deviate from the district proportion of blacks according to our measure. For whites and Hispanics, conventional public schools are slightly less likely to deviate and for Asians, conventional public schools are very slightly more likely to deviate. However, the difference between groups tends to be small.

Although these results are enlightening, additional research is needed to identify the reasons for these patterns. It is also important to recognize that student counts tell us nothing about the quality of integration in schools.

RAND *MR1700-2.8*

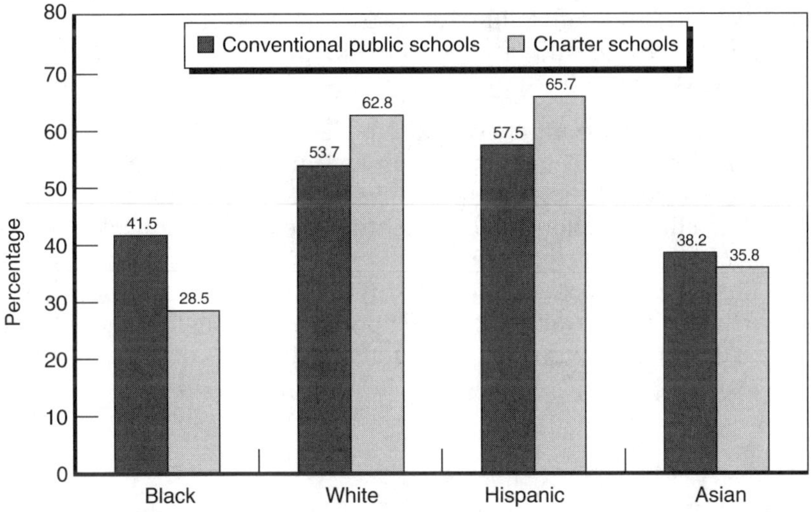

SOURCE: 2001–02 CBEDS data.

Figure 2.8—Percentage of Schools That Deviate from the District Mean, by Racial Group and Direction

---

We report only the weighted results, which tended to be similar to the results from the restricted sample.

SUMMARY

- According to survey responses, the charter school admissions processes differ little from admissions processes in matched conventional public schools. Charter schools are more likely than matched conventional public schools to interview applicants, but most charter school principals report that they use the interview for diagnostic purposes rather than to determine eligibility for admission.
- According to the principal surveys, charter schools are more likely than matched conventional public schools to focus their services on specific student populations.
- Comparing the average racial makeup of charter students to that of conventional public school students within the same school districts, and controlling for district heterogeneity, we find that charter school students are more likely to be black and less likely to be Hispanic or Asian, but no more or less likely to be white.
- It is also important to compare the level of integration in charter schools relative to that in conventional public schools. For blacks, conventional public schools are somewhat more likely than charter schools to deviate from the district's racial makeup according to our measure. For whites and Hispanics, conventional public schools are slightly less likely to deviate and for Asians, conventional public schools are very slightly more likely to deviate. However, the difference between groups tends to be small.

Chapter Three

ACADEMIC OUTCOMES

Richard Buddin and Ron Zimmer

INTRODUCTION

Many charter school advocates argue that charter schools will do a better job of teaching students, because they have more flexibility than conventional public schools that are burdened by central administration (Nathan, 1996; Miron and Nelson, 2000; Danner and Bowman, 2002; Koehler et al., 2003). This flexibility may translate into higher student achievement if charter schools or teachers better meet the needs of their students. In addition, other attributes of charter schools themselves may translate into a better learning environment that may indirectly improve student achievement.

But flexibility and a different learning environment do not automatically translate into improved achievement. Parents, principals, and teachers may have different incentives and opportunities in charter schools than in conventional public schools, but it is not clear whether these differences will lead to more rigorous instruction and higher academic test scores. Charter schools may pursue goals other than academic achievement or they may emphasize material that is not well measured on standard achievement tests. In short, charter schools are not designed to be rescaled replicas of conventional public schools. Indeed, they may differ from other schools in many dimensions that may have direct and indirect implications for student achievement.

The main goal of this chapter is to assess how well charter schools are doing on standardized achievement tests administered in California public schools. The analysis focuses on two main questions.

1. How does the academic performance of students in charter schools compare with the performance of comparable students in conventional public schools?
2. How does academic performance vary across students attending different types of charter schools? Do students in start-up schools do better or worse than students in conversion schools? Are students in schools with nonclassroom-based instruction performing at achievement levels above or below those in schools that offer instruction in a classroom setting?

The key issue for answering these types of questions is controlling for the academic potential of students attending different types of schools. In many cases, charter schools are in low-income, urban areas and serve a disproportionate share of at-risk students. The analysis must adjust for these types of factors that affect student performance to compare the performance of different types of schools.

The analysis relies on "naturally" occurring variation between students enrolled in charter and conventional public schools. Ideally, an experimental design might assign students randomly to different types of schools. This design would provide a thorough method for disentangling the contributions of different types of schools to academic achievement. This type of controlled experiment was not possible for evaluating charter schools. Indeed, an endemic feature of charter schools is that parents are able to choose between charter and conventional public schooling alternatives.

We used three approaches to compare the academic achievement of students in charter and conventional public schools. The approaches use different methods and datasets to adjust test scores for the characteristics of students attending various types of schools. Each approach has important limitations, and using all three gives a more complete picture of academic outcomes in charter schools than is possible with any single approach. Each approach is described in a separate section of the chapter.

- *School-level performance.* This approach compares school-level test scores between charter and conventional public schools over the past several years. The data include information on the demographic and socioeconomic status (SES) of students at each school.
- *Statewide nonlongitudinally linked student-level data.* Student test scores, demographic information, and SES data are available for all students for school years 1997–98 through 2001–02. We develop an analytic model to separate the effects of school type on student achievement after controlling for the attributes of students attending each type of school.
- *Longitudinally linked student-level data.* These data were available from only a few districts in the state, but they allow us to track student progress over time and across schools within each district.[1] Analysis of these data provides a value-added estimate of the contribution of charter schools to student achievement.
- *Competitive effects of charter schools.* An additional section examines the competitive effects of charter schools on conventional public schools in California. The chapter concludes with a summary of key findings.

SCHOOL-LEVEL PERFORMANCE

The first approach relies on a school-level comparison of the API for California schools from 1999 through 2002. The API is a composite measure of academic performance at each school. The numeric index or scale ranges from a low of 200 to a high of 1,000 and is constructed from the percentile scores of students in different grades and in different test areas.[2] The index initially relied on test infor-

---

[1]California's current student data system does not identify individual students. This limits the ability of researchers to track student progress from year to year or from school to school. Stecher and Bohrnstedt (2000) found that this data limitation complicated their efforts to assess how class size reduction affected student achievement in California and argued that student identifiers would be a major improvement to the state's data collection system.

[2]The API assigns weighting factors to students in different ranges of achievement. Scores are divided into five performance bands based on a 20 percentile range of scores. Weighting factors assign a 300 unit increase in weight for improving a student from the lowest (1 to 19th percentile) band to the next lowest (20 to 39th percentile) as

mation from the Stanford 9 achievement test, but the index has been modified in recent years to include test scores from the California Standards Test.[3] Changes in the composition of the API mean that the score reflects different factors from year to year. The CDE does compute a so-called "growth API" each year that is based on the index formula for the previous year. The calculated growth API is used to compute test score performance at a school for adjacent years on a common scale.

The CDE uses the API and growth API measures to assess the performance of schools in the state at a point in time and from year to year. Each school is given a target each year, and the state assigns various rewards and penalties for schools that depend on API scores. The scores are also well publicized and provide parents with a measure of how well their neighborhood school is doing relative to other nearby schools.

The CDE reports API scores as well as the demographic composition for each school. The school-level variables include ethnicity (percentage black, American Indian, Filipino, Hispanic or Latino, Pacific Islander, and white), the percentage of students who are English Learners, the percentage who participate in the federal free or reduced-price school lunch program, and the percentage who first attended the school in the present year. Academic achievement varies substantially across different types of students, so a school's API is tied to the background of the students attending the school.

A key weakness of the API measure for the charter analysis is the high degree of aggregation in the API. This aggregation may mask variations of important characteristics within a school. Therefore, a school-level analysis cannot capture the variation in how the school performs across different subjects and grades and provides only an imprecise control for the variation of student characteristics within

---

compared with only a 125 unit increase for improvement from the fourth band (60 to 79th percentile) to the highest band (80 to 99th percentile). The weights are designed to encourage schools to focus on low-achieving students. The complex formula of the API has been analyzed in Rogosa (2000), who shows that the measure is highly correlated with the percentage of students at a school who are at or above the 50th percentile for a weighted sum of test scores in various achievement areas.

[3]A detailed discussion of the computation of the index in each year is available from CDE at http://www.cde.ca.gov/psaa/api/.

the school. In essence, school-level data may not pick up the nuances of school characteristics and can provide only an incomplete picture of why outcomes can vary across schools.

A more pragmatic problem with the API measure is that the index is not computed for many charters schools in California. API was not computed for about 25 percent of charter schools whereas it was not computed for only 6 percent of conventional public schools. The above-normal missing rate for charter schools is related to several factors.

Many charter schools in California are new. API comparisons require two successive years of API scores, and the measure was introduced in 1999. The full panel of API scores is not available for many of the new schools.

The state does not compute the API for many charter schools because of an excess of parental waivers, which is defined as when the school's proportion of students excused at parent request compared to its Standardized Testing and Reporting (STAR) program enrollment on the first day of testing is equal to or greater than 10 percent. When a school's proportion of parental waivers is equal to or greater than 10 percent but less than 20 percent, the CDE conducts standard statistical tests to check whether the pupils tested at the school were representative of the entire school's population.[4]

In addition, CDE has changed the formula for computing API each year since the index was adopted in 1999, so the standard index cannot be compared over time. The growth API, which is based on the formula used in the previous year, can be used only to compare school-by-school changes in API for adjacent years.

Our API analysis compares *changes* in API scores for conventional public schools and charter schools conditional on *changes* in the demographics of students attending each school. The goal is to identify whether charter schools (or some types of charter schools)

---

[4]Many charters did not have a valid API because CDE determined that "an adult irregularity in testing procedure occurred at the school affecting five percent or more of pupils tested." The reasons for not computing an API score are provided by CDE at http://www.cde.ca.gov/psaa/api/api0102/growth/flags02g.htm.

are more or less likely to have achievement gains than are conventional public schools with a comparable composition of students.

An important limitation of the API analysis is that student achievement depends on a wider panoply of factors than student ethnicity, English Learner status, school lunch eligibility, and mobility. Parental involvement, previous educational experience, student motivation, and other factors are likely to affect how well a student does in school. Unfortunately, the list of individual factors collected by CDE is quite limited. The danger is that some schools may seem to be doing well (or poorly) given the changes in the observed factors affecting student achievement because the composition of the students is changing in some way that is not being measured.

On average, the year-to-year comparisons of API show increases in every year for both elementary and secondary schools. Table 3.1 shows that the size of the growth has declined over time and has consistently been much greater for elementary schools than for other schools. The median API in 2001 was 682 with the index ranging from 587 at the 25th percentile to 775 at the 75th percentile. Rogosa (2000) provides a metric for translating changes in student percentile scores into changes in API: Percentile point increases of one, two, three, and four in the Stanford 9 achievement scores imply increases of about 7, 17, 24, and 31 API points, respectively. The trends in API reflect a substantial improvement in measured student achievement, especially for elementary students.

To analyze the performance of charter schools, we used two approaches. We first compared the performance of all charter schools with API scores to the performance of all conventional public schools with an API score. A second approach compares the performance of

Table 3.1

Average Annual Growth in API for All California Schools, by Grade Level

Year	Elementary	Secondary
1999–00	38.4	18.0
2000–01	20.6	8.6
2001–02	14.9	5.1

NOTE: The table is constructed from CDE's API database.

all charter schools with API scores to conventional public schools with API scores within districts that have some charter schools.

The analysis that compares all charter schools to all conventional public schools shows that charter schools did neither better nor worse than conventional public schools over each of these years. The analysis compared changes in API scores for charter and conventional public schools after adjusting for changes in the demographics of students attending each school. The results show that the average growth rate for charter schools in each of the three years was not significantly different from that of other schools with similar changes in demographics.[5] The result was consistent for both elementary and secondary schools.[6]

Similarly, the results indicate that type of charter had no statistically significant bearing on API in any of the years. API growth did not differ between conversion and start-up schools. In addition, growth was insensitive to whether the charter school offered some nonclassroom-based instruction.[7]

However, this approach may have limitations, which suggests that we should also use an alternative approach to restrict the comparison. Suppose that charter schools are started in struggling districts with poor academic performance, and suppose that parents in high-performing districts have little incentive to create charter schools. Then, charter schools might do well relative to conventional public schools in districts with charter schools, but they might not do as well as schools in high-performing districts with no charter schools. This type of reasoning suggests that we need a second analysis to compare the performance of charter schools against that subset of conventional public schools in districts with some charter schools.

We redid the API analysis for the subset of districts with some charter schools. We again examined the changes in API score from year to

---

[5]The main analysis is based on school-to-school comparisons adjusting for the size of the school. Additional analysis was performed to assess whether the results were sensitive to school size. These results also suggested that charter schools had no statistically significant effect on API growth.

[6]The results are described in Appendix C and documented in Tables C.1 and C.3.

[7]The results are documented in Tables C.2 and C.4.

year. Although controlling for changes in school demographics and an annual trend, charter schools (or type of charter school) had no statistically significant effect on school performance in districts with some charter schools, which is consistent with the results in our first analysis. These API results show that the API performance of charter schools is neither better nor worse than that of comparable conventional public schools in districts with some charter schools or in all other districts in the state.

As discussed above, these API results should be viewed cautiously, since the measure is highly aggregated. Missing data for charter schools is also an important concern. In our view, both of these issues are better addressed with the individual-level data that are analyzed in the next two sections.

STATEWIDE NONLONGITUDINALLY LINKED STUDENT-LEVEL DATA

The remaining two approaches rely on individual test score data. The CDE collected individual-level Stanford 9 test scores and demographic data for all tested students in the state for the school years 1997–98 through 2001–02.[8] The database consists of about 20 million student records from 1998 through 2002. The file includes information on student ethnicity, English Learner status, school lunch eligibility, and student mobility as well as a measure of parental education. Parent's education is an important indication of a student's SES that may complement the information available for school lunch eligibility for low-end SES students.[9]

These individual-level data directly link a student's test score with his/her demographic information and provide a better adjustment for how these school composition factors affect school-level outcomes. The analysis provides a more accurate assessment of how

---

[8]Starting in 2002–03, CDE is switching from the Stanford 9 to the California Achievement Tests, 6th Edition (CAT/6). Therefore, our datasets include the full range of test scores for the Stanford 9.

[9]Students were asked to report the education level of the most educated parent or guardian with whom they reside. The categories were non–high school graduate, high school graduate, some college (including AA degree), college graduate, graduate school, and decline to state or unknown.

well charter schools are performing relative to conventional public schools after adjusting for the observed characteristics of students who attend each type of school.

The main limitation of the individual-level data available from the CDE is that they do not provide a student-level identifier to track year-to-year changes in a student's test scores. Individual identifiers are important for this type of analysis because they would allow the analysis to isolate a baseline achievement level for individual students. Baseline achievement would allow the analysis to better adjust for the unmeasured background of students that has an ongoing effect on their achievement.

Test scores are measured in terms of the percentile normal curve equivalent based on the Stanford 9 norming sample. If a student is in the 45th percentile for math in the 3rd grade and the 50th percentile for the 4th grade, then the student's achievement level is growing relative to his/her grade cohort.

Figure 3.1 shows the average percentile score for California students on the Stanford 9 reading and math tests for the years 1998 through 2002. On average, students in charter schools have lower scores than students in conventional public schools. This comparison may be misleading, however, because charter school students are not a random sample of public school students in the state, i.e., charter schools may enroll a disproportionate number of low-achieving students initially or be located in areas with high concentrations of at-risk students. These unadjusted numbers do not account for substantial differences in the background of conventional public school and charter school students.

To account for differences in student population that may affect student achievement, we estimate a statistical model that adjusts for the backgrounds of students attending different types of schools.[10] The results in Figure 3.2 show how charter school status affects test score for a representative student with the typical background characteristics of a California elementary or secondary school student. For

---

[10]The model controls for each student's ethnicity, parental education, English Learner status, and gender as well as whether the current year is the student's first at the school. The analysis also adjusts for overall trends in test score from year to year.

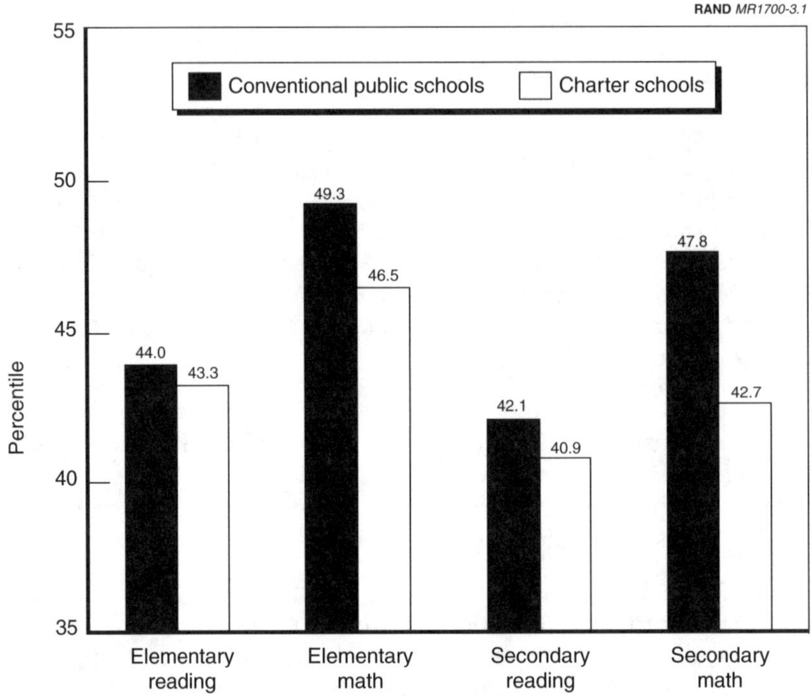

NOTES: The results are based on CDE statewide student-level data. In each case, the scores for students in charter schools are statistically different from those of students at conventional public schools at the 5 percent significance level.

Figure 3.1—Unadjusted Average Stanford 9 Test Scores for Conventional Public Schools and Charter Schools

example, the elementary school math score results mean that a typical elementary school student in the state would score 49.3 in a conventional public school and 47.8 in a charter school. The statistical model is designed to hold constant student background factors that affect achievement and isolate the effect of charter status on achievement.

Figure 3.2 shows that this adjustment for the differences in the background of charter school and conventional public school students narrows the gap between the schools' achievement scores in both reading and math, but some significant differences remain. The

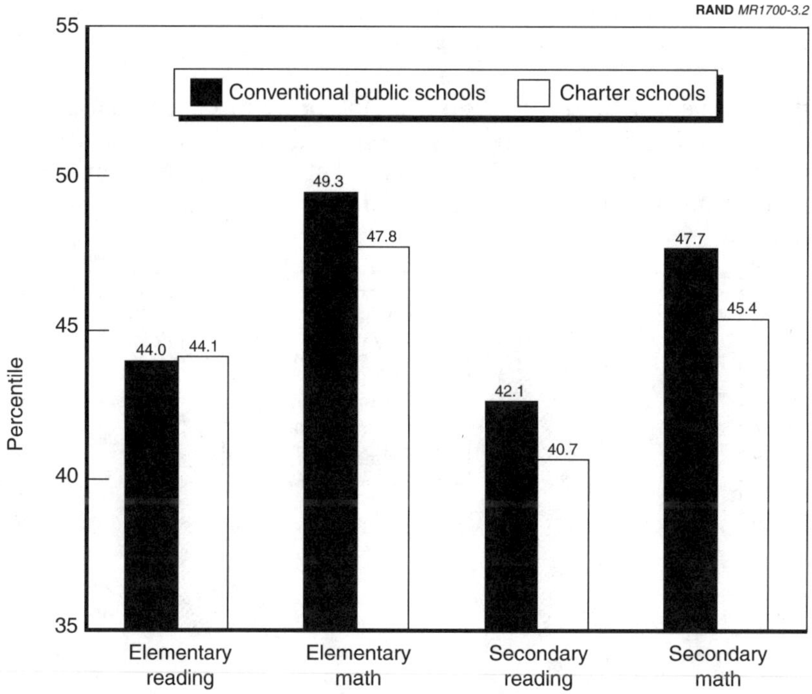

NOTES: The results are based on CDE statewide student-level data. The model is described in Appendix C and the regression results are reported in Tables C.5 and C.6. The differences in the figure reflect coefficients on charter schools that are significantly different from zero at the 5 percent level for elementary math and secondary reading and math. Elementary reading scores do not differ significantly between conventional public schools and charter schools.

Figure 3.2—Adjusted Average Stanford 9 Test Scores for Conventional Public Schools and Charter Schools

elementary school reading score for comparable students in conventional public schools and charter schools is virtually identical, but each of the other scores is lower for charter schools (these differences are statistically significant).

The performance of charter schools is clarified by considering academic achievement in different types of charter schools. Schools with a nonclassroom-based instruction component are much more prevalent in secondary schools than in elementary schools and much more common in start-up schools than in conversion schools.[11] Figure 3.3 shows that 72 percent of charter elementary school students are enrolled in conversion schools and most of those students are taught in schools classified as classroom-based. Start-up schools constitute 28 percent of charter school students in the elementary grades and about half of these students are enrolled in a school

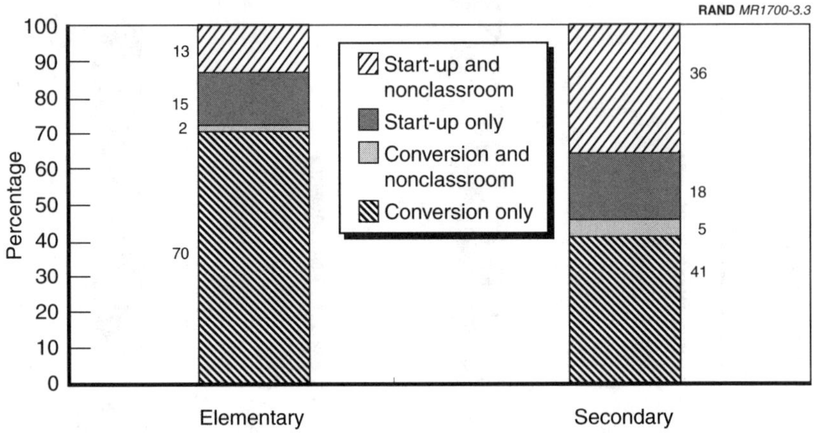

NOTE: The results are based on CDE statewide student-level data.

Figure 3.3—Distribution of Students, by Type of Charter School and Grade Level

---

[11]As mentioned in the introduction, a nonclassroom-based school does not necessarily mean that all students are instructed in nonclassroom-based settings or that the entire instruction of an individual student is entirely nonclassroom-based. Our list of nonclassroom-based schools consists of schools that are part of the state audit of such schools. These schools are audited if "1.) The charter school's pupils are engaged in education activities required of those pupils, and the pupils are under the immediate supervision and control of an employee of the charter school who is authorized to provide instruction to the pupils within the meaning of Education Code Section 47605(1); 2.) At least 80 percent of the instructional time offered at the charter school is at the school site; 3.) The charter school site is a facility that is used principally for classroom instruction; and 4.) The charter school requires its pupils to be in attendance at the school site at least 80 percent of the minimum instructional time required pursuant to Education Code Section 47612.5(a)(1)" (http://www.cde.cagov/charter/regs/sb740covlet0203df.htm).

offering at least some nonclassroom-based instruction. For secondary school students, start-up schools are more common than conversion schools, and two-thirds of start-up school students are enrolled in a school with nonclassroom-based instruction. Schools with a component of nonclassroom-based instruction are more common among conversion schools in secondary schools than in elementary schools.

The data do not distinguish whether a particular student uses any form of nonclassroom-based instruction, but we do know which charter schools offer these programs. The RAND charter school survey collected information on the percentage of students who receive instruction at the school site. Using these responses, we estimate that about 63 percent of students in a school with nonclassroom-based instruction receive at least some instruction away from the formal school site.

Charters that offer nonclassroom-based instruction have much lower adjusted test scores than either other charter schools or conventional public schools. Figure 3.4 shows that students in start-up schools with some nonclassroom-based instruction have test scores about 9 percentile points lower than comparable students in other start-up schools. A much smaller share of conversion schools have nonclassroom-based offerings, but students in these schools score about 5 and 8 points lower in reading and math, respectively, than comparable students in conversion schools with only classroom-based instruction.[12]

However, it should be noted that students in schools offering nonclassroom-based instruction may be different in unique ways from students in conventional public schools that are not captured by our control variables in the analysis. For instance, if such students have been pulled out of conventional public schools because of problems they have in traditional settings, then conventional school students

---

[12]It should also be noted that our analysis did not address the achievement of students receiving nonclassroom-based instruction outside the charter school setting (we had no evidence on the performance of these schools or students). Such students may differ markedly from students in nonclassroom-based charter schools and may have a different level of performance.

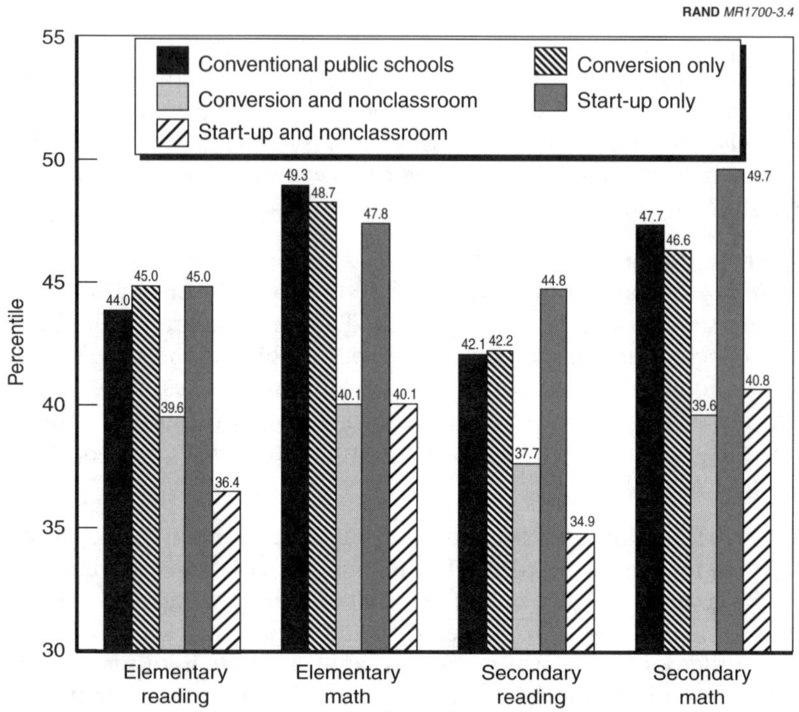

NOTES: The results are based on CDE statewide student-level data. The model is described in Appendix C and the regression results are reported in Tables C.7 and C.8. At the elementary level, math and reading scores for start-up schools only do not differ significantly at the 5 percent level from the scores in conventional public schools. At the secondary level, the reading scores for conversion schools only and conversion and nonclassroom-based do not differ significantly at the 5 percent level from reading scores at conventional public schools. All other comparisons between types of charter and conventional public schools are significant at the 5 percent level.

Figure 3.4—Adjusted Average Stanford 9 Test Scores for Conventional Public Schools, Conversion Schools, and Start-Up Schools, and Whether the Charter Schools Offer Nonclassroom-Based Instruction

who do not have these problems do not make a good comparison group.[13]

[13]The RAND charter school survey found that a statistically higher percentage of non-classroom-based charter schools focus on students with academic and discipline

Examining Figure 3.4, it is evident that the poor test results for students in nonclassroom-based charter schools pull down the average performance of students in charter schools and particularly in start-up schools. The figure shows that start-up secondary schools with only classroom-based instruction outperform conventional public schools by 2 to 3 percentile points in reading and math. In conversion and start-up elementary schools with classroom-based instruction only, test scores are 1 point higher in reading, but these schools trail behind conventional public schools by about 1 point in math (0.5 points lower in conversion schools and 1.5 points lower in start-up schools). Start-up schools appear lower-performing than conversion schools on average, because so many of them offer nonclassroom-based instruction. Among elementary schools with classroom-based instruction only, conversion and start-up schools perform similarly (the same scores for reading and start-up schools scoring 1 point lower in math), but start-up schools outpace conversion schools by about 3 points in both reading and math in secondary grades. In schools with some nonclassroom-based instruction, conversion schools do better than start-up schools in reading, start-up schools do better at secondary school math than conversion schools, and test scores are the same for both in elementary school math.

These results, however, do not take into account the tenure of the school. The number of charter schools has increased rapidly in recent years, and two factors suggest that new charter schools may have different academic outcomes than established ones. The first factor is an experience effect where new charter schools may have lower test scores initially as they refine their programs and build relationships with teachers and parents. This initial performance might not represent how well charter schools are doing in general and pull down the average performance of charter schools. The second factor is a vintage effect where new charter schools of a certain type are inherently different from the established ones. For example, new start-up schools might try a new teaching technique, so their

problems than classroom-based charter schools. This does not provide evidence of unobservable differences, but it does provide a possible explanation.

performance might be higher or lower than that of established start-up schools.

The test score evidence shows that the performance of new charter schools differs somewhat from that of established ones. For each type of charter school, we compared the scores of comparable students in charter schools that are less than three years old (new charter schools) with those of established ones. For elementary school students, new conversion schools have reading test scores about 1.4 percentage points lower than established conversion schools. In new start-up schools with nonclassroom-based instruction, test scores in reading and math were 4.9 and 7.0 points higher, respectively, than for similar established start-up schools with nonclassroom-based instruction. The scores for conversion schools with nonclassroom-based instruction (a very small group) and for start-up schools with only classroom-based instruction did not differ significantly between new and established schools.

At the secondary school level, new schools generally performed better than established ones. New conversion schools had test scores that were about 2 points higher than scores for similar established conversion schools. New start-up schools with nonclassroom-based instruction had test scores 5 and 4 points higher in reading and math, respectively, than similar established charter schools with nonclassroom-based instruction. In contrast, new start-up schools with only classroom-based instruction had test scores 1 and 2 points lower in reading and math, respectively, than scores for similar established start-up schools.

The relative success of many new charter schools raises important questions of how they differ from established schools and whether these strong achievement results will persist. Although the analysis controls for observed background factors that are known to affect achievement, the strong performance of new start-up schools may reflect important unobserved differences in the students attending new and established start-up schools. For example, if a greater number of motivated parents are drawn to new schools than to established ones, then this factor might explain the pattern that we observe in the data. These issues could be better separated if we had longitudinally linked student data and a baseline achievement measure for a student before entering a charter school. In the next section, we examine charter school performance with longitudinally linked student data, but we do not have a sufficient variety of charter school types to further explore the issues of new and established start-up schools.

LONGITUDINALLY LINKED STUDENT-LEVEL DATA

The last approach uses individual-level data collected for this study from six school districts with large numbers of charter schools. The variables are similar to those of the individual-level data provided by CDE, but the district data include an individual identifier that allows the tracking of individual achievement scores from year to year.[14]

The analysis using individual student tracking data provides our best estimates of the effects of charter schools. By tracking student scores over time, the analysis adjusts for unmeasured student factors that may predispose a student's success or failure in a particular school. The analysis assesses whether students in charter schools are performing better or worse than comparable students in conventional public schools, given each student's background characteristics. The approach isolates the contribution of charter status to student achievement.

A limitation of the approach is that the data were available for only a limited number of districts. As part of the study, we tried to acquire data containing student identifiers from ten prominent districts with charter schools, but four were unable to provide data. It was beyond the scope of the project to collect data from all districts with any charter schools.

The district-level data contain only a few charter secondary schools or schools offering nonclassroom-based instruction. Table 3.2 shows

---

[14]Rouse (1998a, 1998b) uses a similar methodology to examine the effects of private school vouchers on student achievement in Milwaukee. Hanushek et al. (2002) use longitudinally linked student data to examine the effects of charter schools on academic performance in Texas schools. They find that the academic performance of students in charter schools is not significantly different from that of similar students in conventional public schools.

Table 3.2

Profile of School Districts

Chula Vista Elementary
Elementary school students only 34 conventional, 4 conversion, 1 start-up No nonclassroom-based instruction In 2002, 13,138 conventional and 2,573 charter school students tested (grades 2 through 5)
Fresno Unified
Only 84 charter school students in secondary school, so restricted analysis to elementary schools 62 conventional, 2 conversion, 1 start-up Start-up offers nonclassroom-based instruction In 2002, 24,628 conventional and 482 charter school students tested (grades 2 through 5)
Los Angeles Unified
Substantial charter representation in elementary and secondary school Elementary: 476 conventional, 21 conversion, and 6 start-up No nonclassroom-based instruction In 2002, 234,107 conventional and 9,977 charter elementary school students tested
Napa Valley Unified
Few charter students in secondary schools (1 charter middle school), so restricted analysis to elementary schools 17 conventional, 3 conversion, 0 start-up No nonclassroom-based instruction In 2001, 3,856 conventional and 1,167 charter school students tested (grades 2 through 5)
San Diego City Unified
Substantial charter representation in elementary and secondary schools Elementary: 124 conventional, 2 conversion, and 6 start-up; secondary school: 44 conventional, 4 conversion, and 2 start-up 1 start-up school offers nonclassroom-based instruction In 2001, 38,686 conventional and 972 charter elementary school students tested and 44,378 conventional and 4,315 secondary school students tested
West Covina Unified
Only 1 charter school that includes grades K–8; no secondary school charters, so restricted analysis to elementary schools Elementary: 25 conventional, 0 conversion, and 1 start-up Start-up does not offer nonclassroom-based instruction In 2002, 2,833 conventional and 497 charter school students tested (grades 2 through 5)

NOTE: The table was constructed from district student-level data.

a profile of the districts that provided data with student-level identifiers. Only Los Angeles Unified and San Diego City Unified had substantial numbers of students in charter secondary schools, so our analysis was restricted to elementary schools except for those two districts. Nonclassroom-based instruction is offered only in one start-up school in Fresno Unified and one in San Diego City Unified. As a result, our analysis of the district-level data is not representative of the various charter schools in the state and we cannot compare the performance of schools offering classroom and nonclassroom-based instruction.

The results in Figure 3.5 show that the patterns of academic achievement are quite similar for conventional public and charter schools. In math, charter school students score 0.7 and 0.4 percentile points lower in elementary and secondary school, respectively, than do students with comparable backgrounds in conventional public schools. The reading scores of charter secondary school students are 0.7 percentile points higher than for comparable

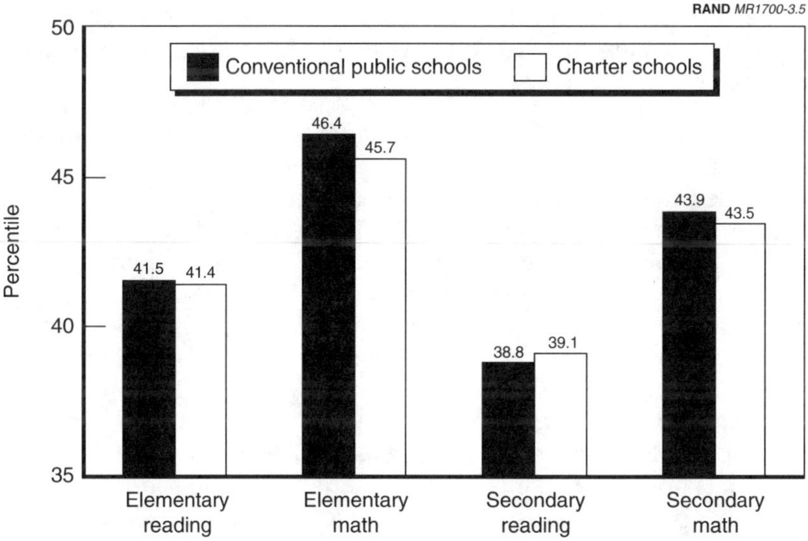

NOTES: The results are based on pooled district student-level data. The model is described in Appendix C and the regression results are reported in Table C.9. The difference between elementary school reading scores in conventional public and charter schools is not statistically significant at the 5 percent level. Other comparisons between conventional public and charter schools are statistically significant at the 5 percent level.

Figure 3.5—Adjusted Average Stanford 9 Test Scores for Pooled District Data

students in conventional public schools. For elementary school students, charter status has no statistically significant effect on reading scores.

Overall, the analysis shows that charter school students are keeping pace with comparable students in conventional public schools. The longitudinal tracking of students from school to school provides precise controls for student characteristics that affect student achievement. The district-level results suggest that much of the difference in achievement from statewide individual data (see Figure 3.2) was related to unobserved student factors. The stronger controls for these unobserved factors with longitudinal data virtually eliminate the small differences in the analysis of the statewide data. Longitudinal data are not available for the whole state, however, so some of the differences between Figures 3.2 and 3.5 may reflect differences between the districts providing longitudinal student data and other districts in the state.

We also examine how charter type affects academic performance using the student-level data from the school districts. The district contained few nonclassroom-based schools, so we were unable to examine this factor with the longitudinally linked data. Only in the large Los Angeles Unified and San Diego City Unified districts were there sufficient numbers of conversion and start-up schools to examine whether these types of schools had differing effects on student achievement. In both cases, the focus was restricted to elementary schools.[15] In Los Angeles Unified, elementary school reading scores for conversion and start-up schools were not statistically different from scores for conventional public schools. Math scores for conversion schools were 0.6 percentile point above the scores for conventional public schools, but start-up schools scored 1.5 percentile points below conventional public schools.[16] In San Diego City Unified, the gap between conversion and start-up schools is wider. In reading, conversion school students scored 2.2 percentile points higher than comparable students in conventional public schools,

[15]The details are documented in Appendix C, and the results are reported in Table C.15.

[16]The start-up school effect in math is measured imprecisely, so the effect is not significantly different from that of conventional public schools. The start-up school effect is significantly less than that of conversion schools, however.

whereas start-up school students scored 1.7 percentile points lower than comparable students in conventional public schools. Math students in start-up schools scored about 2.9 percentile points lower than comparable students in either conversion or conventional public schools.

Summarizing across the three methods, we generally found comparable scores for charter schools relative to conventional public schools. Only when charter schools are broken down by charter type do significant differences appear. Most strikingly, we found that nonclassroom-based schools performed significantly lower than conventional public schools and classroom-based schools performed slightly higher in certain subjects.

However, it should be noted that our analysis examines student achievement only as measured by test scores. Obviously, the quality of schools cannot be entirely captured through test scores. Other important indicators of school performance could include dropout rates or parental satisfaction.[17] Because of data limitations and budget constraints, we were not able to focus on these outcomes.[18]

COMPETITIVE EFFECT OF CHARTER SCHOOLS

A potential factor distorting the measured performance of charter schools is the effect that they may have on the performance of conventional public schools. Charter school advocates often argue that competitive pressure from charter schools may induce conventional public schools to improve their performance (Bettinger, 2002). If achievement does increase at conventional public schools, then the gap between charter and conventional public school achievement

---

[17]Gill et al. (2001) suggest that by examining parental satisfaction, it is possible to capture the indirect effects of a variety of dimensions including discipline, safety, and opportunities for parental involvement. In their review of the literature, they find that charter schools generally have a very high level of parental satisfaction relative to conventional schools. However, there is a possible selection bias in these prior studies that is generally not accounted for. Charter school parents choose the school their children attend, whereas parents in conventional public schools often take a more passive role in school selection. Therefore, charter school parents may be justifying their choice when rating their parental satisfaction.

[18]However, our survey suggested that there are no significant differences in dropout rates between charter and conventional public schools.

scores would understate the total effect of charter schools on student achievement.

There is little direct evidence on how conventional public schools respond to charters. Bettinger (2002) examines the effects of Michigan charter schools on neighboring pubic schools and finds little or no changes in test scores. Hsieh and Urquiola (2002) examined various measures of student achievement and found no evidence that greater school choice in a voucher program in Chile increased student performance. Cullen et al. (2000) analyzed the effects of open enrollment on high school dropout rates in Chicago public schools. They find that students move in response to open enrollment but that choice does not alter the overall tendency of students to complete high school.

In California, a conventional public school may reexamine its educational program if students are drawn to a nearby charter. Any substantive changes may be limited by school resources, personnel, and district policies, however, so there is no compelling reason to expect a quick transformation.[19]

Because few students enroll in charters, few conventional public schools face the direct pressure of their students leaving for a charter school alternative. Only about 38 percent of all students are enrolled in a district with at least one charter school. The average share of students enrolled in charter schools for these districts is only 3.3 percent. In total, only about 2.5 percent of elementary and secondary school students are enrolled in charter schools.

The indirect effects of charter schools on conventional public schools are harder to quantify. The success of a distant charter school or the mere threat of a charter school movement could create some pressure for improved performance of a conventional public

---

[19]In a review of the literature, Gill et al. (2001) suggest that the competitive effects can manifest in four ways: (1) Market competition of students (and the associated resources) will induce improvement within the schools, (2) innovation will induce imitation, (3) choice programs will drain conventional public schools of the high-achieving students and, therefore, will reduce the positive peer effects within these schools, and (4) choice programs will permit the most motivated parents to exit the system, reducing parental pressure to improve current conventional public schools.

school. These indirect pressures are confounded with other pressures from parents, teachers, administrators, and public officials, however, so the net effect of remote or potential charter schools on conventional public schools is unclear.

One of the most measurable ways in which charter schools can influence conventional public schools is through the competition for students. From our survey, 49.3 percent of our matched conventional public schools said that they have students in the local attendance area who attend charter schools. This competition may stimulate low-performing conventional public schools to improve through operational changes. Table 3.3 displays the responses from matched conventional public schools to a survey question asking what type of an effect charter schools have had on several categories. Generally, conventional public school principals responded that charter schools have had very little effect across the different categories. Only two categories—financial security and ability to attract and retain students—had more than 10 percent of conventional public schools say that charter schools had something other than "no effect."

We also asked the matched conventional public school principals if the charter schools have caused any changes in the operational policies of the school or district. Table 3.4 displays the responses. Again, the principals generally responded that charter schools have not had

Table 3.3

The Effect of Charter Schools on Matched Conventional Public Schools

		How Have Charter Schools Affected Your School? (%)				
	No.	Very Positive	Somewhat Positive	No Effect	Somewhat Negative	Very Negative
Financial security	177	0.6	0.8	81.9	14.4	5.5
Ability to acquire necessary resources	177	0.0	0.5	93.1	6.2	0.2
Teacher recruitment and retention	177	0.0	0.4	94.1	4.4	1.1
Ability to attract and retain students	177	0.0	1.2	84.6	12.7	1.4
Ability to educate students	177	0.0	3.4	95.2	1.4	0.0
Parental satisfaction	178	0.6	7.9	88.0	3.4	0.0

SOURCES: 2002 RAND charter school and matched conventional public school surveys.

Table 3.4

The Effect of Charter Schools on Matched Conventional Public Schools or Their Respective Districts

Effect	No.	% Agree
Restructured compensation to teachers	82	4.7
Restructured hiring/firing/discipline policies of teachers	88	6.2
Changed curriculum	91	4.8
Changed instructional practices	90	11.6
Changed professional development	90	6.7

SOURCES: 2002 RAND charter school and matched conventional public school surveys.

much effect on operational practices. The only category in which more than 10 percent of conventional public schools have made changes is instructional practices, with 11.6 percent of principals responding that they had made a change.

Together, Tables 3.3 and 3.4 suggest that conventional public schools have not felt much of a competitive effect from charter schools and have not changed their operational practices significantly. This would suggest that there would be very little competitive effects in the student achievement of conventional public schools, which provides more confidence in the results provided in this chapter.

SUMMARY

School-Level Analysis of API Scores

- The school-level API analysis does not indicate a significant difference between charter and conventional public schools. However, many charter schools were missing from the dataset and the aggregation at the school level reduces the precision of our analysis.

Statewide Nonlongitudinal Student Data

- The statewide student-level analysis shows that charter elementary and secondary school students are performing slightly lower than their conventional public school counterparts in math.

They have comparable reading scores at the elementary grade level, but they do slightly worse at the secondary grade level.

- The results also show that the performance of charter schools varies substantially with the type of classroom offerings available. Charter schools that offer nonclassroom-based instruction have much lower test scores for comparable students than either conventional public schools or other charter schools.
- Secondary school students in start-up schools with only classroom-based instruction outperform their counterparts in both conventional public schools and conversion schools.
- Elementary school reading scores for comparable students in conversion and start-up schools are 1 percentile point higher than for comparable conventional public school students, but elementary school math scores are about 1 point lower for these charter schools than for conventional public schools.
- Achievement results differed little with charter age for most types of schools. Among start-ups with nonclassroom-based instruction, however, students in new schools were outperforming comparable students in established schools.

Longitudinally Linked Student Data

- Charter school students tended to do slightly worse in math than comparable students in both elementary and secondary schools.
- In reading, charter secondary school students scored slightly higher than comparable students in conventional public schools, but charter school status has no statistically significant effect on elementary school reading scores. Even the statistically significant difference in achievement by charter status is less than 1 percentile point, however, so the main theme of the analysis is that charter schools are keeping pace with conventional public schools.
- Data limitations meant that district-level data were not useful for comparing different types of charters.

Competitive Effects of Charter Schools

- Public school principals reported that charter schools had no effect on their operations.

Chapter Four

AUTHORIZATION, GOVERNANCE, AND OVERSIGHT OF CHARTER SCHOOLS

Derrick Chau, Glenn Daley, and Brian Gill

INTRODUCTION

Chapter Two described the students who go to charter schools, and Chapter Three reported on their academic performance. This chapter turns to our third research question, which addresses the relationship between chartering authorities and the charter schools that they authorize. One rationale underlying the charter school law is that these schools are to have more operational autonomy than conventional public schools in exchange for greater accountability for results. The governance and oversight sections of this chapter directly explore this issue by investigating the patterns of autonomy and accountability of charter schools relative to their chartering authorities.

The analysis in this chapter relies primarily on results from the survey of chartering authorities and secondarily on the interviews conducted as part of the case studies of charter schools and chartering authorities.[1] To a lesser extent, we also use results from the surveys of charter schools and conventional public schools to provide alternative perspectives on governance and oversight.[2]

---

[1]In both the survey responses and the interviews, chartering authority respondents may be describing their relationships with multiple charter schools.

[2]See Appendix A for further descriptions of these surveys and Appendix B for the mechanisms for examining differences.

AUTHORIZATION OF CHARTER SCHOOLS

Chartering authorities approve the creation of charter schools—a pivotal role in implementing charter school policy. This section describes the chartering authorities and the processes they use to review petitions.[3] It presents data on the outcome of charter school petitions, including rates of approval and denial. A hallmark of charter school policy is that charters can be revoked, so this section also examines the revocation of charters and the closure of charter schools.

Description of Chartering Authorities

Unlike charter school laws in some states (e.g., Massachusetts), California's law allows for more than one type of chartering authority. Potential chartering authorities include school districts, county boards of education, and the state board of education. The state board of education can also charter entire school districts.[4] Until recent changes in the legislation, school districts could even grant charters to schools operating outside districts' geographic boundaries.

Because the California charter school law allows for different types of chartering authorities, understanding the chartering process requires an assessment of the level of charter-granting activity for each type of organization. Figure 4.1 shows that local school districts grant the vast majority of the charters. County boards of education and the state board of education (SBE) have granted only a small percentage of charters. These percentages are similar to those reported in the previous evaluation of California's charter schools and are not surprising, given that changes in the law in 1998 require that charter

---

[3]Section 47605 in the charter school law presents general requirements for submitting and reviewing charter petitions.

[4]California charter school law allows for the creation of districtwide charters in which a district can convert all of its schools to charter schools under certain conditions (see charter school legislation, section 47606). These charter districts can choose to receive funding through either the existing system or charter block grants (see legislation, section 47664). One charter district was included as a case study, which will be referred to when applicable. The evaluation of charter districts was not a focus of this study. This chapter concentrates on the relationship between chartering authorities and individual schools.

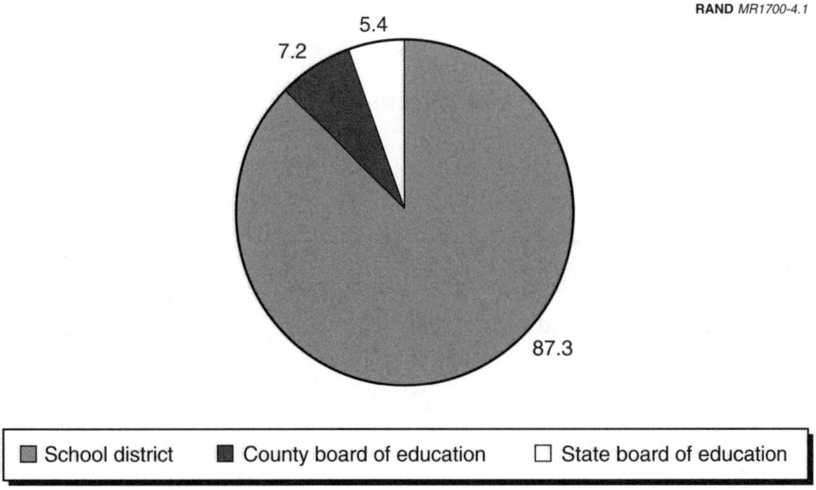

SOURCE: State board of education.
NOTE: The state board of education has granted individual charters and districtwide charters.

Figure 4.1—Percentage of Charters Granted by Different Chartering Authorities (n = 108)

applicants apply to a local school district before applying to a county or state board of education. The SBE can grant charters directly to individual schools and to schools included in districtwide charters. Fifteen schools are operating under seven SBE-approved districtwide charters. The SBE has granted charters directly to only three schools.

California's charter school law is one of the few in the nation that allows local school districts to authorize charter schools outside district boundaries. In the survey of charter school principals, 5.6 percent responded that their schools are operating outside the geographic boundaries of their authorizing school district. Because of concerns over the ability of chartering authorities to oversee such charter schools, the state recently revised the charter school legislation (AB 1994) to limit charters to the boundaries of the chartering authority. Existing charter schools must comply with these changes by either the end of their current charter terms or July 1, 2005, whichever is later. Charter schools operating outside the boundaries of their charter authorizers must apply for a new charter to the correct local district or county or to the state board of education.

The charter-granting activity of chartering authorities can also be assessed by examining how many charters each chartering authority grants. As Table 4.1 shows, most chartering authorities have approved only one charter school. However, a handful of chartering authorities have authorized a large percentage of the charter schools in California. Although only four of the responding chartering authorities have authorized six or more charter schools each, those four authorities oversee the same number of charter schools as the 77 responding authorities with only one charter school. Authorities that have authorized six or more schools are mostly school districts in urban areas that serve large student populations.

Table 4.1

Number of Operating Charter Schools Authorized by Chartering Authorities

No. Authorized	% of Chartering Authorities (n = 113)
1	68.5
2	16.7
3	5.6
4	3.7
5	1.9
6 or more	3.7

SOURCE: 2002 RAND chartering authority survey.

Development and Evaluation of Charter Petitions

Chartering authorities have taken a variety of approaches to the petition and evaluation process, and these have evolved. The charter school law does not specify the role of authorities during the petition and evaluation process, but it outlines the criteria that should be used to evaluate charter petitions.

The development of a charter petition often involves informal interactions between petitioners and the chartering authority before the official submission of the petition. Prospective charter school operators sometimes test the waters by meeting with potential chartering authorities to determine whether the authorities are amenable to sponsoring a charter school. After identifying a potential chartering authority, petitioners may collaborate with it during the drafting of the petition, so that substantial agreement exists before formal submission.[5]

Chartering authorities sometimes take the initiative in the development and revision of charter petitions. One chartering authority in our case studies holds regular informational meetings for people interested in developing a charter school. Developers who draft charter petitions also meet regularly with personnel in this chartering authority. In one charter school we visited, the local school district was the driving force in the development of the charter petition. Personnel in the local district decided to design a "dream school" from the ground up; those personnel were employed by the district to research and write the charter petition and then became the organizers of the charter school when it was approved.

Chartering authorities use criteria based on charter school legislation and develop their own criteria to evaluate charter petitions. The charter school legislation identifies 15 elements required in charter petitions; examples include a description of the educational program, the measurable pupil outcomes to be assessed, and the governance structure.[6] Survey responses indicate that approximately half of chartering authorities have written guidelines or a scoring system to determine whether to approve charter petitions. In our case studies, some of the chartering authorities based their evaluation guidelines and scoring systems on the legislation; others developed their own guidelines. Some did not formalize any guidelines because they did not expect to receive more petitions than the one that was approved. At the end of the process, the charter school legislation requires public hearings and formal action by the governing board of the chartering authority to approve a charter petition.[7]

---

[5]These findings are derived from the case studies rather than the survey, so we cannot tell how many of the state's charter school petitioners have followed such strategies.

[6]See section 47605 in the Education Code, which lists all 15 elements.

[7]See section 47605.b in the Education Code.

In our case studies, chartering authorities often depended on personnel outside the governing boards, with expertise in such areas as finances and educational programs, to investigate the potential of charter petitions and then present findings to the governing boards for decision. Public hearings were generally used as a way to involve parents, community members, and teachers' union representatives in the evaluation of petitions.

Case study respondents indicated that the processes used to evaluate charter petitions have changed over time. They indicated that experience has helped their chartering authorities identify potential problems with charter petitions. Changes in the charter law, such as funding and facilities requirements, have also changed the evaluation process. Chartering authorities that grant many charters have developed more formal structures and rules for the evaluation of petitions.

The Outcomes of Charter Petitions

The majority of chartering authorities with operating charter schools—almost 64 percent—have received only one or two charter petitions, as shown in Figure 4.2,[8] whereas only a few chartering authorities have received a large proportion of the total number of petitions. The three chartering authorities that have received nine or more petitions account for 126 petitions, or 33 percent of the petitions in our sample. The chartering authorities that have received 14 or more petitions are all school districts that operate a large number of conventional public schools.

Of the charter petitions submitted, about 69 percent have been approved, as shown in Table 4.2. About 56 percent of approved petitions and are still operating. About 9 percent of petitions had been approved but the schools were not yet operating at the time of our

---

[8]Chartering authority surveys were distributed only to authorities that currently have operating charter schools. Districts and counties that do not have operating charter schools may also have received charter petitions, but our sample does not include these. For instance, a principal in one of our case studies explained that his charter had been denied by two school districts before it was approved by a county board of education. Those two school districts were not surveyed because they do not have charter schools; however, they have received at least one charter petition.

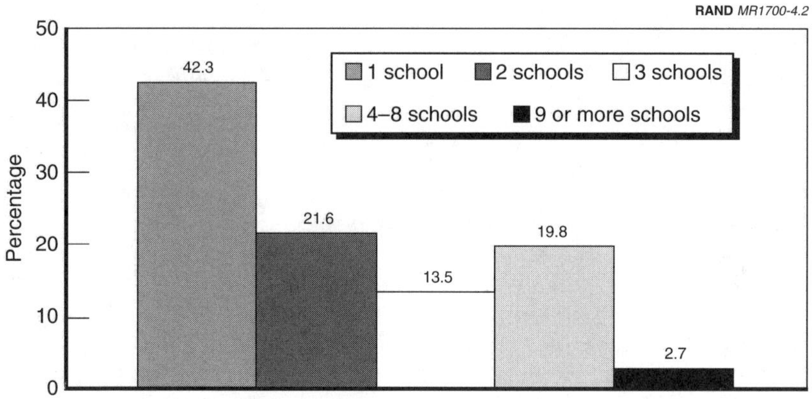

SOURCE: 2002 RAND chartering authority survey.
Sample size: 113 chartering authorities.

Figure 4.2—Distribution of the Chartering Authorities, by Number of Petitions Received

Table 4.2

Outcome and Number of Petitions Submitted to Chartering Authorities That Have Operating Charter Schools

Outcome of Petition	No. of Petitions	% of Petitions
Approved and still operating	228	56.4
Approved but not yet operating	36	8.9
Approved but later revoked	5	1.2
Approved but later closed	12	3.0
Pending	49	12.1
Denied	42	10.4
Not valid because it was withdrawn before approval	29	7.2
Other	3	0.7

SOURCE: 2002 RAND chartering authority survey.

NOTE. The total number of charter petitions for this item (404) was based on the sum of all responses to the outcomes of petitions. This is greater than the number of petitions cited in Table 4.1 (380). Percentages were based on the total for this item (404).

Sample size: 108 chartering authorities.

survey. These are most likely charter schools that were approved after the fall of 2001 and did not begin to serve students until the fall of 2002. Issues related to the denial of petitions as well as the revocation or closing of charter schools are discussed in the following sections.

Closed or Revoked Charter Schools

As shown in Table 4.2, only about 4 percent of approved charter petitions have resulted in closed schools or revoked charters.[9] This study did not investigate the reasons for charter school closures as distinct from revocations. However, a national report on charter school closures found that most in California resulted from mismanagement or financial problems (Center for Education Reform, 2003). In our survey of chartering authorities, we learned that the situations that have prompted revocations included financial irregularities, failure to comply with terms of the charter, failure to comply with state or federal laws, and parental complaints.

Denied Charter Petitions

Chartering authorities with operating charter schools have denied approximately 10 percent of charter petitions. However, this percentage understates the true rate of denials, because the survey does not include chartering authorities that have denied all applications. This percentage also masks informal denials and petitions that were never formally submitted because they were informally discouraged or rejected during the presubmission interactions between petitioners and chartering authorities.

In the original 1992 charter school law, chartering authorities were not required to provide reasons for denying charters. Amendments to the law now require written reasons for denial of a charter petition, describing the specific facts to support at least one of five reasons for denial presented in Education Code 47605.b. These reasons and their frequencies of use appear in Table 4.3. The five reasons for

[9]The revocation of a charter does not necessarily mean that the school ceases to exist; some conversion schools have been converted back to conventional public schools.

Table 4.3

Number of Times Chartering Authorities with Operating Charter Schools Cited Reasons for Denying Petitions

Reason for Denial	No. of Times Reason Used to Deny a Petition
Unsound educational program	26
Demonstrably unlikely to succeed	24
Did not contain reasonably comprehensive descriptions of the required 15 elements (A–O elements)[a]	22
Did not contain an affirmation of each of the four conditions described in Education Code 47605.d[b]	11
Inadequate number of required signatures	2
Other	3

SOURCE: 2002 RAND chartering authority survey.

NOTE: Chartering authorities could cite multiple reasons for the denial of petitions.

[a]Refers to the 15 required elements of a charter petition as specified in Education Code 47605, including descriptions of the educational program, the governance structure, and the method by which student outcomes will be measured.

[b]Refers to the conditions described in Education Code 47605.d, which include operating principles that are nonsectarian and nondiscriminatory as well as requirements related to open student enrollment and admissions.

denial are rather broad to allow chartering authorities latitude in their decisions. Additional research would be necessary to elaborate further on specific reasons for the denial of petitions.

GOVERNANCE OF CHARTER SCHOOLS

We turn now to the governance of charter schools in terms of their relationships with chartering authorities. A main policy element of the charter school law is the greater governing responsibility and freedom allowed to these schools as compared to conventional public schools. One indicator of the effective implementation of the charter school law would be schools that are indeed more autonomous than their conventional public school counterparts. Our research finds that charter schools do tend to have more autonomy but that the degree of such autonomy varies among schools.

Dependent and Independent Charter Schools

The terms "dependent" and "independent" do not appear in the charter school law and have no formal definitions, yet they are widely used in California to describe relationships that charter schools have with their chartering authorities. In preliminary interviews and discussions with our advisory panel of charter school experts, we allowed respondents to provide their own definitions of dependent and independent schools. This allowed the respondents to answer items relating to governance and oversight differently for their dependent and independent charter schools.[10]

As part of our survey, we did ask the chartering authorities to define dependent and independent charter schools. In their responses, many defined dependent charter schools as relying on the district for services and receiving funds through the district. Many authorities defined independent charters as being fiscally autonomous from their chartering authorities and receiving funds directly from the state. These definitions were similar to the ones in the previous evaluation of California's charter schools, which stated that dependent charter schools were subject to district policies and procedures, except where they sought waivers, whereas independent charter schools made most of their own programmatic, personnel, and financial decisions. Although neither legally specified nor universally acknowledged, these working definitions appear to be justified by our findings on charter school operations discussed in following sections.

Our survey of chartering authorities indicates that approximately 43 percent define their charter schools as either dependent or independent. The other 57 percent do not define their relationships with charter schools using these terms. Only about 7 percent of chartering authorities have granted charters to both dependent and independent charter schools, not surprising since most chartering au-

[10]We grouped undefined charter schools with independent charter schools to reduce the complexity of survey items for respondents. If undefined charter schools are more like dependent than independent schools, this would understate any differences between them. However, we found strong differences between them in spite of this potential underestimation. In survey questions on governance, we did not make distinctions between start-up and conventional public schools or between classroom-based and nonclassroom-based schools.

thorities have granted only one charter. About 18 percent of chartering authorities have only independent charter schools, and a similar percentage have only dependent charter schools.

Legal Liability in Charter Schools

The greater independence envisioned for charter schools also means greater responsibility, which also implies liability. Liability affects governance, since the party bearing the liability will typically insist on more authority. When the charter school law was passed in 1992, charter schools were new organizations whose legal relationships with the existing education system had no clear precedent.

One means of clarifying these relationships was the development of the memorandum of understanding (MOU), usually separate documents from the charters, that define liability of charter schools and their chartering authorities. About 67 percent of charter schools responded that they have MOUs with their chartering authorities. In interviews, personnel in charter schools and chartering authorities explained that MOUs are designed to be comprehensive in addressing issues related to the regular operation of schools. Some of the issues addressed in these MOUs pertain to personnel, facilities, special education, fiscal control, and school governance. In several case studies, charter school principals stated that they do not have MOUs with their chartering authorities, and legal liability for problems fell on the schools.

Table 4.4 indicates that independent or undefined charter schools are much more likely than the chartering authority to assume liability.[11] In strong contrast, legal liability for dependent charter schools either falls mostly on chartering authorities or is shared by both schools and authorities.

Special education claims are the area where both types of charter schools accept the least liability relative to their chartering authorities. Legal liability surrounding special education claims may differ from liability in the other areas because Special Education Learning

[11]These answers represent the perceptions of survey respondents and are not legal expert opinions or case decisions. Very little case law has developed in this area, so these perceptions of relative liability are largely untested in court.

Table 4.4

Placement of Legal Liability Between Charter Schools and Chartering Authorities for a Variety of Areas According to the Charter, Memorandum of Understanding, or Other Written Policies

(in percent)

	Charter School	Chartering Authority	Both	Not Specified in Writing	Don't Know
Independent or Undefined Charter Schools (n = 86)[a]					
Health and safety issues	67.4	13.9	13.9	4.6	0
Harassment claims	66.3	13.9	10.5	8.1	1.2
Financial obligations	64.4	19.5	13.8	1.2	1.2
Civil rights issues	62.8	13.9	12.8	9.3	1.2
Special education claims	34.9	31.4	32.6	1.2	0
Dependent Charter Schools (n = 33)					
Health and safety issues	27.3	30.3	33.3	3.0	6.1
Harassment claims	28.1	28.1	18.7	18.7	6.2
Financial obligations	33.3	35.4	24.2	3.0	3.0
Civil rights issues	27.2	30.3	18.1	18.1	6.0
Special education claims	9.1	39.4	39.4	6.1	6.1

SOURCE: 2002 RAND chartering authority survey.

[a]In the survey, chartering authorities responded to the questions for dependent and independent or undefined charter schools. Many chartering authorities do not define charter schools as either dependent or independent.

Plan Areas (SELPAs), rather than chartering authorities, have responsibility for governing special education for most charter schools. Issues related to special education services and governance are discussed in greater detail in Chapter Eight.

Charter School Autonomy

Our surveys asked chartering authorities and school principals about their levels of control over various areas of school operations. This section first presents results from the survey of chartering authorities, which indicate that chartering authorities overall exercise less control over charter schools than over conventional public schools. Chartering authorities also have less control over all areas of governance for independent charter schools than for dependent ones. The section ends with results from principals confirming that charter schools overall are provided with greater autonomy than conventional public schools.

Table 4.5 shows that chartering authorities exercise less control over charter schools than over conventional public schools. The small percentages of chartering authorities that exercise more control over

Table 4.5

Levels of Chartering Authority Control over Independent and Dependent Charter Schools Compared to Control over Conventional Public Schools for Different Types of School Operations
(percentage of chartering authorities responding for each type of charter school)

	No.	No Control	Less Control	Same Control	More Control
Independent					
Student disciplinary policies*	87	60.9	23.0	16.1	0
Professional development	87	56.3	27.6	16.1	0
Staff hiring, discipline, and dismissal*	87	55.2	23.0	21.9	0
Student assessment policies except state-mandated tests*	87	49.4	23.0	27.6	0
Staff salaries and benefits*	87	47.1	20.7	32.2	1.1
Budgetary expenses, other than salaries and benefits*	87	47.1	20.7	32.2	0
Curriculum**	86	40.7	39.5	19.8	0
Special education*	86	23.3	22.1	50.0	4.7
Dependent					
Student disciplinary policies*	3	24.2	36.3	36.3	3.0
Professional development	3	27.3	30.3	39.4	3.0
Staff hiring, discipline, and dismissal*	3	15.2	33.3	45.5	6.1
Student assessment policies except state-mandated tests*	3	5.1	33.3	48.5	3.0
Staff salaries and benefits*	33	21.2	18.2	54.6	6.1
Budgetary expenses, other than salaries and benefits*	32	12.5	21.9	55.3	9.4
Curriculum**	33	18.2	39.4	39.4	3.0
Special education*	33	0	12.1	75.8	12.1

SOURCE: 2002 RAND chartering authority survey.

*Indicates percentages that are statistically different from matched conventional public school percentages at the 1 percent level.

**Indicates percentages that are statistically different from matched conventional public school percentages at the 5 percent level.

charter schools indicate that most charter schools have at least the same amount of control over various school operations as conventional public schools do. Especially in the areas of student disciplinary policies and professional development, the majority of chartering authorities are providing charter schools with more control than conventional public schools.

Chartering authorities exercise more control over dependent charter schools than over independent and undefined charter schools. For both dependent and independent schools, chartering authorities retain a greater degree of control over special education than other areas. In addition, about 70 percent of chartering authorities with dependent charter schools require collective bargaining contracts for their school teachers, whereas only about 26 percent of chartering authorities with independent or undefined charter schools require their teachers to be covered by such contracts. Overall, these results indicate that dependent and independent charter schools have significantly different relationships with their chartering authorities, and that dependent charter schools are operated much more like conventional public schools than are independent or undefined charter schools.

It is important to consider not only the views of chartering authorities but also the perspectives of individual school principals regarding control over governance. Results in Table 4.6 indicate that charter school principals perceive that they have a greater degree of control than do the principals of matched public schools for all of the items included on the survey.[12] The majority of charter school principals responded that they have full control (a rating of 4) for all six areas of control.

In spite of the near universal perception of greater control on the part of principals, case studies of charter schools and interviews with chartering authority personnel indicate that charter schools vary greatly with respect to their degrees of control. The degree of autonomy granted to charter schools is negotiated on an individual basis between charter schools and their respective chartering authorities. For instance, one start-up school was provided almost complete

---

[12]The charter school principal survey did not ask whether schools had independent or dependent relationships with their chartering authorities.

Table 4.6

Levels of School Control on a Scale of 1 (No Control) to 4 (Full Control)

Area of Control	Charter School	Matched Conventional Public School
Staff salaries and benefits	2.9*	1.5
Curriculum	3.6*	2.6
Budgetary expenses, other than salaries and benefits	3.6*	2.9
Staff hiring, discipline, and dismissal	3.5*	2.8
Student assessment policies (except state-mandated tests)	3.6*	3.1
Student disciplinary policies	3.7*	3.2

SOURCES: 2002 RAND charter school and matched conventional public school surveys.

*Indicates percentages that are statistically different from matched conventional public school percentages at the 1 percent level.

autonomy over all aspects of school operations and curriculum. Another was converted from an existing conventional public school to preserve its unique curriculum while the chartering authority maintained control over all other school operations. As a district administrator explained, “everything looks the same just like our other schools” except for the curriculum. Other case studies provide examples between these two extremes of autonomy.

To summarize, charter schools appear to have more control over their own operations than do conventional public schools, but they vary considerably in their degree of control over specific areas. Independent charter schools (and those not identified as dependent or independent) have more autonomy than dependent charter schools. More specifically, independent charter schools are more likely to be legally liable for school operations and to have greater control over most areas of school operations, with special education being the notable exception.

OVERSIGHT OF CHARTER SCHOOLS

A challenge facing chartering authorities is the monitoring and oversight of schools. Because charter schools have more autonomy than conventional public schools, chartering authorities must develop new mechanisms for holding them accountable for elements defined in their charters. A recent study conducted by the California State Auditor (2002) was critical of the quality of oversight by several chartering authorities. In contrast to that report, the present study surveyed all chartering authorities with operating charter schools. This evidence indicates that chartering authorities monitor dependent and independent charter schools in different ways.

Characteristics of Chartering Authority Oversight of Charter Schools

Oversight of charter schools can include school visits, evaluations of educational goals, and demands for information from schools. This section examines the extent to which chartering authorities use these procedures and explores whether some types of charter schools receive greater scrutiny than others.

Our interviews show that the primary tool for measuring achievement of educational goals is standardized tests, but other tools are also employed. Personnel in several chartering authorities reported using a variety of other methods of assessing charter school progress toward educational goals, such as the Academic Performance Index, graduation rates, and other methods that districts use to oversee their conventional public schools. In one chartering authority, personnel with expertise in special education and curriculum methods visit charter schools as a way to assess progress toward educational goals.

Our survey asked respondents in chartering authorities about a number of different methods they may use to monitor charter schools. Survey responses indicate that chartering authorities conduct financial audits of their charter schools at least once per year. They conduct scheduled and unscheduled visits with dependent charter schools more often than with independent or undefined charter schools. In addition, chartering authorities tend to monitor site-based start-up schools more often than others, regardless of their independent or dependent status. Both survey and case study data indicate that chartering authorities use unscheduled visits more often than scheduled visits. These unscheduled visits were used for informal monitoring of school practices rather than for formal reviews of school progress. For example, one chartering authority respondent interacts with a charter school daily through visits, phone calls, or electronic mail to ensure that "the charter is not disconnected from the" chartering authority.

Most chartering authorities make oversight an additional duty for full-time staff, which is not surprising, since most authorities oversee only one charter school. About 70 percent of chartering authorities have full-time staff assigned part time to charter school oversight. Less than a quarter of chartering authorities have full-time staff who oversee only charter schools. A similar percentage have part-time staff assigned to charter school oversight. Personnel assigned to oversee charter schools typically have additional responsibilities such as overseeing special education programs, serving as a principal or administrator in a charter school, or teaching at a charter school.

As Table 4.7 shows, a higher percentage of authorities require information from dependent charter schools than from independent or undefined charter schools, in some cases a much higher percentage, in almost every category of information. The requirements for information from both independent or undefined and dependent charter schools are highest in the categories related to school finances, such as student attendance, financial reports, and liability insurance, and in the categories where districts are otherwise held accountable to the state, such as standardized test scores and teacher credentialing.

Chartering Authority Actions Toward Charter Schools

Many types of situations have prompted chartering authorities to take actions toward charter schools, as shown in Table 4.8. Chartering authorities frequently act on complaints, especially from parents. One chartering authority used these complaints to support the revocation of a charter. Parent complaints regarding the governance structure of a charter school led another chartering authority to require that the school clarify the role of its advisory board.

Many chartering authorities have taken actions related to finances and compliance. In three cases, financial irregularities resulted in

Table 4.7

Types of Information That Chartering Authorities Require from Independent or Undefined and Dependent Charter Schools

Type of Information	% Requiring Information from Independent or Undefined Charter Schools	% Requiring Information from Dependent Charter Schools
Student attendance data	90.7	96.4
Financial reports or budgets	85.3	96.4
Standardized achievement test data	82.7**	100.0
School calendar and schedule	81.3	89.2
Evidence of liability insurance	76.0	67.9
Evidence of teacher credentialing	74.7**	92.9
Curriculum information	68.0	85.7
Evidence of adequacy/safety of facilities	54.7	57.1
Student demographic information	53.3**	78.6
Student admission data	50.7*	82.1
Graduation/promotion rates	37.3	53.6
Number of dropouts	37.3	42.9
Student discipline information	26.7	46.4
Number of transfers	21.3**	42.9
Parent satisfaction survey	21.3	25.0
Student grades	18.7*	46.4
Portfolios of student work	17.3	28.6

SOURCE: 2002 RAND chartering authority survey.

NOTES: In the survey, chartering authorities responded to the questions for dependent and independent or undefined charter schools. For conventional public schools, many of these categories of information are routinely maintained by districts rather than by schools. If a district also maintains such information for its dependent charter schools, it might not have considered the information to be a reporting requirement in responding to this question. Thus, the percentages for dependent schools might be underestimated.

*Indicates percentages that are statistically different at the 1 percent level.

**Indicates percentages that are statistically different at the 5 percent level.

the revocation of charters. In interviews, personnel in several chartering authorities indicated that financial problems associated with their charter schools would be grounds for the revocation of charters. These problems could include financial mismanagement, negative financial effect on the district because charter schools were attracting a large percentage of students from the district, or declining school revenue resulting from declining student enrollment in the charter school. Overall, chartering authorities used these situations more often than others to justify the revocation of charters.

Table 4.8

Number of Chartering Authorities Taking Actions at Least Once for Different Situations

Situation	Investigation of School	Increased Support or Resources	Increased Supervision of School	Revocation of Charter	Other Disciplinary Action
Complaints from parents	27	14	13	1	6
Complaints from teachers	11	8	4	0	4
Complaints from teacher unions	5	2	0	0	1
Administrative					
Financial irregularities	18	13	17	3	3
Failure to comply with state or federal laws	16	5	7	2	3
Failure to comply with terms of the charter	16	4	10	3	3
Educational					
Declining enrollment	9	11	9	0	1
Low test scores	11	10	12	0	1
Student disciplinary incidents	10	9	6	0	2
Credit or unit irregularities	12	5	5	0	1
High dropout rates	5	3	1	0	0

SOURCE: 2002 RAND chartering authority survey.

NOTE: Chartering authorities could cite more than one action for each situation.

Regarding educational issues, chartering authorities have investigated schools because of low test scores, declining enrollment, student disciplinary incidents, credit irregularities, and high dropout rates. These situations have prompted chartering authorities to increase support and resources as well as supervision. Declining enrollment particularly concerned several chartering authorities, because it would directly affect the income of the charter school and would jeopardize the school's financial viability.

In general, chartering authorities have begun to develop oversight mechanisms for holding their charter schools accountable. The monitoring and information requirements placed on independent charter schools by their chartering authorities are less stringent than those placed on dependent charter schools. Additional research would be necessary to determine the reasons for these differences. The continued and strong control of chartering authorities over dependent charter schools implies that these schools have more direct accountability to their authorities for school operations. On the other hand, independent charter schools rely less on their chartering authorities for school operations, and these schools may be being held accountable to other organizations such as state and county organizations.

SERVICES PROVIDED BY CHARTERING AUTHORITIES

In addition to granting and overseeing charters, most chartering authorities provide administrative services to charter schools, as shown in Table 4.9. These services are generally provided to conventional public schools by school districts.

SUMMARY

Below, we highlight some of the major findings from this chapter.

Authorization

- The vast majority of charters are granted by school districts; only a few are authorized by county or state boards of education.

Table 4.9

Chartering Authority Provision of Administrative Services to Charter Schools

Type of Service	% of Charter Schools Receiving Services (n = 252)	% of Chartering Authorities Providing Services (n = 106)
Payroll	67	66
Assistance in meeting federal or state regulations	65	79
Administrative support to apply for and maintain categorical funding	58	70
Bookkeeping	54	60
Budget preparation	48	58

SOURCES: 2002 RAND charter school and chartering authority surveys.

- About two-thirds of chartering authorities have only one charter school, but a small number of authorities account for a substantial proportion of charters.
- Petition evaluation processes vary substantially. Some have formal processes that explicitly incorporate statutory requirements and others do not. Many authorities have so few applications that they have little need for formal processes.
- Informal interactions between potential charter petitioners and chartering authorities have played an important role in assessing attitudes toward chartering, developing petition details, and reaching agreements in principle even before formal petitions are submitted.
- Authorities with approved charter schools report that formal denials are rare.

Governance

- As the law intends, charter schools have greater control over decisions and policies than conventional public schools do.
- Compared to independent or undefined charter schools, dependent charter schools have less autonomy and are operated much more like conventional public schools.

- Independent or undefined charter schools tend to accept more legal liability than their chartering authorities, whereas dependent charter schools tend to accept about the same legal liability as their chartering authorities. Both independent and dependent charter schools have less control over, and less liability for, special education than other areas of operations.

Oversight

- Independent or undefined charter schools have less monitoring and oversight than dependent charter schools, both in terms of the information demanded and the frequency of monitoring activity.
- For independent or undefined charter schools, only a few categories of information are routinely demanded by chartering authorities.
- The most common causes of specific regulatory action by a chartering authority are complaints from parents and financial irregularities.
- The most common action taken by chartering authorities in response to a specific concern is an investigation of the school. Other common responses include increased supervision and increased support.
- Chartering authorities report revocation of only five charter schools and closure of a handful of others.

Services

- Most charter schools rely on chartering authorities to assist with a variety of administrative services.

Chapter Five

CHARTER SCHOOL FINANCES AND FACILITIES

Cathy Krop

INTRODUCTION

This chapter discusses charter school funding, including the charter school funding model, charter school participation in categorical aid programs, private donations to charter schools, and charter school expenditures. In addition, the chapter describes charter school facilities including types of charter school facilities, how charter schools finance facilities, and facilities challenges. Finally, we examine other fiscal challenges facing charter schools. The analysis is based on the data from the chartering authority, charter school, and conventional public school surveys along with CBEDS and J-200 data.

CHARTER SCHOOL FUNDING

Conventional public schools in California generally receive funding through two means: (1) revenue limit funding, which is general purpose money allocated on the basis of average daily attendance (ADA) at a school and (2) categorical aid, which is generally more restricted funding for particular students or programs and is based on application and eligibility. In contrast, charter schools are funded under the charter school funding model.[1] The charter school funding model is

[1]Before AB 544 (effective January 1, 1999), charter schools were funded under the traditional revenue limit model. AB 544 required that the California Department of Education propose a funding model for charter schools that would provide operational

a block grant funding system that was established to meet the legislative requirement to provide each charter school operational funding equal to total funding received by a school district serving a similar population.[2] In addition, the model was to provide funding in a simple manner.[3]

The charter school block grant funding model contains two block grants: (1) a general purpose entitlement in lieu of revenue limit funding and (2) a block grant in lieu of some categorical funding. Similar to the revenue limit allocation, both block grants are provided on an ADA basis calculated separately for each of four grade ranges. The general purpose block grant is based on comparable revenue limit funding. The funds are unrestricted and may be used for any school purpose. The categorical block grant is provided in lieu of funding for many state categorical aid programs.[4] Charter schools are exempt from the program requirements of the individual state categorical aid programs included in the block grant calculation. The federal government does not allow charter schools any flexibility in the use of federal funds, so they must fully comply

---

funding equal to total funding received by a school district serving a similar pupil population. The model was to provide funding in a simple manner and, at the option of the charter school, through local or direct allocation of funds. The new funding model, established by AB 115 in the 1999–00 state budget "education trailer bill," created a charter school block grant. All new charter schools—those assigned numbers after June 1, 1999—are funded under the charter school funding model. Charters that were previously assigned numbers were allowed to continue to operate through the 2001–02 school year under a district apportionment or to be funded through the charter school funding model. The exception to this is districtwide charter schools, which retain the option to be funded under the revenue limit model or the charter school funding model.

[2]Except that a charter school may not be funded as a necessary small school or a necessary small high school whereas conventional public schools may be funded as necessary small schools. The California Education Code (42280–42289) sets out a small school funding formula, based on a calculation that includes the number of students and the number of full-time teachers, that allows small schools to receive additional basic revenue limit funding.

[3]California Education Code 47630.

[4]Therefore, a charter school is not eligible for separate funding for any state program included in the block grant. Charter schools must apply separately for categorical aid programs not included in the block grant.

with the conditions of federal programs. As with the general purpose entitlement, the funds provided in the categorical block grant may be used for any purpose determined by the charter school.[5]

Table 5.1 shows the charter school block grant funding rates for the 2001–02 school year. In general, the general purpose entitlement is equal to the revenue limit funding provided to conventional public schools for the 2001–02 school year. It should be noted that the total funding per ADA shown in Table 5.1 is not the total funding received by charter schools. Many of the largest federal and state categorical aid programs fall outside the state categorical block grant and are applied for separately, as is discussed in greater detail below.

The charter school may choose to be funded through a local or direct allocation of funds. Under local funding, the charter school has its funds deposited in the appropriate fund or account of the authorizing local educational agency. Under direct funding, the charter school has its funds deposited in the appropriate fund or account of the charter school. The decision on whether to be locally or directly funded does not affect the amount of block grant funding provided

Table 5.1

Charter School Block Grant Estimated Funding Rates per Student in Average Daily Attendance, 2001–02
(in dollars)

	Grade			
Source	K–3	4–6	7–8	9–12
General purpose	4,421	4,478	4,600	5,341
Categorical	309	317	232	294
Total	4,730	4,795	4,832	5,635

SOURCE: California Department of Education.

[5]These exemptions were intended to simplify the process of obtaining and maintaining categorical aid for charter schools as well as to provide charter schools greater freedom in decisions over the use of the funds.

to the charter school.[6] In addition, regardless of the funding decisions a charter school makes, the oversight responsibilities of the chartering authority do not change. The chartering authority is still responsible for assuring that the charter school is meeting all the terms of its charter, including an annual audit.[7]

Meeting Legislative Requirements

Two important questions raised by the charter school funding model are to what extent it meets the legislative requirements to provide each charter school operational funding equal to total funding received by a school district serving a similar population and whether it provides funding in a simple manner. According to our surveys, the majority of charter school principals and chartering authority representatives strongly agree or agree that the funding model is simple (see Figure 5.1).[8]

Figure 5.2 shows that charter school principals are fairly evenly split over whether the charter school funding model provides operational funding equal to total funding received by a school district serving a

---

[6]In general, local funding tends to be a more popular option with conversion schools and those that rely on a district for fiscal services. In addition, some districts prefer local funding if they intend to help charter schools with cash flow, because of the sense of control or recourse by handling the state dollars and passing them through. Direct funding tends to be a more popular option with start-up charter schools, possibly giving them a greater sense of control as the money goes directly to them. As a practical matter, the decision to be locally or directly funded may affect the level of administrative support in applying for and managing categorical aid programs that are not included in the block grant. This will be discussed in greater detail below. In addition, regardless of how the charter school is funded, the chartering authority may charge for the actual costs of supervision, not to exceed 1 percent of a charter school's revenues. This limit becomes 3 percent if the charter school obtains "substantially rent-free facilities from the chartering authority."

[7]According to our survey, the majority of chartering authorities (70 percent) and charter school principals (77 percent) strongly agree or agree that adequate oversight is provided of their charter schools' funds. This is consistent across locally and directly funded charter schools.

[8]Specifically, 70 percent of charter school principals strongly agree or agree and 75 percent of chartering authority representatives strongly agree or agree. We examined this question separately for conversion and start-up charter schools, small and large charter schools, and classroom-based and nonclassroom-based charter schools. In all cases, the majority of charter schools strongly agreed or agreed with this statement.

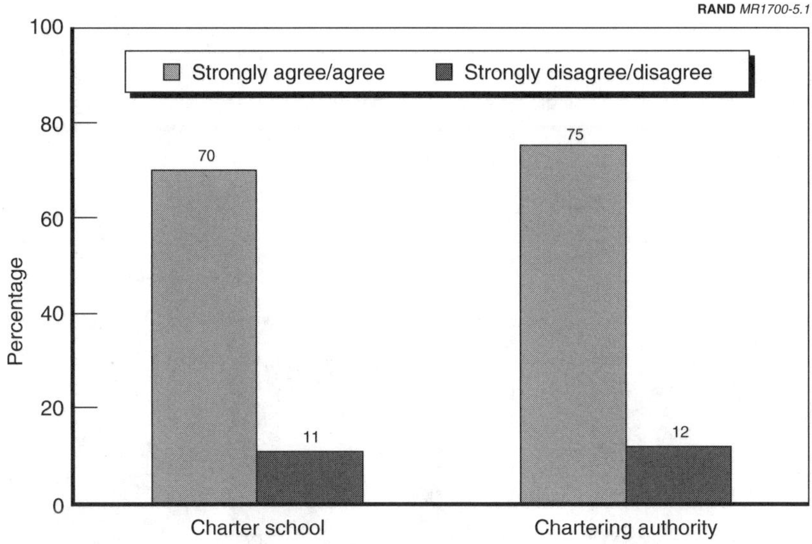

SOURCES: 2002 RAND charter school and chartering authority surveys.
NOTE: Responses marked "Uncertain" are not shown in this figure.

Figure 5.1—The Charter School Block Grant Funding Model Satisfies the Legislative Requirement to Be Simple

similar population.[9] Thirty-nine percent of charter school principals strongly agree or agree and 38 percent of charter school principals disagree or strongly disagree that the charter school model provides equal funding. The majority of chartering authority representatives strongly agree or agree (58 percent) that the charter school model does provide equal funding.

---

[9]AB 544 required that the California Department of Education propose a funding model that would provide each charter school operational funding equal to total funding received by a school district serving a similar population. Responses by principals as to whether this condition has been met are likely a rough estimate. First, charter school principals do not observe other public school finances and so it is difficult to make comparisons. In addition, it is not entirely clear what "operational funding" includes and different principals may interpret this differently.

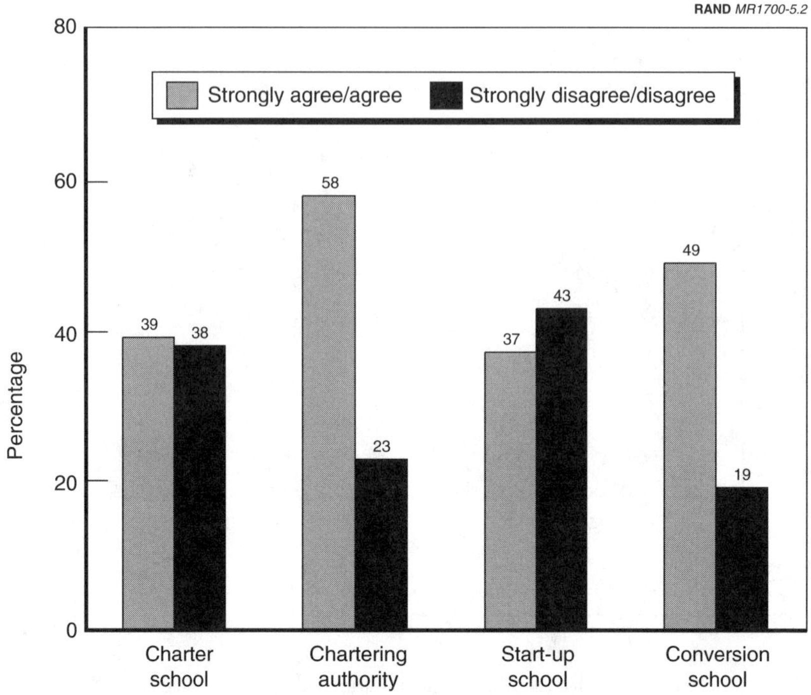

SOURCES: 2002 RAND charter school and chartering authority surveys.

Figure 5.2—The Charter School Block Grant Funding Model Provides at Least as Much Operational Funding as Would Be Available to a Similar District Serving a Similar Pupil Population

Looking at the charter school principal responses in greater detail, start-up charter school principals in particular strongly disagree or disagree that the charter school model provides equal funding.[10] As Figure 5.2 shows, 43 percent of start-up charter school principals

---

[10]We also examined responses separately for large and small charter schools and classroom-based and nonclassroom-based charter schools. In general, there were not large differences between responses for these groups and responses for charter schools as a whole. The exception is that nonclassroom-based charter schools were less likely to disagree or strongly disagree with the statement about equal funding (25 percent strongly disagree or disagree) than charter schools as a whole.

strongly disagree or disagree that the charter school model provides equal funding whereas only 19 percent of conversion charter school principals strongly disagree or disagree. These responses seem to be driven in part by charter school categorical aid funding and charter school facility funding, as will be discussed below.

Participation in Categorical Aid Programs

In the past, many charter schools have had great difficulty getting their legally entitled share of state and federal categorical funds (Sugarman, 2002; Powell et al., 1997). The charter school categorical block grant is intended to simplify the process of obtaining and maintaining state categorical aid for charter schools as well as to allow charter schools freedom in the use of the funds. This is very desirable for charter schools both because the cash is more likely to be received in a timely manner and because charter schools can avoid the applications and reporting involved in obtaining funds from a large number of small categorical aid programs (Sugarman, 2002). Charter school operators are often unsophisticated in completing the forms and carrying out the procedural activities that have taken districts years to master. In addition, charter schools may not have the economies of scale to operate categorical aid programs on their own. Approximately 30 state categorical aid programs are currently included in the categorical block grant.[11] It is important to note that several state categorical aid programs and all federal categorical aid programs—including several of the largest size categorical aid programs such as K–3 Class Size Reduction, Transportation, Special Education, and Title I funding for disadvantaged pupils—fall outside the categorical block grant and require that charter schools apply separately and adhere to the statutes and regulations that govern the programs.[12]

[11]Some of these programs are the Agricultural Vocational Education Incentive Program, Apprentice Education, Beginning Teacher Support and Assessment System, College Preparation Programs, Demonstration Programs in Intensive Instruction, Education Technology, and California Mentor Teacher Program.

[12]Nonblock grant programs include all federally funded programs such as Title I funding for disadvantaged pupils, and other criteria-based state programs such as K–3 Class Size Reduction. In addition, a charter school may not participate in new categorical aid programs established in 1999–00 and beyond, unless the authorizing legislation specifically includes eligibility for charter schools.

The categorical block grant rates have declined over time largely because of the removal of state programs from the block grant and the expiration of or reduction in programs that previously contributed to the block grant. Table 5.2 provides the categorical block grant funding rates for the 2000–01 and 2001–02 school years. Categorical block grant funding is expected to decline sharply in the 2002–03 school year because of several factors. These include removing instructional materials funding from the block grant and requiring that schools apply separately for such funding,[13] shifting funding for several categorical aid programs—including some in the charter school block grant—across fiscal years because of state budget shortfalls, and expiration of or reduction to other programs that previously contributed toward the block grant.

Through the charter school and conventional public school surveys, we sought to address a number of questions related to charter school participation in categorical aid programs *outside the block grant*. First, do charter schools participate in programs outside the block grant? If charter schools choose not to participate in these programs, why? And what are the barriers to participation in specific categorical aid programs?

Comparing all charter schools to a matched sample of conventional public schools suggests that charter school participation in many categorical aid programs is at a significantly lower rate than participation at conventional public schools. Specifically, we asked charter school and conventional public school principals about nine relatively large state and federal categorical aid programs outside the block grant: whether they are currently receiving funding, have an

Table 5.2

Categorical Block Grant Funding, 2000–01 and 2001–02
(in dollars)

	Grade			
School Year	K–3	4–6	7–8	9–12
2000–01	328	338	246	313
2001–02	309	317	232	294

SOURCE: California Department of Education.

[13]This change is discussed below.

application pending, are ineligible to apply, are not applying but eligible, or do not know whether they are eligible. Figure 5.3 shows the percentage that reported currently receiving funding for each categorical aid program. There are statistically significant differences in participation for all programs except the desegregation program.

We also examined participation in categorical aid programs separately for start-up and conversion schools.[14] Participation may vary for these groups for several reasons. The decision to be locally or directly funded as a practical matter may affect the level of administrative support necessary to apply for and manage the programs outside the block grant. Start-up charter schools may be less likely than conversion schools to participate in categorical aid programs. Most start-up schools are directly funded. Charter schools that choose to be funded locally must apply for categorical aid programs that are not included in the block grant through the approving local educational agency, unless legislation for individual programs specifically allows charter schools to apply separately. Locally funded charter schools can work with their approving local educational agencies to ensure that they are included in those agencies' applications for programs for which the charter schools are eligible and in which they choose to participate. In particular, conversion charter schools that are chartered by their local district already have the mechanisms in place to be included in the sponsoring district's applications for categorical aid programs.

In contrast, start-up charter schools do not have a history of participation in categorical aid programs and are more likely to be directly funded. A charter school that is directly funded may apply individually only for state or federal funds not included in the block grant.

---

[14]We also examined these differences separately for small versus large and classroom-based versus nonclassroom-based charter schools. Although some differences did occur between small and large charter schools, the driving force of the differences appears to be start-up versus conversion status. We did regression analyses to examine differences in participation in categorical aid programs outside the block grant for start-up and conversion charter schools controlling for school size. The statistically significant differences generally held. In addition, classroom-based and nonclassroom-based schools show differences in participation in programs outside the block grant largely because nonclassroom-based charter schools report that they are "ineligible to apply" to many of the programs outside the block grant.

RAND MR1700-5.3

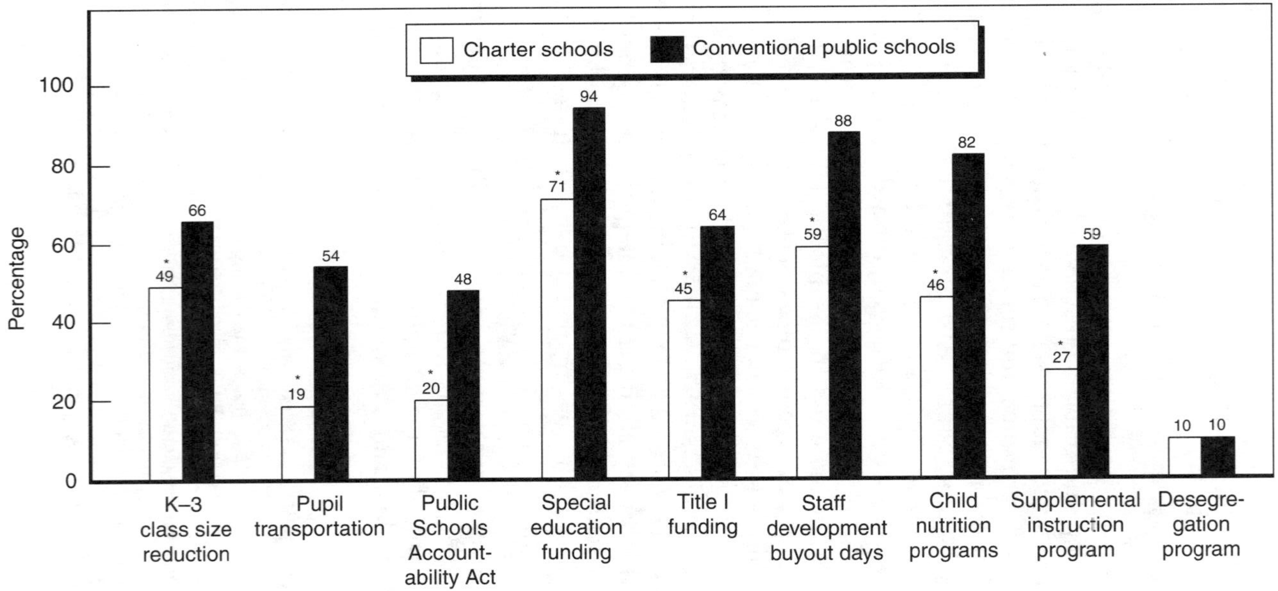

SOURCES: 2002 RAND charter school and matched conventional public school surveys.

*Indicates percentages that are statistically different from matched conventional public school percentages at the 5 percent level.

Figure 5.3—Percentage of Charter Schools and Matched Conventional Public Schools Currently Receiving Funding from Various Categorical Aid Programs

The school may not be included in the application or eligibility of the authorizing entity for any categorical aid programs. An election to receive funding directly applies to all funding the charter school receives, including other state and federal categorical aid.

Figure 5.4 shows quite clearly that the differences in participation between charter schools and matched conventional public schools shown in Figure 5.3 are attributable to start-up schools, not conversion schools. Figure 5.4 shows the percentage of principals who reported currently receiving funding for start-up schools, conversion schools and matched conventional public schools for each individual categorical aid program. Start-up schools have statistically significant lower participation rates than matched conventional public schools for every categorical aid program. By contrast, conversion schools in general have similar participation rates in categorical programs as matched conventional public schools and, in some cases, have higher participation rates.[15]

In addition to examining the percentage of charter and matched conventional public schools that currently receive funding, additional information is gained by determining whether schools are eligible but not applying and whether schools do not know whether they are eligible. Figures 5.5 and 5.6, respectively, show the percentage of start-up school, conversion school, and matched conventional public school principals who reported that their schools were "eligible but not applying" or "don't know whether eligible or not" to specific categorical aid programs outside the categorical block grant.

In general, no more than 5 percent of conventional public school principals responded that their schools are "eligible but not applying" to the individual categorical aid programs. Similar results are seen for conversion schools. Start-up schools are generally more likely than either conversion or conventional public schools to be "eligible but not applying" to the individual aid programs. In particular, there are large differences in "eligible but not applying" for the child nutrition programs and Title I. Both programs provide, on average, relatively large per-pupil funding to participating schools.

---

[15]There is a statistically significant difference between matched conventional public schools and conversion schools for participation in special education funding and the desegregation program.

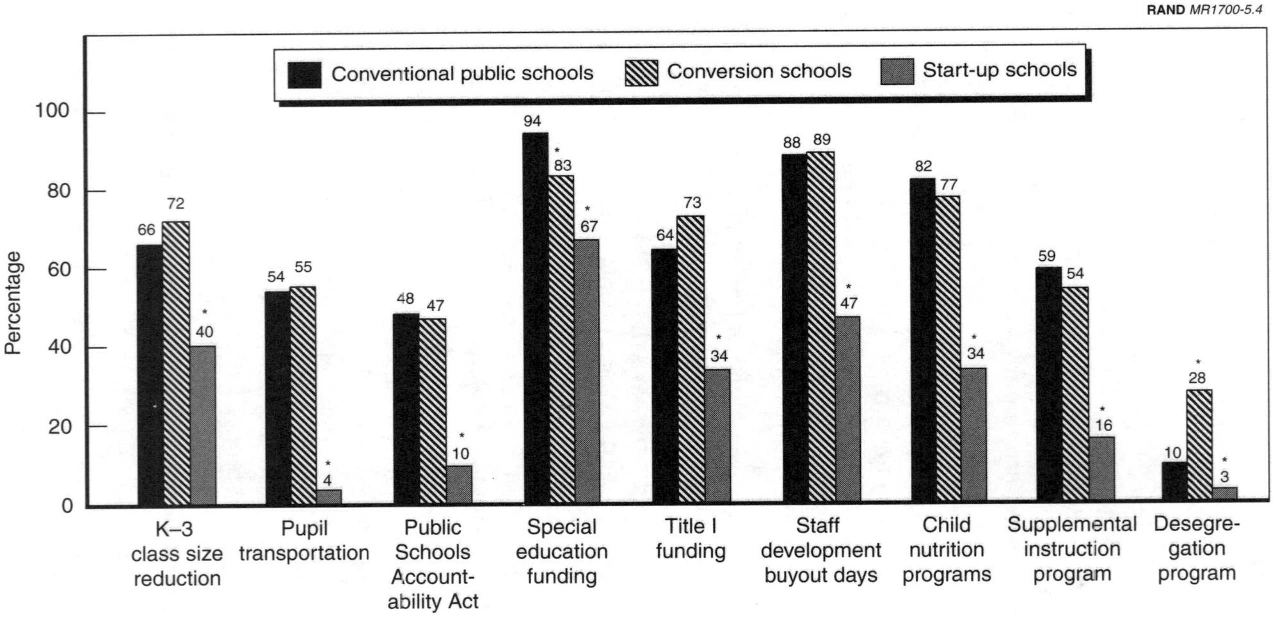

SOURCES: 2002 RAND charter school and matched conventional public school surveys.

*Indicates percentages that are statistically different from matched conventional public school percentages at the 5 percent level.

Figure 5.4—Percentage of Conversion Schools, Start-Up Schools, and Matched Conventional Public Schools Currently Rceiving Funding from Various Categorical Aid Programs

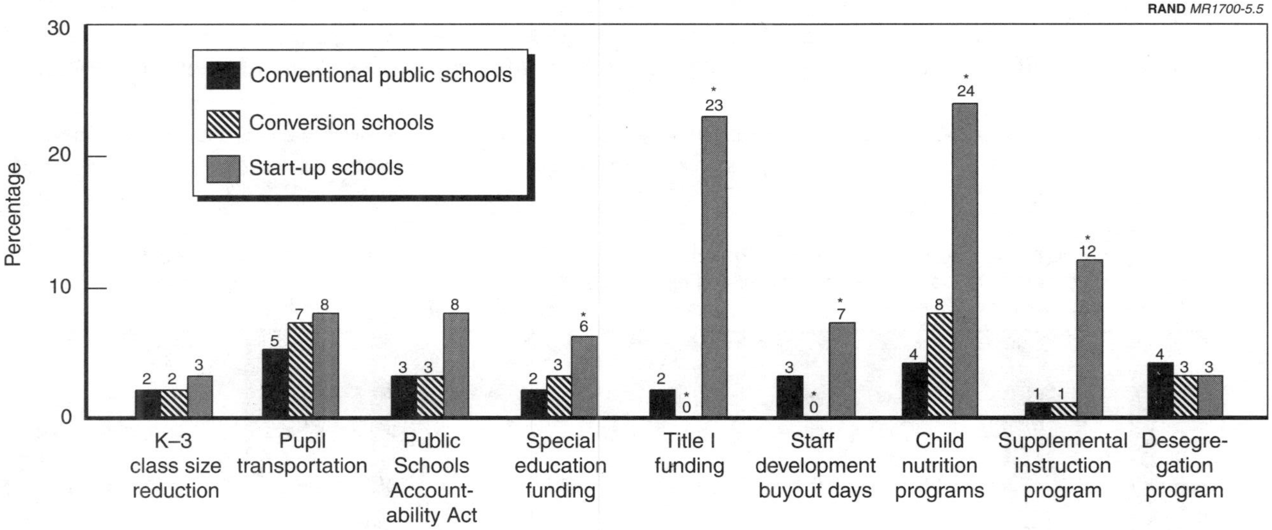

SOURCES: 2002 RAND charter school and matched conventional public school surveys.

*Indicates percentages that are statistically different from matched conventional public school percentages at the 5 percent level.

Figure 5.5—Percentage of Matched Conventional Public Schools, Conversion Schools, and Start-Up Schools "Eligible for Categorical Aid Funding But Not Applying"

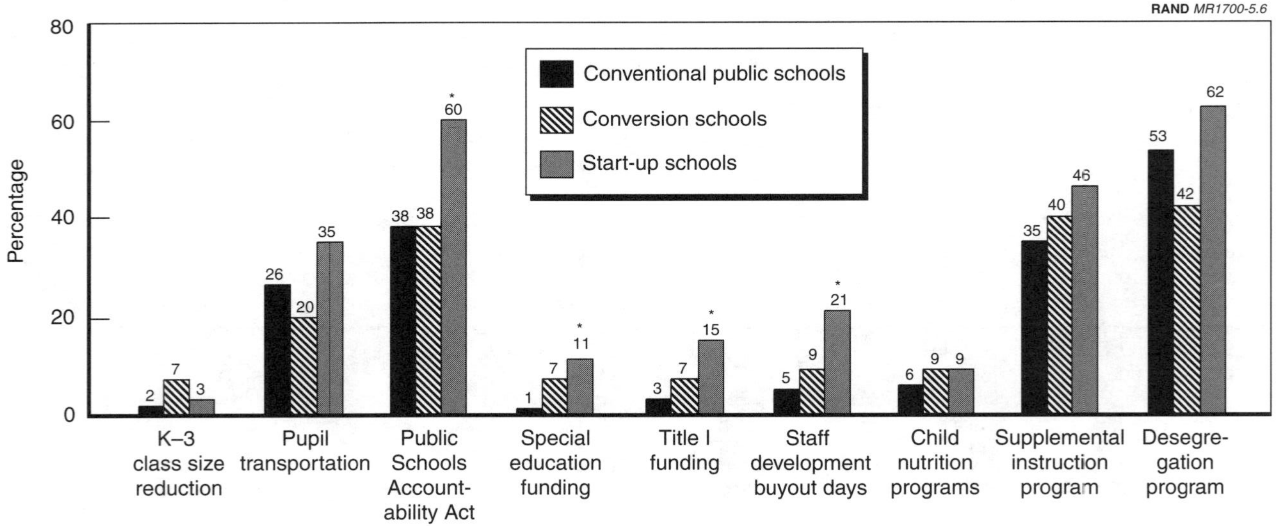

SOURCES: 2002 RAND charter school and matched conventional public school surveys.

*Indicates percentages are statistically different from matched conventional public school percentages at the 5 percent level.

Figure 5.6—Percentage of Conventional Public Schools, Conversion Schools, and Start-Up Schools That "Don't Know Whether Eligible or Not" for Categorical Aid Funding

Our case study results suggest that participation in child nutrition programs can pose a problem to charter schools, particularly those that do not have a sponsoring district willing to include them in their child nutrition program. Charter schools have neither economies of scale nor administrative resources to support such a program on their own. In addition, several of the schools we visited did not have kitchen facilities. Some of these charter schools were actively trying to link up with other districts to be included in their child nutrition programs.

Similarly, Title I is a federal aid program with extensive statutes and regulations that govern requirements relating to receipt of funding. Those charter schools without links to a district chartering authority willing to include them in the district's Title I program likely cannot participate alone. When asked in the charter school survey to agree or disagree with the statement "our school has given up pursuing certain categorical funds because they are too complex," about 25 percent of conversion schools strongly agreed or agreed and 48 percent of start-up schools strongly agreed or agreed.

Turning to the issue of knowledge about categorical aid programs, Figure 5.6 again shows that conversion schools and conventional public schools are generally similar in the percentages that "don't know whether eligible or not" for the various categorical aid programs. Again, start-up schools show considerably larger percentages of those who "don't know whether eligible or not" than either conventional public schools or conversion schools.

Added together, those who responded that they are "eligible but not applying" and "don't know whether eligible or not" result in considerably lower participation in categorical aid programs outside the block grant for start-up schools than conversion schools or conventional public schools. This suggests that the removal or exclusion of programs from the block grant could have a sizable effect on start-up schools.

It is worth noting that individual categorical aid programs outside the block grant have program-specific rules and regulations governing them that influence the policy levers available to increase charter school participation. Some categorical aid programs, such as Title I, are purely federally funded. The state is limited in its ability to include such programs in the charter school categorical block grant. Therefore, policy levers to increase charter school participation are limited to such areas as increasing charter school administrators' information on the programs and how to participate. Other programs, such as class size reduction and child nutrition, are funded through various mixes of state and federal support and may allow the state some more flexibility to include all or parts of the programs in the block grant. Other categorical aid programs, such as instructional materials, are purely state funded with the state having the ability to decide whether to include the programs in the categorical block grant. Block granting of state categorical aid programs alone would not result in equal participation of charter schools and conventional public schools in categorical aid programs. Some of the difference in categorical aid program participation and funding between charter schools and conventional public schools is due to federal programs that cannot be block granted.

PRIVATE DONATIONS TO CHARTER SCHOOLS

Private donations may play a role in charter school funding for several reasons. Public schools call on a variety of private givers to provide a spectrum of goods and services. Recent research suggests public schools have increasingly sought private support (both financial and in-kind) in recent years (Zimmer et al., 2001; Brunner and Sonstelie, 1997). However, private financial contributions still account for a relatively small share of total resources for the vast majority of public schools, and the source and type of those contributions vary a great deal across public schools.

Private donations may play a unique role in charter schools. For example, charter schools, particularly newly created ones, face a number of start-up costs—ranging from books and materials to facility needs. In addition, some charter schools have distinct educational focuses that may be used to identify and attract donors. Further, some charter schools may choose not to participate in various federal or state categorical aid programs because of the restrictions and regulations that govern the programs and may seek to substitute these funds with private donations. For example, one case study charter school intended to forgo state instructional materials funding because the state-adopted materials did not match the school's educational program. Instead, the school was going to seek private funds to cover instructional materials. Finally, charter schools may be able to gain private funding for programs for which public schools cannot charge similar fees.

There is little systematic public data quantifying how much money or in-kind services public schools receive from private donors. To address the role of private donations in charter school funding, we asked both public school and charter school principals how much private funding their schools received for the 2001–02 school year. On average, matched conventional public schools and charter schools received about $83 and $433, respectively, in private funding per pupil for the 2001–02 school year. Figure 5.7 shows the breakdown of private dollars to conventional public and charter schools.

RAND *MR1700-5.7*

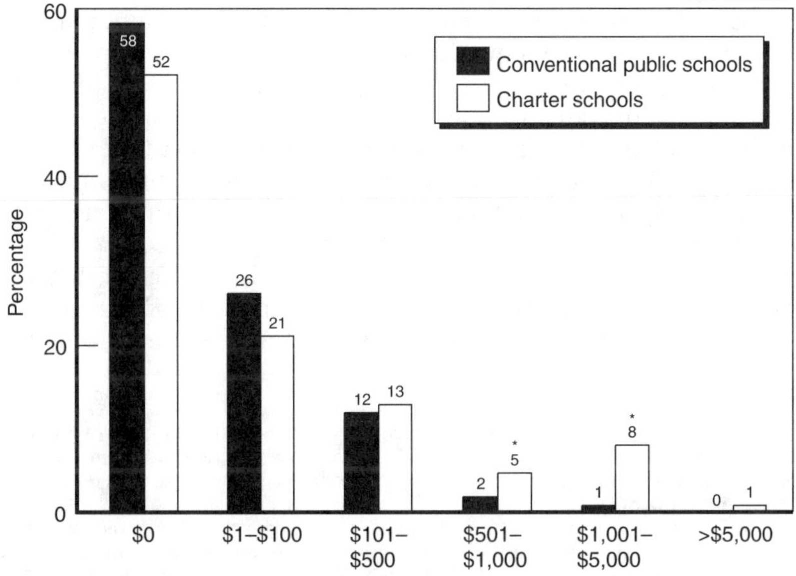

SOURCES: 2002 RAND charter school and matched conventional public school surveys.

*Indicates percentages that are statistically different from matched conventional public school percentages at the 5 percent level.

Figure 5.7—Private Funding per Pupil in Conventional Public and Charter Schools, 2001–02

It suggests that public schools serving similar populations receive less private funding than do charter schools. Fifty-eight percent of matched conventional public schools receive no private funding whereas 52 percent of charter schools do. In addition, those charter schools that receive private funding receive on average more than matched conventional public schools.

We also examined whether private funding to charter schools might be tied to whether the charter school is a conversion or start-up school.[16] Figure 5.8 displays these results.

In general, start-up schools receive more private funding per pupil than do conversion schools, \$576 per pupil compared to \$56 per pupil.[17] Most likely this results in part because start-up schools have greater start-up expenses and facility needs. Conversion schools generally have facilities, supplies, and materials to begin instruction and so might not have as great a need for private support, particularly in the early years. In addition, possibly start-up schools seek private donations to fill some of the gap in categorical funding described in the previous section. Ideally, we would like to know if private funding merely helps to compensate for the fact that start-up schools need to pay for facilities and conversion schools do not. Unfortunately, we do not know this gap in facility funding, so we do not know how it compares to the reported difference in per-pupil private funding. In addition, we do not know how much of this private funding is for operating or capital expenditures. Finally, we do not know if private funding consists of one-time gifts or ongoing

[16]We also examined private funding separately by years since the charter was granted. One thought is that charter schools might receive more private funding in the early years to cover start-up expenditures including facilities. Or possibly, charter schools receive more private funding after they have been in existence for several years and have build a reputation of results and stability. Those charter schools receiving the most per pupil (\$1,335 per pupil) were those that had been granted their charter one year earlier. Those charter schools that received the least per pupil were those that were granted charter status eight or nine years earlier, possibly because these are generally conversion schools. Those charter schools that were granted in the last year or between two and seven years ago show no pattern in private donations based on the age of the charter school.

[17]It is important to note that even the average private funding per pupil for start-up schools amounts to under 10 percent of average statewide revenues per pupil to conventional public schools.

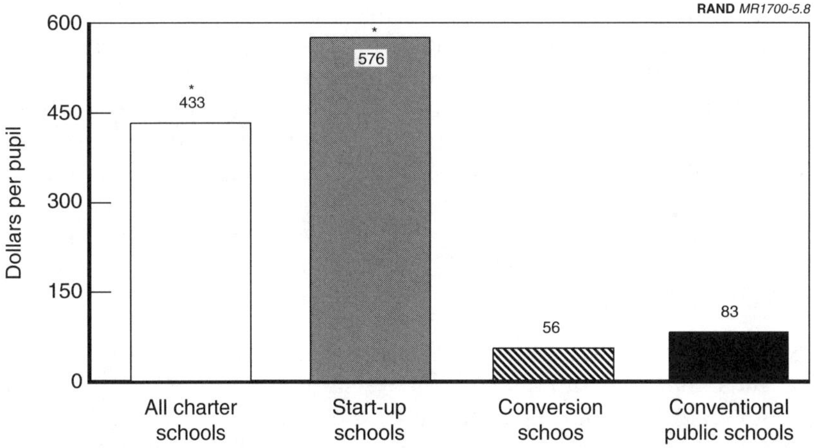

SOURCES: 2002 RAND charter school and matched conventional public school surveys.

*Indicates percentages that are statistically different from matched conventional public school percentages at the 5 percent level.

Figure 5.8—Private Donations per Pupil to Charter Schools and Conventional Public Schools, 2001–02

contributions. These limitations are important to address before drawing conclusions from these results.

CHARTER SCHOOL EXPENDITURES

Having examined charter school revenues, we now turn to charter school expenditures. A number of interesting questions relate to expenditures, such as how do charter schools spend their resources, how does spending differ among types of charter schools, and how do their expenditures differ from conventional public school expenditures. These questions are difficult to answer given current data sources. First, there are no systematic state data collected at the school level on expenditures. Instead, data are collected and reported at the district level. Even if there were systematic, reliable charter school expenditure data at the school level, these data could be compared only to public school district averages. Further, it is also difficult to collect expenditure data for individual charter schools. For example, some locally funded charter schools rely on a district to pay for some large expenditures and others do not. Data reported by the charter school may or may not include expenditures that are assumed by the district, and charter schools may not be able to accurately report such expenditures. In addition, charter school expenditures are influenced by large capital expenditures in a given year.[18] Without a detailed cost study—one that correctly apportions overhead, administration, and personnel to the "right" schools—it is difficult to document and compare school expenditures.

Because systematic charter school or conventional public school finance data are not collected by the state, we addressed questions about charter school expenditures through a "supplemental" survey, as described in Chapter One.[19] In addition to other items, we asked charter schools to report their total expenditures, teacher salary and benefit expenditures, and other staff salary and benefit expenditures for the 2001–02 school year. These numbers should be interpreted with caution given the limitations discussed above.

Charter schools reported an average total expenditure per student of $6,204 for the 2001–02 school year.[20] In addition, we looked at how average total expenditures per pupil, average teacher salary and benefit expenditures per pupil, and average other staff salary and benefit expenditures per pupil differ among different types of charter schools.[21] Charter schools report average teacher salary and benefit expenditures of $2,841 per pupil and average other staff salary and benefit expenditures of $1,075 per pupil. Table 5.3 documents these

---

[18]The expenditure numbers reported by charter schools in our survey do not separate capital expenditures from operating expenditures.

[19]We piloted a similar survey with conventional public school principals, and they were unable to answer questions about financial data specific to their school.

[20]The mean expenditures throughout this section are influenced by several high outliers, often resulting from the inclusion of capital expenditures in total expenditures. In the cases of extreme outliers, we called the survey respondents to confirm the reported numbers. The median total expenditure reported by charter schools is $5,408 for the 2001–02 school year. The standard deviations for total expenditures per pupil are as follows: all charter schools, $4,984; start-up schools, $4,658; conversion schools, $6,084; classroom-based schools, $5,708; and nonclassroom-based schools, $3,281.

[21]Chapter Seven discusses how teacher salaries and benefits differ between conventional public schools and charter schools.

Table 5.3

Charter School Expenditures per Pupil, 2001–02
(in dollars)

Type of Charter School	Total Expenditures per Pupil	Teacher Salary and Benefit Expenditures per Pupil	Other Staff Salary and Benefit Expenditures per Pupil
All charter schools	6,204	2,841	1,075
Start-up	6,168	2,729	1,006
Conversion	6,366	3,237	1,340
Classroom-based	6,926	3,233	1,315
Nonclassroom-based	4,973	2,217	720

SOURCE: 2002 RAND charter school supplemental survey.

expenditures for start-up and conversion schools, and classroom-based and nonclassroom-based charter schools.

Table 5.3 suggests that, on average, start-up schools spend less overall per pupil as well as less per pupil on teacher salaries and benefits and other staff salaries and benefits than conversion schools.[22] In addition, start-up schools, on average, allocate about 60 percent of their total expenditures to teacher and other staff salaries and benefits compared to about 72 percent for conversion schools. This may be due to start-up schools' need to allocate relatively large shares of their expenditures to such items as facilities and start-up costs.[23] In addition Table 5.3 shows that, on average, nonclassroom-based schools spend about $2,000 less per pupil than classroom-based schools because of their lower revenues.[24]

---

[22]Chapter Three suggests that classroom-based start-up schools appear to hold their ground in terms of academic outcomes compared to a matched sample of conventional public schools. Per-pupil expenditure data may suggest that they hold their ground while given less resources. In addition, the lower level of resources to nonclassroom-based schools may be of interest given the findings of Chapter Three. Given the limitations of these expenditure data, as reported above, a more detailed cost study would need to be conducted to draw any conclusions.

[23]Sugarman (2002) suggests that start-up schools often have to redirect perhaps 20 percent or more of their core funding to pay for space.

[24]Senate Bill 740 of the 2000 legislative session authorized the state board of education to cut the funding for nonclassroom-based schools. The regulations establish a range of spending, operational, and other criteria that such schools must meet to receive full funding. In addition, they are ineligible for a number of categorical aid funds outside the block grant. In the supplemental survey, these schools report mean and median revenues per pupil of $5,385 and $4,793, respectively. Classroom-based

The previous section suggests that charter schools have lower rates of participation in and, therefore, revenues from several large categorical aid programs outside the block grant than a matched sample of conventional public schools. In addition, statewide average per-pupil expenditure data suggest that charter schools as a whole may have lower per-pupil expenditures than conventional public schools.[25] An accurate estimate of the difference in per-pupil spending between charter schools and conventional public schools is difficult to arrive at given current data sources. First, average statewide per-pupil expenditures, at the time of publication, were not available for the 2001–02 school year. In addition, as mentioned above, we are able to compare charter school reported expenditures only to district averages. Further, there are limitations with the charter school survey expenditure data as suggested above. With that said, a possible inference from the charter school survey data, which would need to be affirmed through a systematic collection of detailed conventional public school and charter school costs, is that charter schools as a whole receive less revenue from categorical aid programs and spend less per pupil than conventional public schools do.

FACILITIES

Acquiring and funding school facilities has been a stumbling block for many charter schools (Sugarman, 2002; Powell et al., 1997). Charter schools do not have access to similar revenue sources for facilities as conventional public schools. Conventional public school districts pay for facilities by issuing bonds, an avenue unavailable to many charter schools.[26] In addition, charter schools pay for facility ex-

---

schools report mean and median revenues per pupil of $7,181 and $6,199, respectively.

[25]Sources of statewide average per-pupil expenditures include the California Department of Education and the National Education Association (NEA).

[26]In addition, charter schools often do not have access to state or district bond monies or other capital resources for school improvements or building of new facilities. Unless the charter provides that its facilities must comply with the Field Act, charter schools are exempt from it. Often bond monies or other state or federal facility monies are dependent on Field Act compliance. Conversion charter schools generally comply with the Field Act, but start-up schools may not.

penses that conventional public schools do not.[27] These expenses may include rent on facilities, utilities, maintenance, and off-site storage facilities.[28] Finally, it is often difficult for charter schools to find suitable facilities and they face landlords who are cautious about leasing facilities to new entities and to charters that are granted for only a few years.

In response to these obstacles, the provision of charter school facilities will undergo tremendous change in the 2003–04 school year. Under previous law, charter schools largely had to find their own facilities. Conversion schools generally already had facilities that they had been occupying as a conventional public school. Start-up schools generally had to acquire facilities. The prior law stated that a school district in which a charter school operates (which is not necessarily the approving district) shall permit a charter school to use, at no charge, facilities not being used by the district for instructional or administrative purposes, unless historically used for rental purposes, provided the charter school shall be responsible for reasonable maintenance (EC 47614, as repealed on November 7, 2000, as a result of Proposition 39).

Recent legislation, Proposition 39 and Senate Bill 740, will require that districts provide facilities for eligible charter schools and will allow reimbursements of facility costs for schools in low-income areas. Proposition 39, passed in November 2000, will take effect in November 2003 for most districts.[29] Proposition 39 directs school districts to provide facilities for charter schools that have an in-district ADA[30] of 80 or more. The charter school does not need to be currently lo-

---

[27]This does not mean that public school facilities are cost-free. There is an opportunity cost if facilities are not rented out or used for another valuable purpose.

[28]For conventional public schools, these expenses are often paid at the district level, where economies of scale may be realized.

[29]Proposition 39 could take effect earlier on a district-by-district basis if districts pass local bond measures. If a district passes a local bond measure, Proposition 39 would take effect July 1 following its passage. In general, eligible, currently operating charter schools had to submit their detailed requests for facilities by October 1, 2002. New charter schools had to submit their charters by November 14 and facility requests by December 31, 2002.

[30]"In-district" refers to students who would be otherwise eligible to attend the districts' schools, with the exception of in-district transfers and parental employment-based eligibility.

cated within the district, nor does the charter have to have been granted by the district where the eligible students live. The district is required to provide space only for the in-district students.[31] The law states that facilities must be "reasonably equivalent" to facilities that the students would otherwise attend in noncharter schools in that district. Districts may charge the charter school an amount equivalent to what they spend per student on facilities from their general fund.[32] In addition, charter schools are responsible for providing maintenance and upkeep. Nonetheless, these costs should prove to be significantly lower than market or even discounted lease rates for most schools and thus should provide substantial relief to schools struggling under facilities costs.[33]

Senate Bill 740 is another legislative measure designed to alleviate some of the facilities burden on charter schools. This measure was implemented for the first time in the 2002–03 school year. The legislation created a small charter facilities aid program for schools in low-income areas. Eligible schools receive a cash reimbursement after the close of the fiscal year. As the law was originally written, only schools that were physically located in the attendance area of a public elementary school in which 70 percent or more of pupil enrollment was eligible for free or reduced-price lunches were eligible for funding. Current law allows schools in which more than 70 percent of the charter school students are eligible for free or reduced-price lunch to be eligible for this funding.[34] Schools that occupy district- or county-owned facilities, provided under either Proposition 39 or

[31]Although there is no requirement that the district house the other students, if the district has room and is so inclined, it may choose to negotiate a separate agreement for additional space with the charter school.

[32]Since most districts pay facility construction costs from nongeneral funds, the general fund share is likely to include only maintenance and upkeep costs, which should be relatively modest. The exception is in overcrowded or otherwise fiscally overburdened districts, where limited general fund monies may have been expended on facilities.

[33] See Charter School Development Center (2002).

[34]CDE has implemented the program to reimburse schools for 2001–02 using the new criteria, so schools that had 70 percent eligibility were eligible for 2001–02 reimbursements. CDE has recently completed the apportionment for the program and all eligible schools were funded at the full level. A total of 54 eligible charter schools received a total of $5,259,645 for reimbursement of 2001–02 costs. The status of funding for current and future years is a subject for budget discussions.

otherwise, are not eligible for these funds. For schools that are eligible, $750 per classroom-based ADA would be available, up to but not exceeding 75 percent of the school's facilities rent and lease costs. This funding depends entirely on each year's state budget, and the money for this reimbursement is not appropriated until the following fiscal year budget is passed.

We surveyed chartering authority representatives about whether they currently pay for charter school facility costs, how they pay for those costs, and whether they are struggling with financing charter school capital expenditures. In addition, we asked charter school principals about how they arrange for facilities and whether they are struggling with financing capital expenditures. Their responses provide a baseline for changes that will come into effect from Proposition 39 and Senate Bill 740 largely in the 2003–04 school year. At the same time, in our case studies, we asked chartering authority representatives and charter school principals how they expect to be affected by these measures.

According to our survey, 38 percent of chartering authorities currently pay for charter school facility costs. Of those that do, the majority rely on general fund revenues to pay for them. Specifically, 84 percent of chartering authorities that pay for charter school facility costs use general fund revenues, 12 percent use school bonds, 14 percent use grant applications, 5 percent use parcel taxes, and 16 percent use other means. In addition, 40 percent of chartering authority representatives state that they currently provide space within existing noncharter school facilities for instructional use by charter schools.

Charter schools appear to use multiple means to obtain facilities. As Figure 5.9 shows, 42 percent of charter school principals report that their facilities are provided by a district, free or at a nominal cost (with most of these being conversion schools). In addition, 30 percent of charter schools lease their facilities from a commercial source (with most of these being start-up schools). About 12 percent of charter schools used two different means to provide facilities (e.g., leased from a commercial source and donated by sponsors) and about 2 percent of charter schools used more than two means to provide facilities.

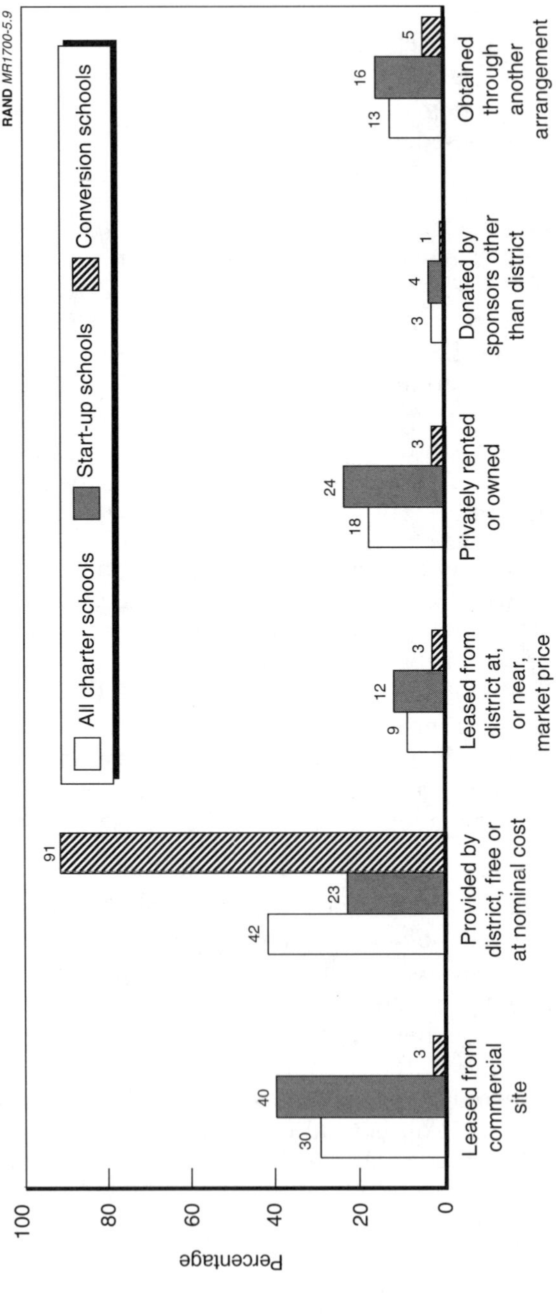

SOURCE: 2002 RAND charter school survey.

NOTES: We asked charter schools to check all that apply. Therefore, adding across all response categories for start-up schools, for example, will result in more than 100 percent.

Figure 5.9—Acquisition of School Facilities, by Type of Charter School

In addition, we asked charter school principals and chartering authority representatives whether they were struggling with financing charter school capital expenditures. Sixty-two percent of charter school principals strongly agreed or agreed with the statement "Our school is struggling with financing capital expenditures" (68 percent of start-up schools and 46 percent of conversion schools). By comparison, 37 percent of chartering authority representatives strongly agreed or agreed with the statement "This chartering authority is struggling with financing our charter school's capital expenditures." Although currently the majority of charter schools are struggling with financing capital expenditures, the majority of chartering authorities are not struggling. This is not surprising given that currently charter schools bear the majority of responsibility regarding facilities.[35] Again, these responses provide a baseline for changes in charter school facility rules and regulations and will likely change once Proposition 39 and Senate Bill 740 are fully implemented.

The case study site visits provide some insights into how charter schools and chartering authorities might be affected by Proposition 39 and Senate Bill 740. Although districts are not legally allowed to reject a charter petition because of difficulty in complying with Proposition 39, case study schools stated that they fear that some districts may begin to scrutinize charter petitions more closely to avoid those with potential facility requirements. In addition, some case study schools stated that this new requirement might cause some districts to call a halt to chartering, even though California law is supposed to make it difficult for districts to refuse a charter sought by an applicant with reasonably sensible plans for its school. As suggested in Chapter Four, there is evidence from our case study schools that some chartering authorities deny all petitions, whether formally or informally. In addition, charter schools that are not chartered by their local district and have a poor relationship with their local district wonder how the new law will play out.

---

[35]We also looked at the charter school responses based on when the charter was granted. One possibility is that capital expenditures are more of a struggle in the early years of a charter. The charter school responses were consistent across different lengths of time since the charter was granted.

OTHER FISCAL CHALLENGES

In addition to the challenges surrounding categorical aid and facilities as discussed above, the case study charter schools identified other fiscal challenges that were not directly addressed through the survey but may deserve additional attention.

Case study charter schools mentioned start-up costs as being a fiscal challenge. These are funds needed to launch the school, to hire staff, and to outfit the school with furnishings and curriculum materials in preparation for its initial enrollment of what is often an uncertain number of pupils. Start-up costs are often a serious problem, especially for newly formed community groups that seek to create charter schools (Sugarman, 2002).

In addition, several of the case study charter schools mentioned concerns related to fiscal flexibility and fiscal autonomy. For example, the decline in the categorical block grant over time was mentioned as being problematic as was the recent removal of the instructional materials component of the block grant. Charter schools had received a "no strings attached," pro-rata share of instructional materials funds through the categorical block grant and did not need to purchase state-adopted materials. Under recent changes, charter schools will now need to apply separately for instructional materials money and must use state-adopted materials to receive funding. Presumably, some charter schools will be able to apply separately for the funding and purchase state-adopted texts and materials. Charter schools offering unconventional programs, however, will presumably have to forgo such funding. The instructional materials changes could be particularly problematic for those charter schools that do not use state-adopted texts or materials, have already purchased other materials for the 2002–03 school year, and were counting on block grant funding to help pay for them. Several charter schools raised the concern that increasingly schools are eligible for separate categorical aid only if they follow a traditional path, even if their charter was granted to follow a nontraditional path or to educate nontraditional students. Several case study charter schools also stated that fiscal flexibility was a cornerstone of the charter idea for them, and they are concerned that this flexibility is waning.

In a related vein, charter schools expressed concern about maintaining fiscal autonomy. The basic idea behind charter schools is that they are supposed to be autonomous. And yet, there is at the same time understandable concern that some charter schools will not be financially sound, might not properly spend on their pupils the public money they get, or might go broke in the middle of a year and leave families in the lurch. These concerns have led to recent changes in auditing, monitoring, reporting, and other requirements.[36] A concern raised among charter schools is how to balance making charter schools accountable while maintaining their fiscal autonomy and not overburdening them with substantial amounts of paperwork.

Finally, case study charter schools discussed at length a variety of fiscal challenges they faced stemming from special education. These were generally expenditures that charter schools had taken on that would not typically fall to a conventional public school. These included extensive legal expenditures in cases where the school was found to be out of compliance with special education as well as the provision of special education services that would normally be provided by a district but for which the individual charter schools had to contract out. Special education issues, including special education finances, are discussed in Chapter Eight in this report.

SUMMARY

The major findings from the finance and facilities chapter are summarized below.

- A majority of charter schools and chartering authorities agree that the charter school block grant funding model meets the legislative requirement to be simple.
- Charter school respondents are divided over whether the block grant funding model provides at least as much operational

---

[36]In the final days of the legislative session, AB 1994 was amended to mandate that charter schools report fiscal information to the state. Charter schools would also be required to report financial data to the state superintendent and the charter-granting agency in a format prescribed by the state superintendent.

funding as would be available to a similar public school serving a similar pupil population.

- Charter schools have significantly lower participation than conventional public schools in categorical aid programs outside the block grant. For particular categorical aid programs, a sizable share of charter schools are "eligible but not applying," in part because of the requirements that accompany the programs. In addition, for several programs, a sizable percentage of charter school principals say that they "don't know whether eligible or not." Conversion schools have a much higher rate of participation than start-up schools in categorical aid programs outside the block grant.
- The majority of charter schools are struggling with acquiring and financing facilities. In the 2001–02 school year, the majority of chartering authorities do not pay for charter school facility costs. However, many of these issues are addressed by recent legislation.

Chapter Six

ACADEMIC ENVIRONMENTS OF CHARTER AND CONVENTIONAL PUBLIC SCHOOLS

Laura Hamilton

INTRODUCTION

This chapter addresses several topics related to the instructional activities and environments of charter schools and their conventional public school counterparts. It deals with questions related to professional development for teachers, curriculum and instruction, student assessment, parent involvement, and student discipline. Because any effect of charter schools on the academic achievement of students who attend them is likely to occur in large part as a result of the teaching and learning environments in those schools, it is important to examine these environments to understand the extent to which students' learning experiences in charter schools differ from those of students in conventional public schools. The results presented in this chapter are intended to illustrate some of these differences. Although these findings cannot provide definitive information on the source of any charter school "effect" on achievement, they suggest some specific differences that could be the subject of future studies.

We might expect curriculum, instruction, and other aspects of the instructional environment to differ between charter and conventional public schools for a number of reasons. One stated goal of charter schools, according to many advocates as well as their founders, is to foster innovation by freeing charter schools from the constraints imposed by district and state regulations (RPP International, 1999). Existing literature on the academic environments of charter schools suggests that innovation in curriculum, instruction, governance, parent participation, and other aspects of school operation is common (Corwin and Flaherty, 1995; Finn et al., 2000). At the same time, the fact that charter schools in California are expected to implement the state standards and demonstrate success on the state testing program may result in fewer curricular differences between charter and conventional public schools than would emerge if charter schools were not subject to the state's accountability requirements. We discuss this issue further below.

Parent involvement in charter schools has been studied to a greater extent than some of the other topics examined in this chapter, and studies of charter schools in California suggest that parent involvement tends to be greater in charter schools than in conventional public schools (Ascher et al., 1999; Becker et al., 1997). This may reflect the fact that many charter schools are schools of choice and therefore serve students whose parents are especially motivated, but there is also evidence that many charter schools are more effective than conventional public schools at engaging parents (Finn et al., 2000). Because some types of parent involvement have been associated with positive academic outcomes for students (see, for example, Bryk et al., 1990), higher levels of such involvement in charter schools may be one source of any positive charter school effect on student learning.

Principals' perceptions about student disciplinary problems, the final topic addressed in this chapter, are primarily relevant for understanding ways in which perceived problems related to student behavior may influence the academic environment and for examining the degree to which charter schools serve easier-to-teach student populations, as some critics contend. Differences in students served are also addressed in other chapters, particularly Chapters Two and Eight.

In the following sections, we present results from the surveys and, where applicable, the case studies, for each of the main topics described above. Below, we summarize key findings and discuss limitations and implications. It is important for readers to keep in mind throughout the discussions of results that the means presented in this chapter mask important variations among both charter schools and conventional public schools.

PROFESSIONAL DEVELOPMENT

The professional development information we collected through our surveys is limited to general information that could be easily obtained from principals and chartering authorities. Because we did not survey teachers, we could not ask questions about specific content or perceived effectiveness of the professional development. Instead, the questions focus primarily on rates of participation and methods for funding professional development activities.

Chartering Authorities' Involvement in Professional Development

Two questions on the chartering authority survey addressed professional development offered to teachers. The first asked respondents to characterize this professional development in terms of who participates. Respondents were asked to select from the options listed in Figure 6.1; they could select more than one option or could select none, since some programs may be optional for both charter and noncharter teachers, a scenario that is not represented among the options in our list. Figure 6.1 shows that more than half of the responding chartering authorities reported professional development programs that were mandatory for noncharter school teachers but optional for charter school teachers. Other responses were less common. These results suggest that although most authorizers offered certain professional development programs that were unavailable to charter school teachers, for the most part teachers in both types of schools had access to professional development opportunities.

The other question on the chartering authority survey asked respondents to report who pays for professional development for charter school teachers. The vast majority of chartering authorities report that charter schools are at least partly responsible for funding professional development, whereas only a third of the chartering authorities pay for some professional development themselves (Figure 6.2).

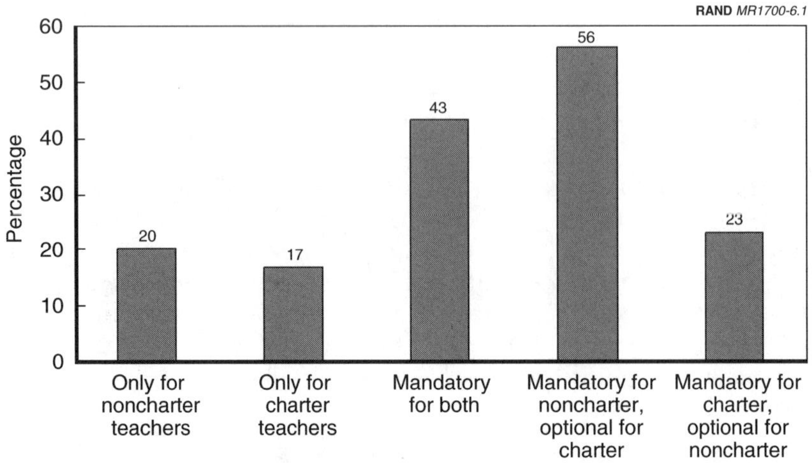

SOURCE: 2002 RAND chartering authority survey.
Sample size: 94.

Figure 6.1—Percentage of Chartering Authorities Offering Professional Development to Charter School and Noncharter School Teachers

These results are consistent with other research that suggests that charter schools are often responsible for paying for professional development (Horn and Miron, 1999; Center for Applied Research and Educational Improvement, 1998). Together, the results presented in Figures 6.1 and 6.2 show that chartering authorities are making professional development activities available to charter school teachers, but that much of the funding burden rests with the charter schools themselves.

Teacher Participation in Professional Development

The principal surveys provided information on teacher participation in professional development activities. First, we asked principals to report the percentages of teachers at the school who participated in various types of professional development over the last year. Figure 6.3 shows the differences in the percentages of charter schools and matched conventional public schools reporting that more than half of their teachers participated in the professional development

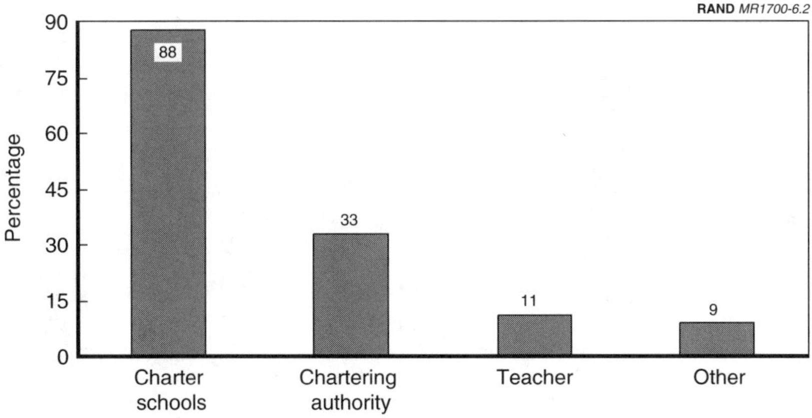

SOURCE: 2002 RAND chartering authority survey.
Sample size: 112.

Figure 6.2—Responsibilities for Paying for Professional Development

activities listed on our survey. Large teacher participation rates were more commonly reported by charter than by conventional public schools, with a statistically significant difference observed for courses for college credit and for mentoring, shadowing, peer observation, or coaching programs, which are often referred to as forms of "informal" professional development. Informal professional development has been shown to contribute to teaching effectiveness to a greater degree than the more formal workshop- and course-based forms (Garet et al., 2001), so this difference is noteworthy. In both types of schools, however, participation rates are reported to be highest in workshops and conferences. We examined participation rates in start-up and conversion schools and found that none of the differences between charter school types was statistically significant.

Principals and teachers at all nine case study schools reported strong emphasis on professional development, especially informal activities such as collaboration and mentoring. Charter school teachers who had spent time in conventional public schools typically claimed that the amount and quality of staff collaboration were higher in charter schools. In a number of schools, these activities were made possible through creative management and staffing plans or as a result of

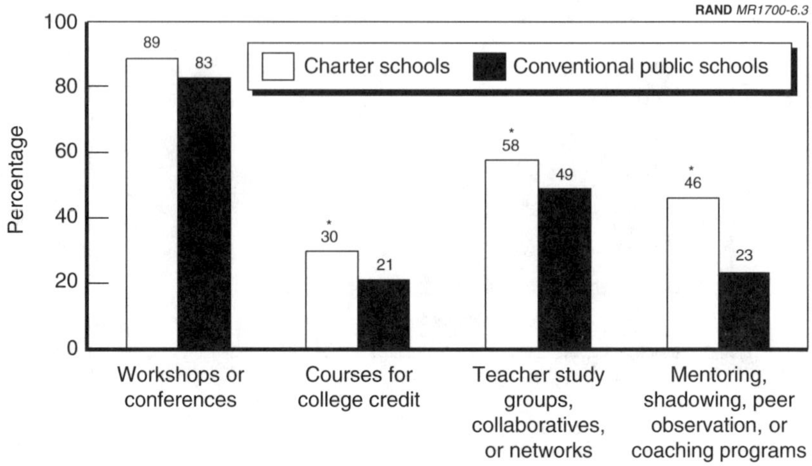

SOURCES: 2002 RAND charter school and matched conventional public school surveys.

Sample sizes: 249 charter schools and 180 conventional public schools.

*Indicates percentages that are statistically different from matched conventional public school percentages at the 5 percent level.

Figure 6.3—Percentage of Respondents Reporting That More Than Half of Their Teachers Participated in Professional Development Activities

teachers spending unpaid time to engage in them. For example, one school employed a full-time director of instruction who observed in classrooms on a daily basis and who oversaw an extensive feedback and mentoring program. At another, teachers reported spending lunch hours, breaks, and after-school time to share ideas and materials. A third school had implemented a salary review process in which professional development participation was considered in the determination of teacher raises, thereby providing an incentive for participation. Despite the apparent widespread use of informal professional development and the belief that charter schools provided better informal professional development opportunities than did conventional public schools, a number of teachers stated that they would have liked more time and resources for these types of activities.

We also examined the support structures that schools have enacted to ensure that teachers are able to participate in professional development activities. A large majority of both types of schools provided professional development time during teachers' regular contract hours—93 percent for charter schools and 96 percent for matched conventional public schools (this difference was not statistically significant). Among charter schools, conversion schools were slightly more likely than start-up schools (100 percent versus 90 percent) to provide paid time.

Figure 6.4 suggests that charter and matched conventional public schools use similar methods for providing teachers with time for

RAND *MR1700-6.4*

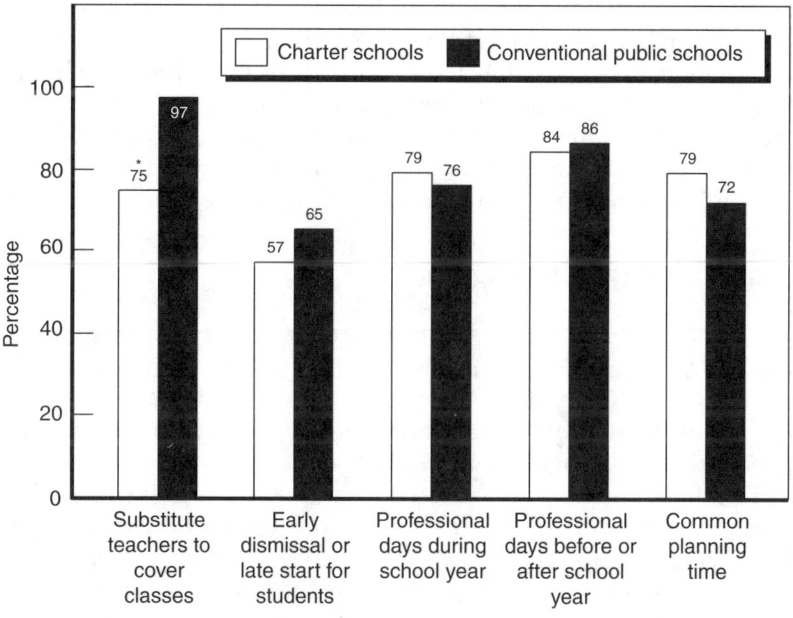

SOURCES: 2002 RAND charter school and matched conventional public school surveys.

Sample sizes: 235 charter schools and 173 conventional public schools.

*Indicates percentages that are statistically different from matched conventional public school percentages at the 5 percent level.

Figure 6.4—Methods for Providing Teachers Professional Development Time During Regular Contract Hours

professional development. The only statistically significant difference between them is that charter schools were less likely than conventional public schools to report using substitute teachers to cover classes. Almost all conventional public schools said that they used this approach, whereas only three-quarters of charter schools did. Our surveys do not indicate the reasons for the differences, but they are likely to stem in part from lack of access to substitute pools by some charter schools. Start-up and conversion schools reported similar emphasis on each of these methods except for substitute teachers and early dismissal or late start for students, both of which were significantly more likely to be used by conversion schools.

The results reported in this section suggest that charter schools are providing a variety of forms of professional development and that rates of teacher participation are at least as high as, and in some cases higher than, those in matched conventional public schools. Unfortunately, because we do not have any information on the quality of these experiences or on how teachers respond to them, it is impossible to determine whether this professional development is positively influencing the instruction that students receive.

CURRICULUM AND INSTRUCTION

Because we did not survey teachers and because our principal surveys had to cover a large number of topics, we were not able to obtain detailed information about curriculum and instruction. Our curriculum-related questions were limited to a few that addressed specific types of programs and time spent on various subjects. We discuss these survey responses below and then present some additional information obtained through the case studies. Readers should keep in mind that because the survey results are reported by principals rather than teachers, their accuracy may be limited, particularly for topics that involve teachers' choices about how to allocate time. These results provide some information on the ways curricular offerings differ across school types.

Programs and Scheduling Modifications

The first set of questions focused on specific programs. Both conventional and charter school principals were asked whether their schools offered bilingual programs and gifted and talented education (GATE) programs.[1] Both programs were approximately twice as likely to be offered by matched conventional public schools as by charter schools (Table 6.1).[2] These results should not necessarily be interpreted as indicating that charter schools are less likely than conventional public schools to meet the needs of students who would benefit from bilingual or GATE programs. In particular, our case study results suggest that some charter schools are committed to providing appropriate education to gifted students even in the absence of a formal program. One principal, for example, expressed a belief that all children benefit from a curriculum designed for gifted students, and stated that the school chose to offer such a curriculum to all students rather than to only a few. She noted that this created some tension with parents, some of whom thought a separate GATE program should be offered. Table 6.1 also displays the percentage of start-up and conversion schools offering the programs. Statistically significant differences were observed for both GATE and bilingual programs.

Table 6.1

Curriculum Programs in Charter Schools, by School Type

	Matched Conventional Public Schools (n = 182)	Charter Schools (n = 252)	Start-Up Schools (n = 182)	Conversion Schools (n = 69)
Bilingual program	49	26*	17	51**
GATE program	82	38*	27	65**

SOURCES: 2002 RAND charter school and matched conventional public school surveys.

*Indicates charter school percentages that are statistically different from matched conventional public school percentages at the 5 percent level.

**Indicates conversion school percentages that are statistically different from start-up school percentages at the 5 percent level.

---

[1]Principals were also asked about special education programs, which are discussed in Chapter Eight.

[2]It is worth noting that GATE funding is included in the categorical block grant. So, although charter schools may provide some sort of program for this population, they are not eligible for the targeted GATE program funds and do not need to comply with specific program requirements as a conventional public school would.

We also asked respondents whether their schools had implemented block scheduling or other modifications to the conventional public school day. Table 6.2 shows that the use of block scheduling and before- and after-school enrichment programs was similar across charter and conventional public schools, but that academic intersessions were more frequently offered by conventional public schools than by charter schools. Among charter schools, conversion schools were more likely than start-up schools to offer block scheduling and enrichment programs and were less likely to offer intersessions or summer school designed to provide extra assistance.

Although the results reported here seem to suggest that charter schools are less likely than matched conventional public schools to offer certain programs that are designed to meet the needs of specific students, we do not know the reasons for this, nor do we know whether charter schools are offering less formal programs that are designed to meet the same needs. The case study results regarding GATE programs, discussed above, reveal the importance of gathering more-detailed information about program offerings than was possible with our surveys.

Table 6.2

Scheduling Modifications, by School Type

	Matched Conventional Public Schools (n = 137)	Charter Schools (n = 251)	Start-Up Schools (n = 181)	Conversion Schools (n = 69)
Block scheduling	26	37	43	21**
Before- or after-school enrichment	76	69	64	83**
Academic intersessions or summer school to provide extra assistance for meeting expectations	83	55*	45	76**
Academic intersessions or summer school for acceleration	47	29*	26	36

SOURCES: 2002 RAND charter school and matched conventional public school surveys.

*Indicates charter school percentages that are statistically different from matched conventional public school percentages at the 5 percent level.

**Indicates conversion school percentages that are statistically different from start-up school percentages at the 5 percent level.

Courses and Academic Program Requirements

The next several questions were directed at respondents whose schools offered instruction at specific grade levels. First, we asked those whose schools included fourth grade to indicate how many hours of instruction were offered in each of several subjects to the typical fourth-grade student. Table 6.3 indicates the percentage who reported not offering each subject and the percentage who reported teaching it for five hours or more per week. As we mentioned above, readers should keep in mind that these principals' reports may not always accurately represent how teachers allocate their time. Validity of these responses may be particularly problematic for elementary schools that typically do not have specified times allocated to each subject. Nevertheless, the directions of differences between school types are likely to be reasonably accurate.

Although charter school principals reported offering approximately the same amount of instructional time in math, English/language arts, and other subjects as principals at conventional public schools, charter schools did report offering statistically significantly more instruction in foreign languages and fine arts. Among charter schools,

Table 6.3

Hours of Instruction Offered Each Week (4th Grade Only)

	Matched Conventional Public Schools (n = 112)		Charter Schools (n = 172)	
	None	5–6 Hours or More	None	5–6 Hours or More
English/language arts	0	92	0	88
Mathematics	0	89	0	88
Computer skills	9	3	18	7
Social studies	0	25	0	33
Sciences	1	20	0	20
Foreign languages	88	0	52*	6*
Fine arts	13	4	4*	7*
Physical education	3	11	2	13

SOURCES: 2002 RAND charter school and matched conventional public school surveys.

*Indicates percentages that are statistically different from matched conventional public school percentages at the 5 percent level.

although not shown in Table 6.3, conversion schools offered significantly more instruction than start-up schools in English/language arts, computer skills, and foreign languages.

We asked the same set of questions for principals whose schools offered instruction in seventh grade. The only statistically significant difference observed was for mathematics, which charter school principals reported offering in greater quantity than did conventional public school principals (Table 6.4). Conversion schools offered more instruction in foreign languages than start-up schools. Aside from this, no statistically significant differences were observed between charter school types.

Principals of charter schools in our case studies suggested that on average they offer a longer instructional day than conventional public schools do, and they noted that they spend at least some of the extra hours on instruction in subjects that tend to receive little attention, particularly at the elementary school level. It would be worthwhile in future studies to examine the school day schedule in detail

Table 6.4

Hours of Instruction Offered Each Week (7th Grade Only)

	Matched Conventional Public Schools (n = 64)		Charter Schools (n = 143)	
	None	5–6 Hours or More	None	5–6 Hours or More
English/language arts	0	70	0	81
Mathematics	0	61	0*	79*
Computer skills	14	11	13	7
Social studies	0	42	0	49
Sciences	0	42	0	45
Foreign languages	68	9	50	6
Fine arts	14	10	17	9
Physical education	5	33	7	26

SOURCES: 2002 RAND charter school and matched conventional public school surveys.

*Indicates percentages that are statistically different from matched conventional public school percentages at the 5 percent level.

to understand these time allocation differences. In addition, the previous two tables make it clear that curricular offerings vary widely for both charter and matched conventional public schools, with some schools offering, for example, no instruction in fine arts and others offering more than five hours per week.

Some of the differences in curriculum offerings between charter and conventional public schools may stem from a greater level of flexibility and autonomy among charter school teachers, which results largely from the lack of district mandates imposed on charter schools. Case study teachers frequently expressed appreciation for the fact that they had input into curricular decisions, and many of them had worked with their colleagues to develop new curriculum programs or to create supplemental materials to accompany purchased curricula. In addition, staff at some schools asserted that their schools offered a broader curriculum than is typical in conventional public schools. The fact that this breadth reduced the time available to devote to tested subjects created some tension, however. One principal stated:

> In the past, we did not place as much importance on the [state's content] standards. However, our API rating was dropping tremendously. So we were forced to look at standards and try to incorporate them into the curriculum. But I must stress that the arts and physical education are completely overlooked. We want to make sure to keep those subjects alive here.

This tension is discussed further in the section on student testing.

For schools offering instruction in 12th grade, we asked about the years of instruction in each subject required for high school graduation. These numbers are presented in Table 6.5. Charter schools on average required slightly more instruction in computer science than did their conventional public school counterparts; otherwise there were no differences. The similarity between school types probably reflects, at least in part, the need to comply with the admissions requirements set by the University of California and the California State University systems.

Table 6.5

Years of Instruction Required (12th Grade Only)

	Matched Conventional Public Schools (n = 58)	Charter Schools (n = 91)
English/language arts	3.4	3.2
Mathematics	2.1	2.3
Computer science	0.4	0.7*
Social sciences, social studies	2.8	2.9
Physical or biological sciences	1.9	1.9
Foreign languages	0.7	0.8
Fine arts	0.9	1.0
Physical education	1.8	1.8

SOURCES: 2002 RAND charter school and matched conventional public school surveys.

*Indicates percentages that are statistically different from matched conventional public school percentages at the 5 percent level.

We also asked respondents whose schools included 12th grade to specify the number of Advanced Placement (AP) courses their schools offered. We instructed them to count multiple sections of a single course only once, so the reported number should indicate the number of different courses offered. Conventional public schools reported offering an average of 7.6 courses, significantly more than the 1.3 offered by the average charter school. This difference may result in part from the larger enrollment in conventional public schools, but it does suggest that students in charter high schools may lack access to some AP courses.

Computers

We asked respondents to specify the number of computers available for instructional purposes in the school. Both charter and matched conventional public schools reported a computer-to-student ratio of approximately one to four with no significant difference.

This section discusses only a small fraction of the program and curricular elements that are of interest when trying to understand the instructional environments of charter and conventional public schools. There is some evidence that although charter schools report fewer formal programs for GATE, bilingual, and advanced placement students, charter elementary schools are somewhat more likely than conventional public schools to offer instruction in arts and foreign language. The case studies provide more details on curricular offerings and suggest that many charter school teachers and principals are committed to offering a rich, innovative curriculum that adequately serves all of their students. Again, charter schools often look very different from one another on these measures, so it is impossible to provide any generalizable descriptions of curriculum in charter schools.

STUDENT TESTING

California's Standardized Testing and Reporting program is designed to provide information that teachers and administrators can use to evaluate their own effectiveness and to change instructional programs as needed. STAR is part of a broader state accountability system that is intended to create incentives for schools to improve and to provide assistance to schools that show persistently poor performance. Although charter schools are subject to the same testing and accountability provisions as conventional public schools, some charter schools may have program emphases that result in a decreased emphasis on the state's standards and testing system. Charter school administrators and teachers in a study by Ascher et al. (1999) indicated that they experienced some tension between the need to meet state standards and their desire for autonomy, and many of them indicated that they made some curricular and instructional decisions as a result of state standards and testing. Examining the degree to which charter schools focus on STAR in their instructional activities and planning is important for understanding differences in operations between charter and conventional public schools and for interpreting any differences that are observed in test scores between the two types of school.

Our principal surveys included two sets of questions regarding the school's responses to STAR. Table 6.6 shows the proportions of charter and conventional public school principals who said they used STAR data for specific purposes. We limited these analyses to schools that participated in STAR testing in 2001. Charter schools reported significantly lower rates than conventional public schools for all six of our listed uses of STAR data. Even so, these activities

Table 6.6

Percentage of Schools Reporting Various Responses to STAR Data

Response	Matched Conventional Public Schools (n = 181)	Charter Schools (n = 252)	Start-Up Schools (n = 142)	Conversion Schools (n = 68)
Realign curriculum	89	71*	65	90**
Reassign students to supplemental instruction	91	70*	65	79**
Determine next year's instructional focus	94	71*	68	87**
Allocate resources	80	62*	57	77**
Identify problems with teaching	82	68*	68	69**
Shape content of professional development	93	71*	65	84**

SOURCES: 2002 RAND charter school and matched conventional public school surveys.

*Indicates charter school percentages that are statistically different from matched conventional public school percentages at the 5 percent level.

**Indicates conversion school percentages that are statistically different from start-up school percentages at the 5 percent level.

were not uncommon in charter schools, with approximately two-thirds or more reporting that they engaged in these actions.

The table also shows the percentages for start-up and conversion schools. As with many of our other items, conversion schools more closely resembled matched conventional public schools than did start-up schools on most indicators. Conversion schools were statistically significantly more likely than start-up schools to report all uses except "identify problems with teaching." It should also be noted, though not shown on these tables, that the percentage of start-up schools that participated in STAR in 2001 was smaller than the percentage of conversion schools that participated.

The other set of questions focusing on STAR asked principals to report whether they had taken each of three actions in response to the STAR testing program. These analyses were also limited to schools that participated in STAR in 2001. Charter schools were less likely than matched conventional public schools to have held staff meetings that focused on STAR and to develop a school plan for improving STAR performance (Table 6.7). There was no statistically significant difference in the percentages of charter and conventional public schools that reported implementing test-preparation activities.

Table 6.7

Percentage of Schools Reporting Various Responses to STAR Data, by Charter School Type

Response	Matched Conventional Public Schools (n = 143)	Charter Schools (n = 204)	Start-Up Schools (n = 142)	Conversion Schools (n = 68)
Hold staff meetings that focus on STAR	88	79*	73	92**
Develop school plan for improving STAR performance	82	66*	59	89**
Implementing test-preparation activities	78	73	74	74

SOURCES: 2002 RAND charter school and matched conventional public school surveys.

*Indicates charter school percentages that are statistically different from matched conventional public school percentages at the 5 percent level.

**Indicates conversion school percentages that are statistically different from start-up school percentages at the 5 percent level.

Among start-up and conversion schools, conversion schools were more likely than start-up schools to report engaging in the first two listed actions but, again, no difference was observed for test preparation.

Together, these results suggest that the instructional environments in some charter schools may be less heavily influenced by the state testing program than is the environment in the typical conventional public school, but large numbers of charter schools do make an effort to tailor their programs to the need to increase their STAR scores. Some of the differences between start-up and conversion schools may result from the fact that the newer start-up schools have less experience with the STAR program and have not yet determined how it will be incorporated into their educational programs; we can expect these numbers to change as these schools become more involved in the state's accountability system.

Teachers and principals at the case study schools gave mixed responses regarding the role of the state's standards and accountability system in shaping their instructional programs. At three schools, staff indicated that although they acknowledged the importance of incorporating the standards into instruction and of attaining high test scores, these factors did not have a strong influence on instruction in their schools. One teacher who had previously taught in a conventional public school stated that "In [traditional] public schools everything was about the Stanford 9. Here, that is not true." A principal in another school noted that the school was more accountable to its chartering authority than to the state, and that "the state is depending way too much on the API to see performance of schools." Most of the staff at these schools asserted that their curricula were in fact reasonably well aligned with the state standards, despite the decisions of the staff to avoid placing a heavy emphasis on standards and testing.

At the remaining six schools, staff described the instructional environment as being strongly shaped by the state standards and tests. Staff in a Montessori school reported having chosen a specific Montessori curriculum because it was ostensibly aligned with the state standards. At another school, the standards were posted on the walls in each classroom, and teachers described the standards as being the primary driver of classroom practices. Staff at all of these schools expressed frustration at having to meet test-score goals while being expected to implement innovative programs. One teacher said that the state seemed to be sending the message that the school should "innovate but fit in a box." Some teachers were particularly concerned about their obligation to meet the needs of students who traditionally do not perform well on such tests as the Stanford 9, particularly students whose first language was not English.

Curricular changes in response to standards and test scores were common among the schools we visited. At a school that offered a bilingual program organized around social studies themes, staff mentioned their frustration at having to respond to a drop in the school's Academic Performance Index. This school had recently adopted a new emphasis on literacy in response to the drop in scores, resulting in a shift away from the social-studies-based curriculum around which the school was originally conceived. Teachers at this school strongly believed that their approach was effective but that they had not been given enough time to prove it. In addition, some expressed the opinion that the narrow focus of the state's testing program actually harmed students by limiting their exposure to information about other cultures. Such opinions were not uniform across the case study schools, however; many teachers and principals stated that although it was sometimes difficult to offer a broad curriculum while meeting state standards, it was in fact a manageable task.

Several principals mentioned the innovation/accountability tension as one of the primary challenges faced by charter schools. One described the challenge as follows:

> We are struggling with questions of loss of innovation and a measurement of flexibility for the schools. I wish there were a way to have a bit more freedom so we could see over time how the school could actually help the students. Perhaps we should figure out new ways in which the schools can be held accountable, but this would take a bit of faith on the policymaker's part to afford us this freedom.

This principal, like many others we interviewed, did not deny the importance of holding charter schools accountable for student performance but thought that the current system was too rigid and narrowly focused. Although for the purposes of the present study we did not visit conventional public schools, these sentiments are similar to many that have been expressed by conventional public school staff in other studies and in media reports.

These findings, although far from definitive, suggest that imposing standards-based accountability on charter schools may be an effective approach for promoting a reasonable degree of emphasis on content that the state considers important but at the same time may frustrate some staff who want to offer innovative curriculum or instruction. Large proportions of survey respondents reported using the state's testing program to shape instruction, and staff at all of our case study schools were aware of the need to meet state standards even though they varied in the relative emphasis they placed on them. It would be valuable to monitor charter schools' efforts to respond to accountability requirements, especially as the provisions of the new federal educational accountability legislation take hold.

PARENT INVOLVEMENT

The fourth major topic examined in this chapter is parent involvement. Opportunity for parent participation is often believed to be one of the strengths of charter schools, and studies suggest that charter schools tend to be effective at engaging parents. Our surveys included a set of questions that asked principals to indicate whether their schools offered specific types of parent involvement opportunities, and the level of parent participation in each.

Table 6.8 provides the percentages of respondents in charter and conventional public schools who reported using various means of facilitating parent participation and the reported rates of parent participation. Figure 6.5 shows the reported participation rates in each activity. The summaries of participation rates include only those respondents who said that their school used a particular approach or activity. Charter schools were statistically significantly more likely than matched conventional public schools to use contracts between parents and school, although more than two-thirds of conventional public schools reported engaging in this practice. However, it is not clear how principals defined the term "contract," which makes these results difficult to interpret. Of the charter schools that did use contracts, almost all of them reported high rates of parent participation, whereas participation rates in conventional public schools were lower. It is not clear from our survey results why the participation

Table 6.8

Percentage of Charter and Matched Conventional Public Schools Offering Parent Involvement Opportunities

	Matched Conventional Public Schools (n = 184)	Charter Schools (n = 253)
Open house or back-to-school night	98	92*
Parent-teacher conferences	80	87
Special events (e.g., science fairs, concerts)	90	81*
Parent education workshops	69	67
Contract between school and parent	68	80*
Parents volunteering in school	92	92
Parents involved in instructional issues	88	73*
Parents involved in governance	91	89
Parents involved in budget decisions	91	77*

SOURCES: 2002 RAND charter school and matched conventional public school surveys.

*Indicates percentages that are statistically different from matched conventional public school percentages at the 5 percent level.

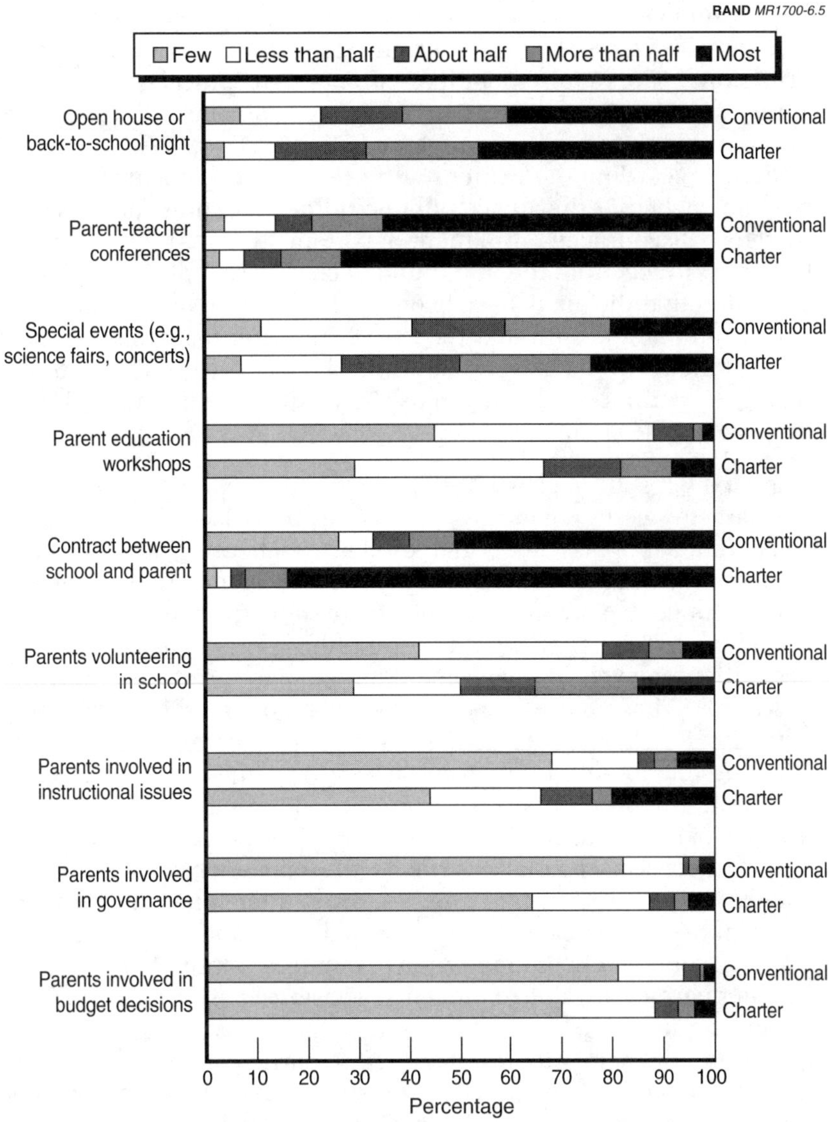

SOURCES: 2002 RAND charter school and matched conventional public school surveys.

Figure 6.5—Rates of Parent Participation in Charter and Matched Conventional Public Schools

rates would vary, or what principals meant by "participation"—e.g., whether this referred to simply signing the contract or meeting its provisions. The requirement that parents sign contracts may affect access to charter schools and could potentially contribute to the problem of "skimming" discussed in Chapter Two. Without more evidence regarding the content of these contracts, however, we do not know whether they placed undue burden on some families and therefore discouraged enrollment of certain students. An examination of contracts from the first round of charter schools in California suggested that they may have been used as a way to ensure compliance from parents, and that the use of such contracts may exclude some students from charter schools (Becker et al., 1997), but without seeing the contracts currently in use by schools in our study, it is impossible to determine their effects.

Our survey results suggested that several other parent involvement mechanisms were statistically significantly more likely to be used by conventional public schools than by charter schools. These included open houses or back-to-school nights, special events such as science fairs or concerts, and parent involvement in instructional issues and in budget decisions. It is not clear that these results necessarily reflect different levels of involvement among parents at the two types of schools. First, charter schools reported higher *rates* of parent participation for all of these activities, as shown in Figure 6.5. Second, it is impossible to determine from these survey questions the level of involvement of parents. For example, the apparent widespread practice of involving parents in instructional issues, governance, and budget decisions probably reflects the existence of school site councils or other governance bodies. Even though parents formally participate on these bodies, their actual decisionmaking influence is likely to vary widely among schools, and it is impossible to assess whether parents are able to influence decisions in meaningful ways.
The next question on the charter school survey asked whether parents or family members were required to participate or volunteer at the school. Forty-three percent of respondents said that there was some mandatory parent involvement. Start-up schools were statistically significantly more likely to require parent involvement than were conversion schools (48 percent versus 33 percent). A requirement for parent involvement suggests a strong commitment on the part of the school to engaging parents in their children's education

but, again, without knowing the nature of the involvement or how many parents are successfully engaged, it is difficult to interpret these differences.

The case studies revealed a variety of parent involvement mechanisms and approaches, including mandated volunteer time, membership on boards or governance councils, and parent-teacher conferences. One school even required parents to interview before enrolling their children and, because the school was oversubscribed, used the interviews to determine which students would be admitted; the focus was on determining whether the parents were sufficiently informed about and committed to the school's mission. Our visits also revealed some challenges that arose from charter schools' efforts to balance parents' desires for involvement with other needs of the schools. The principal of one school reported that founding parents wanted to "run the school" and "make fundamental changes in conflict with the charter, specifically over issues of student discipline." The school responded by developing a new set of bylaws that limited the representation of parents on the executive board. Staff at several schools said that the fact that parents chose the school facilitated involvement and made teachers more accountable to parents than would be the case in a school they did not choose. The two schools serving primarily Hispanic student populations expressed the most concern about low levels of parent involvement and had instituted programs to provide outreach to families.

STUDENT DISCIPLINE

In this section we discuss two sets of survey questions that elicited principals' assessments of student disciplinary problems. This information is important in part because it affects the instructional environment of the school but also because some critics of charter schools have suggested that any academic success charter schools achieve is a result of easier-to-teach student populations. These questions, along with the discussions of charter school students in Chapter Two and special education in Chapter Eight, shed some light on possible differences in student populations between charter and conventional public schools.

The first set of questions asked principals how many students were suspended or expelled during the past year. We divided these numbers by the school's enrollment to obtain a percentage for each school. Figure 6.6 shows that charter schools reported statistically significantly fewer in-school suspensions but did not statistically differ from conventional public schools in the percentage of out-of-school suspensions or expulsions.

Next we asked principals to specify the percentage of students experiencing problems with each of a set of behavioral and health issues. Figure 6.7 presents the average reported percentages for charter and conventional public schools. There were no significant differences on any of these questions other than student dropout and pregnancy, for which the charter school percentage was statistically significantly higher than the conventional public school percentage. These results indicate that charter and conventional public school principals generally perceive similar degrees of difficulty with each of these issues.

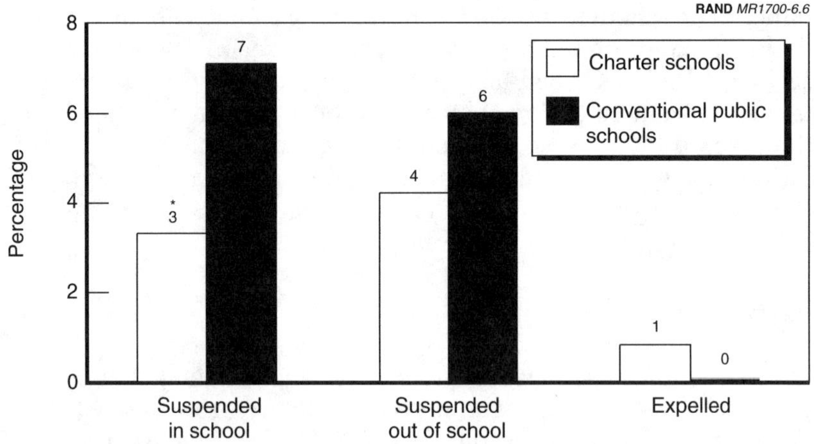

SOURCES: 2002 RAND charter school and matched conventional public school surveys.

Sample sizes: 253 charter schools and 183 conventional public schools.

*Indicates percentages that are statistically different from matched conventional public school percentages at the 5 percent level.

Figure 6.6—Percentage of Students Suspended or Expelled over the Past Year

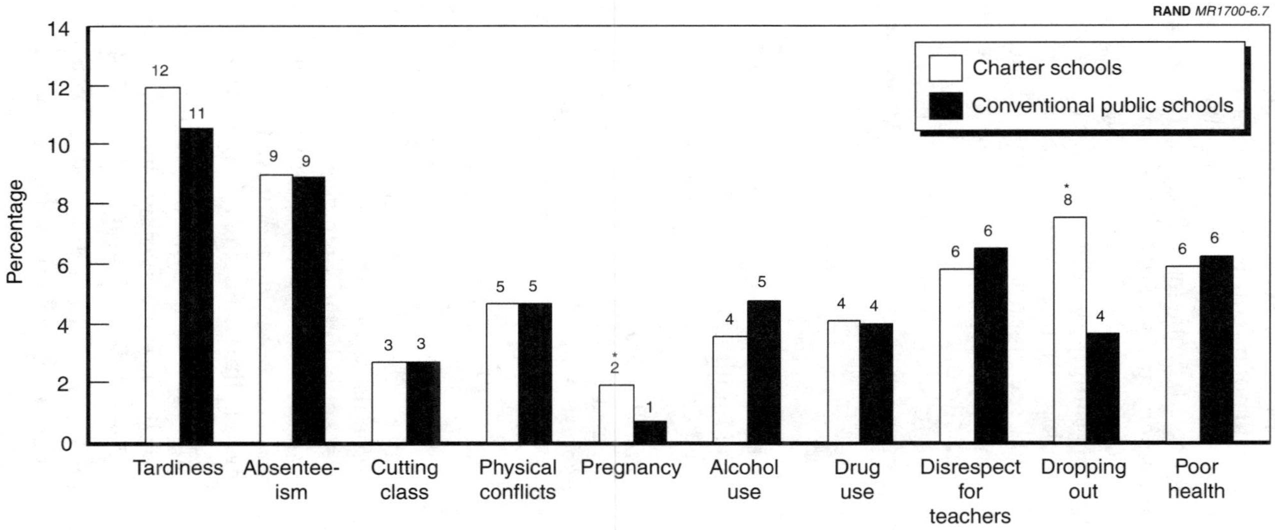

SOURCES: 2002 RAND charter school and matched conventional public school surveys.
Sample sizes: 254 charter schools and 184 conventional public schools.
*Indicates percentages that are statistically different from matched conventional public school percentages at the 5 percent level.
NOTE: Figure numbers have been rounded to the nearest whole number.

Figure 6.7—Percentage of Students Experiencing Behavioral or Health Problems

As with the other survey questions discussed in this chapter, the findings presented here should not be considered definitive evidence of a lack of difference between school types. In particular, the questions about behavioral and health problems are subject to principals' interpretations of the frequency and severity of each problem. It is possible that rates of some of these behaviors may be higher than reported and that principals simply do not view them as major "problems." At the same time, there may be underreporting for some of these behaviors and issues, for a variety of reasons including but not limited to lack of awareness. However, there is no reason to believe that these potential sources of bias would apply to a greater extent to one type of school than to another, and it is unlikely that these results are masking any large differences between school types.

SUMMARY

Here we briefly summarize the main findings presented in this chapter and discuss some of the limitations and implications of these analyses.

- *Professional development:* Charter school principals report higher rates of teacher participation in informal professional development, such as mentoring and shadowing programs, than do conventional public school principals. This difference is noteworthy because there is some evidence that informal professional development is linked to improved student achievement (Garet et al., 2001).
- *Program offerings:* Charter schools are less likely than matched conventional public schools to offer some types of programs (e.g., GATE or summer school), but it is not clear that this translates into differences in how well students are served. Case studies suggest that charter schools look for ways to provide appropriate instruction even in the absence of a formal program.
- *Curriculum:* Charter schools report offering more instruction in noncore subjects such as fine arts and foreign languages than do matched conventional public schools, particularly in 4th grade.
- *Testing:* Charter schools report less influence of STAR on instructional planning and practice than do matched conventional

public schools, but they do not differ in reported involvement in test-preparation activities.

- *Parent involvement:* Charter schools differed from matched conventional public schools in the percentages offering some types of parent involvement activities, and charter schools reported higher rates of parent participation in those activities that were offered.
- *Student discipline:* Reports of disciplinary action and perceptions of behavior problems did not differ between charter schools and matched conventional public schools.

Chapter Seven

STAFFING IN CHARTER AND CONVENTIONAL PUBLIC SCHOOLS

Cassandra Guarino

INTRODUCTION

Charter schools are allowed to diverge from standard district policies with respect to several issues involving the workforce. Statewide regulations regarding teacher qualifications are somewhat more relaxed for charter schools than for conventional public schools, although not all charter schools differ from their conventional school counterparts in this regard.[1] Charter school legislation allows for an even greater relaxation of regulations with regard to the certification and experience of school principals than it does for teachers. In addition, the legislation grants charter school principals the flexibility to employ, compensate, and dismiss teachers without having to submit to the intervention of a district or a teacher's union, although the degree to which charter school principals make use of these exemptions varies.

In this chapter, we examine the extent to which charter and conventional public schools—and different types of charter schools—differ along dimensions related to the qualifications, hiring, compensation,

[1]The Charter Schools Act of 1992 states that "Teachers in charter schools shall be required to hold a Commission on Teacher Credentialing certificate, permit, or other document equivalent to that which a teacher in other public schools would be required to hold. . . . It is the intent of the Legislature that charter schools be given flexibility with regard to noncore, noncollege preparatory courses."

and working conditions of teachers and principals. In addition, we explore principals' perceptions of the importance of the flexibility with regard to staffing that is permitted under the law and the degree to which this flexibility is used. The data to support these analyses come from our surveys of principals and from administrative data from California's Department of Education. In addition, these data are supplemented with insights gathered during our visits to charter school sites.

THE CHARACTERISTICS OF TEACHERS

To investigate the differences in the qualifications of instructional staff between charter and conventional public schools, we analyzed data from the PAIF of 2001–02, a database containing information regarding the characteristics and instructional assignments of all teachers in California. We took data from the PAIF for the subsample of charter and matched conventional public schools that responded to our surveys.[2] We used these data to investigate possible differences between the staffs of charter and matched conventional public schools with respect to credentials, education, and experience. The reason for limiting this analysis to these schools was to maintain our ability to compare charter schools to conventional public schools with similar demographics and to maintain consistency with the rest of the report. We discuss the results of our analysis below.

Teaching Credentials

Although evidence from the literature is mixed on whether credentialing matters in relation to student achievement (e.g., Goldhaber and Brewer, 2000, 2001), politicians and educators across the country often advocate increasing the proportion of credentialed teachers within the classroom, especially in low-income schools (e.g., Darling-Hammond et al., 2001). In this section, we use the PAIF data to examine the extent to which charter and matched conventional public schools use credentialed teachers. The PAIF data can be aggregated to calculate the percentages of teachers in each school who have full credentials, emergency credentials, waivers, and other types of

---

[2]See Appendix A for our weighted adjustments for nonresponse bias.

permits such as district internships, precredentials, etc. Using these data, Table 7.1 shows that approximately 76 percent of charter school teachers possessed a full teaching credential in 2001–02, whereas approximately 88 percent of teachers in matched conventional public schools possessed a full credential[3]—a statistically significant difference. Approximately 21 percent of charter school teachers held

Table 7.1

Percentage of Teachers, by Qualification Type

Qualification	Matched Conventional Public Schools (n = 184)	Charter Schools (n = 257)	Conversion Schools (n = 70)	Start-Up Schools (n = 180)
Full credential	87.5	75.8*	88.0**	67.4
Emergency credential	10.0	21.5*	15.6**	27.4
Waiver	0.8	2.1*	0.9**	3.3
Full credential (core secondary school teachers)	86.4	71.7*	—	—
Subject authorization (elementary school teachers)	95.7	96.0	—	—
Subject authorization (secondary school English teachers)	73.4	53.7*	—	—
Subject authorization (secondary school math teachers)	79.7	50.1*	—	—
Subject authorization (secondary school science teachers)	85.1	57.6*	—	—

SOURCE: California Department of Education PAIF data.

*Indicates charter school percentages that are statistically different from matched conventional public school percentages at the 5 percent level.

**Indicates conversion school percentages that are statistically different from start-up school percentages at the 5 percent level.

---

[3]To obtain a true picture of the amount of instruction delivered by credentialed staff, all percentages were calculated using the number of full-time-equivalent (FTE) teachers (rather than the number of individual teachers) in each category divided by the total number of full-time-equivalent teaching staff, since a significant number of teachers worked part time. The percentage estimates and the statistical comparisons were then calculated according to the procedure described in Appendix B. The regressions were weighted by a weight consisting of the survey school analysis weight multiplied by the total teaching FTE for each school to produce the overall proportion of teachers in the specific categories in charter schools and conventional public schools.

emergency credentials, in contrast to 10 percent of teachers in matched conventional public schools. Again, this difference was significant in the statistical sense. Two percent of charter school teachers and less than 1 percent of matched conventional public school teachers had waivers. The remaining 1 to 2 percent of teachers in both school types were distributed among various types of internships.

Within the group of charter schools, approximately 67 percent of teachers in start-up schools possessed a full credential, in contrast to 88 percent in conversion schools—again, a statistically significant difference. Start-up schools employed larger percentages of teachers with emergency credentials than did conversion schools—27 versus 16 percent, and the difference was statistically significant.

Since the PAIF data allow us to look at the types of teachers teaching various classes and assignments, we are also able to look at the percentage of credentialed teachers teaching *core* subjects in secondary schools. Core subjects are defined as English, mathematics, social studies, science, and foreign language. For secondary schools, approximately 72 percent of charter school core teachers possessed a full credential, whereas 86 percent of core teachers in matched conventional public schools possessed a full credential—a statistically significant difference. Nearly all of the remainder of core teachers in both types of secondary schools possessed emergency credentials.

In addition, we are able to determine the percentage of teachers teaching subjects for which they had obtained a *subject authorization*. In elementary schools, we checked to see what percentage of teachers had either an elementary, self-contained classroom, or multiple-subject credential. In secondary schools, we checked to see what percentage of teachers teaching English, mathematics, and science had secondary or subject-specific classroom authorizations in the subject being taught. Our analysis suggests no significant difference at the elementary school level, with 96 percent of both charter and conventional elementary school teachers in possession of the relevant authorization. At the secondary school level, however, the differences were large and statistically significant. The analysis shows that 54, 50, and 58 percent of charter secondary school teachers teaching English, mathematics, and science, respectively, possessed the relevant subject authorization, in contrast to 73, 80, and 85 percent of secondary school teachers in matched conventional public schools.

It is important to note that the regulation requiring that teachers in core subjects hold the same qualifications that are required in conventional public schools was imposed on charter schools years after the original charter legislation was written. This regulation came in the form of a 1998 amendment to the original 1992 legislation (see Chapter One). It is therefore possible that some start-up schools might lag behind conversion and conventional public schools in the percentages of teachers with full credentials in the time period represented by our data—namely, the 2001–02 school year. Since most start-up schools were formed after 1998, however, it is more likely that funding or teacher supply constraints may be factors producing the differences in the qualifications of teachers in these schools.

Teaching Experience

Another factor often considered to be related to the quality of instruction is the experience level of teachers. Again, using the PAIF data, Figure 7.1 shows that teachers in charter schools were, on average, less experienced than those in noncharter schools. The analysis shows that the average charter school teacher had approximately 10.1 years of experience in contrast to the 13.6 years of experience possessed by the average matched conventional public school teacher—a statistically significant difference.

The experience differential between teachers in start-up and conversion schools was also notable. Teachers in start-up schools possessed, on average, 8.7 years of experience, in contrast to the 11.4 years of experience of the average teacher in a conversion school. In addition, teachers in large charter schools collectively had more experience than those in small charter schools (11 versus nine years).

The experience of teachers in core subjects also differed for charter and noncharter secondary schools. Core teachers in charter secondary schools possessed an average of nine years of experience, in contrast to 13 years of experience for their secondary school counterparts in matched conventional public schools.

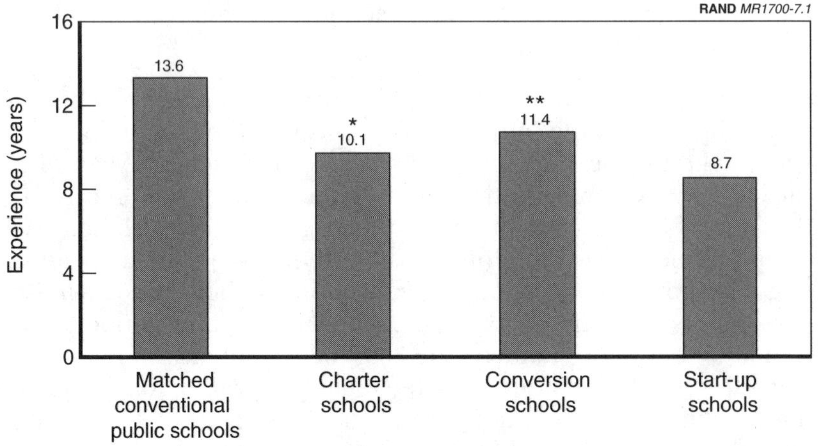

SOURCE: California Department of Education PAIF data.

*Indicates charter school percentages that are statistically different from matched conventional public school percentages at the 5 percent level.

**Indicates conversion school percentages that are statistically different from start-up school percentages at the 5 percent level.

Figure 7.1—Teacher Experience

THE CHARACTERISTICS OF PRINCIPALS

In this section, we examine the characteristics of principals in charter and conventional public schools using responses from our principal survey. The survey asked principals to describe their qualifications, experience, and demographic characteristics. We find a number of differences in the characteristics of charter school and matched conventional public school principals and between principals of different types of charter schools. Whether these differences are correlated with differences in quality is beyond the scope of this study, but they do suggest that either financial constraints cause charter schools to hire principals with fewer educational credentials or that underlying philosophical differences exist between charter and conventional public schools in the value placed on certain attributes of school leaders. One caveat to keep in mind in interpreting these data is that they are based on self-reports.

Credentials and Qualifications of Principals

We found that the principals in charter schools were less likely than principals in matched conventional public schools to report having either a teaching credential or an administrative credential, and the differences were statistically significant. The results of this analysis are displayed in Table 7.2. Eighty-six versus 99 percent of charter and matched conventional public school principals, respectively, reported having a teaching credential, and 61 versus 97 percent reported having an administrative credential. Since the administrative credential generally consists of a master's degree in California, it is not surprising to find that more than 95 percent of matched conventional public school principals reported that they had a master's degree or more, whereas 76 percent of charter school principals reported that they had this level of postgraduate education.

Within the group of charter schools, principals of start-up schools were less likely than principals of conversion schools to have a full teaching credential, an administrative credential, or a master's degree—80, 49, and 71 percent versus 100, 93, and 91 percent, respectively.

We also examined the prior experience of principals. Charter and matched conventional public school principals differed significantly with respect to their prior occupations, as might be expected, given the latitude of charter school legislation on this point. We asked

Table 7.2

Percentage of Principals, by Qualification Type

Qualification	Matched Conventional Public Schools (n = 182)	Charter Schools (n = 251)	Conversion Schools (n = 68)	Start-Up Schools (n = 180)
Full credential	99.2	85.6*	100.0**	80.2
Administrative credential	97.0	61.2*	92.9**	49.1
Master's degree	94.5	76.3*	90.6**	70.8

SOURCES: 2002 RAND charter school and matched conventional public school surveys.

*Indicates charter school percentages that are statistically different from matched conventional public school percentages at the 5 percent level.

**Indicates conversion school percentages that are statistically different from start-up school percentages at the 5 percent level.

principals to tell us which of the following categories described their most recent prior occupation: principal, assistant principal, other school administrative position, teacher, other occupation within the field of education, and other occupation outside the field of education. We also asked whether the prior positions relating to education were in private schools or public schools. Whereas over 73 percent of conventional public school principals answered that they were principals or assistant principals of public schools before taking on their current position, only 40 percent of the charter school principals gave this response. No principals of matched conventional public schools said that they had been administrators in private schools, whereas 6 percent of charter school principals had come from private school administration. Although 12.9 percent of principals in matched conventional public schools came to the principalship from a teaching position, 22 percent of charter school principals had been teachers immediately before taking their current positions, and whereas only one conventional public school principal came from a nonteaching or nonadministrative occupation outside the field of education, 10 percent of the charter school principals (25) came from an occupation outside the field of education. All differences in prior occupation between charter and matched conventional public school principals were statistically significant.

Administrative and Teaching Experience

We also asked principals to tell us the amount of school administration and teaching experience they possessed. As shown in Table 7.3, principals in charter schools had shorter tenures in their current schools than those in matched conventional public schools (3.1 years versus 4.4 years), as would be expected, since so many charter schools are very new. Charter school principals tended to have less total experience in school administration, as well—9.1 versus 11.5 years. Charter and matched conventional public school principals showed no statistically significant difference with respect to classroom teaching experience, however. Both reported an average of about 12 to 13-1/2 years of this type of experience.

Table 7.3

Principal Experience

	Matched Conventional Public Schools		Charter Schools		Conversion Schools		Start-Up Schools	
Experience	No.	%	No.	%	No.	%	No.	%
Tenure at current school	182	4.4	248	3.1*	66	5.2**	182	2.4
Total years of experience as a school administrator	179	11.5	246	9.1*	66	11.4**	180	8.2
Total years of classroom teaching experience	184	13.6	248	12.1	66	12.0	182	12.0

SOURCES: 2002 RAND charter school and matched conventional public school surveys.

*Indicates charter school percentages that are statistically different from matched conventional public school percentages at the 5 percent level.

**Indicates conversion school percentages that are statistically different from start-up school percentages at the 5 percent level.

Within the group of charter schools, principals of start-up schools had shorter tenures and less experience as administrators than those in conversion schools—2.4 and 8.2 versus 5.2 and 11.4 years, respectively. Start-up and conversion school principals did not show a statistically significant difference in the amount of teaching experience they possessed (approximately 12 years for both types of principals).

Principals of small charter schools have shorter tenures and less experience as administrators than those in large charter schools—1.9 and 7.2 versus 4.6 and 13 years, respectively.[4] Principals in small and large charter schools do not show a statistically significant difference in the amount of teaching experience they possess.

---

[4]Multivariate analyses revealed that the importance of school size in relation to the tenure of charter school principals diminished when controlling for the status of the school (conversion or start-up). The importance of school size remained strong in relation to administrative experience, however, even after controlling for status.

In addition to examining the qualifications of principals, we also asked about their demographic characteristics. We found that principals in charter schools were more likely to be female. In fact, the majority (57 percent) of charter school principals were female, compared to 44 percent of matched conventional public school principals, a statistically significant difference. With respect to the race or ethnicity of principals in the two types of schools, we found no differences.

WORKING CONDITIONS AND COMPENSATION OF TEACHERS

According to information provided on our survey of principals, teachers in charter schools reportedly worked an average of five days more per year than those in matched conventional public schools, and the difference was statistically significant. It is important to remember, however, that these data are based on principals' reported estimates. According to their principals, teachers in both types of schools often worked more than the required number of hours per week.

Although we did not have access to data on the salaries of teachers, we asked principals about the use of salary schedules and collective bargaining agreements in setting salaries. The responses from the surveys suggest that charter and matched conventional public schools differed substantially in the use of these instruments. Seventy-eight percent of charter school principals reported that they used a salary schedule, whereas all matched conventional public schools had schedules. Our analysis suggests that about a third of charter schools—32 percent—were engaged in collective bargaining agreements with a teachers' union, whereas 83 percent of the matched conventional public schools reported such an arrangement—a statistically significant difference.

Although a number of the schools we visited used a set salary schedule, merit pay had been instituted in a number of others. In one case, a teacher found this to be objectionable. One school gave standard starting salaries to new teachers but rewarded continuing teachers on the basis of performance. At the time we visited it, this particular school was in the process of developing an explicit set of performance pay criteria.

WORKING CONDITIONS AND COMPENSATION OF PRINCIPALS

In our surveys of school principals, we asked them to specify where their salary fell within a range of salaries. We also asked them to report the number of hours they worked and the number of days they were contractually bound to work each year. We found a number of differences between charter and matched conventional public school principals in compensation and working conditions and between different types of charter schools.

On average, principals in charter schools received a lower salary than did their counterparts in conventional public schools, and the distribution of earnings was quite different. Thirty-four percent of charter school principals reported annual earnings of less than $65,001, compared to only 9 percent of matched conventional public school principals. Ninety percent of matched conventional public school principals earned between $65,001 and $110,000, compared to 63 percent for charter school principals. Twenty-seven percent of matched conventional public school principals earned more than $95,000, whereas only 14 percent of charter school principals earned this amount.

The reported number of hours worked per week did not show a statistically significant difference for the two types of principals—these averaged between 51 and 53 hours during the regular school year and between 27 and 30 hours during the summer. Charter school principals reported working an average of 218 contracted days per year, and noncharter school principals reported working an average of 213 contracted days per year. The difference approached statistical significance at the 5 percent level.[5]

In general, we know from prior research on principal labor markets (Gates et al., 2003) that elementary school principals are more likely to be female and to earn less than secondary school principals, so the

[5]The t-statistic for this difference was 1.85 and the p-value was .0655.

lower grade span of charter schools may explain the differences we find in gender and salary. In addition, the same prior research informs us that principals in smaller schools tend to earn less than those in larger schools. Thus, the smaller average size of charter schools further explains the reported differences in compensation. We also found in our data that start-up school principals tended to be less like matched conventional public school principals than conversion school principals, further accounting for the observed differences along every dimension reported.

Our site visits to charter schools informed us that financial constraints may also contribute to differences in the compensation of principals in some schools. One principal told us that she worked only four days a week to meet budget constraints and that enrollment growth beyond 80 students had been necessary to allow for a principal's salary to be paid. Another school with over 1,000 students, on the other hand, was co-led by two principals with specialized roles, suggesting that economies of scale that could be used to pay for administrators existed when schools were larger.

THE COMPOSITION OF THE INSTRUCTIONAL STAFF

The composition of the instructional staff did not differ in a statistically significant sense in charter and noncharter schools. In both types of schools, approximately 62 percent of the total full-time-equivalent staff were teachers, 15 percent were teacher aides or paraprofessionals, and 7 to 9 percent were special education aides. The remaining staff were noninstructional.

Within the group of charter schools, we found statistically significant differences between start-up and conversion schools only in the percentage of total staff that was made up of special education aides. Only 2 percent of the staff in start-up schools consisted of special education aides, in contrast to 11 percent in conversion schools.

PRINCIPALS' USE AND PERCEPTIONS OF CONTROL

One objective of the charter design was to provide greater control over the operation of charter schools, including salaries and benefits, hiring, firing, and staff discipline. Table 7.4 displays the responses of

Table 7.4

Level and Importance of Control

	Matched Conventional Public Schools (n = 182)		Charter Schools (n = 251)		Conversion Schools (n = 68)		Start-Up Schools (n = 180)	
Item	Level of Control	Importance of Control	Level of Control	Importance of Control	Level of Control	Level of Importance	Level of Control	Level of Importance
Staff salaries and benefits	1.5	2.5	2.9*	3.4*	1.9**	2.7**	3.3	3.7
Staff hiring, discipline, and dismissal	2.9	3.6	3.5*	3.9*	3.0**	3.8	3.7	3.9

SOURCE: 2002 RAND charter school and matched conventional public school surveys.

*Indicates charter school percentages that are statistically different from matched conventional public school percentages at the 5 percent level.

**Indicates conversion school percentages that are statistically different from start-up school percentages at the 5 percent level.

principals to survey questions that ask about the level of control over these items and the importance of this control.

We first examine the extent to which principals perceived that they had flexibility with regard to aspects of employment that shape the teaching staff. In our surveys of both charter and conventional public school principals, we asked them to tell us how much control they felt they had (on a scale of 1 to 4, with 4 being the maximum level of control[6]) over staff salaries. Principals of charter schools reported a statistically significantly greater sense of control over salaries than did the principals of matched conventional public schools. Charter school principals reported an average of 2.9 points on the four-point scale versus 1.5 points for the matched conventional public school principals. In the same manner, we asked principals to rate the level of control they had with respect to the hiring, discipline, and dismissal of the teaching staff. Charter school principals reported an average of 3.5 points on the four-point scale versus 2.9 points for the other group of principals, again a statistically significant difference.

Next, we asked principals the extent to which they deemed their current level of control over these aspects of the teaching workforce to be important to the operation of the school. On average, charter school principals perceived control over salaries and benefits to be more important than did matched conventional public school principals: On a scale of 1 to 4, with 4 being the maximum level of control, charter school principals responded with a mean of 3.4 and matched conventional public school principals responded with a mean of 2.5, a statistically significant difference. Similarly, in rating the importance to the operation of the school of their current level of control over staff hiring, discipline, and dismissal, charter school principals responded with an average of 3.9 points on a four-point scale versus 3.6 points for their conventional public school counterparts—a statistically significant though small difference. It is important to keep in mind that these ratings are entirely subjective. It could be the case that, once given control, all principals would rate the importance of control more highly.

[6]See Question 13 in the charter school survey and the public school survey of principals in Appendix D.

Within the group of charter schools, we found that principals of start-up schools felt that they had a greater level of control over staff salaries and benefits and over staff hiring, discipline, and dismissal than principals in conversion schools (see Table 7.4). Conversion school principals looked similar to the principals of matched conventional public schools in this regard.

With respect to staff salaries and benefits, the principals of start-up schools also felt that control was more important than did the principals in conversion schools. It is interesting to note that the principals in start-up and conversion schools did not differ in their rating of the importance of control over staff hiring, discipline, and dismissal. Thus, it appears that although principals in conversion schools felt that they had less control in this area, they considered such control to be just as important as did start-up school principals.

Several of our other survey questions were devoted to obtaining information about some of the specific ways in which the teaching staff were hired and remunerated and their contractual obligations or working conditions. For example, we asked principals about their perceived importance of certain criteria in considering applicants for teaching positions in their schools. The results are displayed in Table 7.5. The responses in the survey suggest that teaching credentials, a college major in the field to be taught, and passage of the California Basic Education Skills Test (CBEST) were regarded as more or less equally important by charter and conventional public school principals. Charter school principals, however, were more likely than conventional public school principals to report that they valued noneducational skills or real world experience, and conventional public school principals were more likely than charter school principals to report that they valued passage of standardized tests of subject knowledge or extensive college work in the subject area to be taught.

Our site visits to charter schools appeared to confirm the importance perceived by principals of control over salaries and benefits, hiring, discipline, and dismissal of staff. Two principals cited instances in which they had dismissed teachers on the basis of performance. Although a number of principals we interviewed lamented that budgetary constraints made it difficult to match teacher salaries at

Table 7.5

Screening Considerations for Hiring Teachers

	Matched Conventional Public Schools		Charter Schools	
Criteria for Hiring	No.	Level of Importance (1–4 scale)	No.	Level of Importance (1–4 scale)
Full standard credential for field to be taught	176	3.7	248	3.6
At least emergency permit or endorsement for field to be taught	169	3.5	232	3.6
College major in field to be taught	172	3.1	231	2.9*
Passage of CBEST test of basic skills	176	3.8	238	3.8
Passage of Praxis of SSAT[a] test of subject knowledge or extensive college work in the subject area to be taught	173	2.9	230	2.7*
Noneducational skills or real world experience	172	2.7	234	3.0*

SOURCES: 2002 RAND charter school and matched conventional public school surveys.

*Indicates percentages that are statistically different from matched conventional public school percentages at the 5 percent level.

[a]Single Subject Assessment for Teaching.

conventional public schools and one principal told us that she was forced to hire inexperienced staff because of fiscal limitations, some principals claimed that the participatory environment of the school made it very attractive as a workplace and that they were able to draw teachers away from their districts. Three principals said that word of mouth was their best recruitment strategy. Although a number of principals and teachers stated that they hired or preferred to hire only credentialed teachers, one principal told us that many of his teachers came from businesses because they found teaching to be a meaningful career.

In addition, the case studies presented a picture in which principals often used their freedom to create a democratic atmosphere in which important decisions were shared with teachers. In two cases, the principal used flexibility with regard to hiring to grant teachers an equal say in deciding whether to hire particular candidates. Teachers in all of the schools visited said that they felt that they played an important role in decisionmaking, and some teachers in schools that had been converted from conventional public schools felt that they were treated with more respect after conversion. At one school, teachers were directly involved in budget setting and the determination of salaries. This process had led, in the prior year, to a decision on the part of teachers to give themselves smaller raises to devote more of the budget to expenditures on items related to the curriculum.

SUMMARY

In summary, our analysis suggests that the characteristics of teachers and principals differed between charter and conventional public schools along several important dimensions. In addition, these differences were often due to differences between start-up and conversion schools. Our findings can be summarized as follows:

- Teachers in charter schools were less likely than those in matched conventional public schools to have a full teaching credential. In general, the use of emergency credentials was more widespread in charter schools. The difference was driven by the fact that teachers in start-up schools were less likely than those in conversion schools to have a full teaching credential.
- Smaller percentages of secondary school teachers teaching core subjects in charter schools had full credentials or subject authorizations than did those in matched conventional public schools.
- Teachers in charter schools were, on average, somewhat less experienced than those in matched conventional public schools, and teachers in start-up schools were, on average, less experienced than those in conversion schools.
- Teachers in charter schools reportedly worked approximately five days more per year than those in matched conventional public schools.
- Principals in charter schools were less likely to have a teaching or administrative credential than those in matched conventional public schools. They were also less likely to have a master's or doctoral degree.

- Principals in charter schools worked approximately the same number of days per year as those in matched conventional public schools but earned lower annual salaries.
- Principals in charter schools had shorter tenures in their current positions and less total experience in school administration than those in matched conventional public schools. Much of the difference in school administration experience was due to the fact that start-up school principals have less experience than conversion school principals. Charter and matched conventional public school principals also differed with respect to the type of job they held before their current position as principal.
- Principals in charter schools felt that they had greater control over staff hiring, dismissal, salaries, and benefits than those in matched conventional public schools.
- Principals in charter schools valued noneducation-related experience more highly than those in matched conventional public schools; the reverse was true with respect to the value placed on extensive college coursework or standardized tests related to subject matter knowledge.

Chapter Eight

SPECIAL EDUCATION IN CHARTER AND CONVENTIONAL PUBLIC SCHOOLS

Cassandra Guarino and Derrick Chau

INTRODUCTION

Charter schools, although exempt from many state and local regulations, must still abide by federal regulations regarding the education of students with disabilities. A number of studies have indicated that it is a challenge for charter schools to serve special education students (Ahearn et al., 2001; Finn et al., 2000). This chapter explores a number of important issues relating to serving special education students in California's charter schools.

The public school system must identify and educate students with special needs by creating and implementing an Individualized Education Plan (IEP) for each of them. Furthermore, schools are urged to serve these students in the least restrictive setting that is conducive to learning. Two issues of primary concern to special education policymakers, therefore, are the proper identification and the service of students with special needs. A question in the minds of many educators is whether charter schools, with their particular constraints relating to facilities and funding, can identify and serve special education students as well as conventional public schools. Our surveys contained several questions designed to elicit information that would enable us to answer these questions.

IDENTIFICATION OF SPECIAL EDUCATION STUDENTS

In our surveys, we asked school principals to tell us the number of students at their school who had currently been given an IEP. For each school, we then divided this number by the school's reported enrollment figure to obtain the school's percentage of students with IEPs—i.e., its rate of identification of special needs students. As shown in Table 8.1, we compared the rates of identification of students with special needs in charter schools with those of such students in conventional public schools.[1] We found that approximately 7.6 percent of charter school students were given an IEP in contrast to 8.9 percent of students in the conventional public schools in our sample. The difference of 1.3 percentage points approached but did not reach statistical significance at the 5 percent level. The significance of the difference was sensitive to the inclusion of certain schools, however. Two schools in our sample focused on special education services and had student bodies that were primarily made up of students with an IEP. Both were charter schools. After deleting these two schools, we found that the percentage of charter school students with IEPs fell slightly to 7.2, and the difference in the percentage of IEP students between charter and matched conventional

Table 8.1

Percentage of Special Education and Severely Disabled Students

	Matched Conventional Public Schools		Charter Schools		Conversion Schools		Start-Up Schools	
Student Type	No.	%	No.	%	No.	%	No.	%
IEP	176	8.9	249	7.6	183	10.4**	67	5.5
Severely disabled	172	1.1	242	1.3	174	2.3**	69	0.4

SOURCES: 2002 RAND charter school and matched conventional public school surveys and 2001–02 CBEDS data.

**Indicates conversion school percentages that are statistically different from start-up school percentages at the 5 percent level.

[1] To conduct our statistical comparison, we regressed the school-level proportions of students with IEPs on a dichotomous variable indicating charter status in the manner described in Appendix B. In these regressions, weights consisted of the survey analysis weight multiplied by the enrollment figure for each school to produce the overall proportion of special education students in charter schools versus that in matched conventional public schools.

public schools became statistically significant. Thus, the difference in identification rates between charter and noncharter schools was not robust to the inclusion of outliers.

We also asked principals to tell us how many special education students in their schools had severe disabilities (e.g., severe autism, deaf-blindness, severe developmental delay, severe emotional disturbance, severe hearing impairment or deafness, severe mental retardation, multiple disabilities, severe orthopedic impairment, traumatic brain injury, or severe visual impairments or blindness). As shown in Table 8.1, charter schools reported that 1.3 percent of their overall student populations were severely disabled. Conventional public schools reported that 1.1 percent of students overall were severely disabled. The difference was not statistically significant, nor was it sensitive to the inclusion or exclusion of the two special education charter schools.

Within the group of charter schools, identification rates varied considerably according to whether the school was a start-up or a conversion, which is also shown in Table 8.1. Students with IEPs formed 10.4 percent of the student population in conversion schools and only 5.5 percent of the student population in start-up schools. The difference was highly statistically significant.[2] Similarly, the rate of identification of students with severe disabilities was significantly different for start-up and conversion schools. Only 0.4 percent of students in start-up schools were diagnosed with severe disabilities, in contrast to 2.3 percent of students in conversion schools. Thus, conversion schools not only tended to have higher percentages of students with special needs and severe disabilities than did start-up schools, but their percentages appeared to exceed those of matched conventional public schools as well.

A possible explanation for the surprisingly large differences in identification rates between start-up and conversion schools could be that facility or financing constraints for the start-up schools are influencing their ability to serve students with special needs. Although it is difficult to test this hypothesis with our data, we were able to rule out school size as a cause of the differences. Within the group of

---

[2]The results reported in all ensuing tables in this chapter include the two special education charter schools, since the results are not sensitive to their inclusion.

charter schools, our results tended not to vary by the size of the school. The percentages of students with IEPs and with severe disabilities did not differ in the statistical sense between small and large charter schools.[3] It therefore remains an open question as to whether start-up schools are financially or otherwise limited to serving fewer students with special needs. Facility or financial constraints are not the only possible explanation for low identification rates in certain types of schools. These schools may instead choose not to give a marginal student an IEP out of a belief that the stigma of special education may cause more harm than benefit to the child. Thus, philosophical rather than cost-related motives may influence identification rates.

Anecdotal evidence suggests that both types of disincentives to identification may exist in start-up schools. During our site visits, principals of start-up schools often referred to fiscal pressures in conjunction with special education services and sometimes claimed that keeping the level of special education programs on a par with expanding needs was challenging. One principal mentioned a severely disabled special education student whom the school was unable to serve because of a lack of proper facilities. One start-up school principal claimed that her school attracted more than the average number of special education students because their small class sizes were conducive to meeting the learning needs of these children and because the district sometimes sent these students their way.

SPECIAL EDUCATION SERVICE DELIVERY

In addition to examining identification rates, we looked for possible differences in the way charter and noncharter schools deliver special education services. We asked how many special education students were currently being served in each of three possible instructional settings or services in the school: (a) exclusively in general education classrooms, (b) exclusively in separate classrooms (i.e., in self-contained special classrooms or departmentalized special education

---

[3]Small schools were defined as schools with fewer than 200 students, and large schools were defined as schools with 500 or more students. Auxiliary multivariate analyses also showed that enrollment size was not a factor determining identification rates after adjusting for school status (start-up or conversion).

classes), and (c) part of the time in general education classrooms and part of the time in separate classrooms (i.e., pullout programs). We found strong differences between charter and matched conventional public schools in the preferred mode of special education service delivery.

As displayed in Table 8.2, charter schools reported serving a significantly higher percentage of students exclusively in the general education classroom than did conventional public schools, 39 versus 19 percent. Charter schools and conventional public schools reported that 25 percent and 20 percent of their students, respectively, were served exclusively in separate classrooms, but these differences were not statistically distinguishable. Last, charter schools and conventional public schools reported that 37 percent and 61 percent of their students, respectively, were served part of the time in the general education classroom and part of the time in separate classrooms. This difference was large and statistically significant. Clearly, charter schools tended to rely heavily on mainstreaming their special education students, whereas matched conventional public schools tended to rely heavily on pullout programs.

Table 8.2

Service of Special Education Students

	Matched Conventional Public Schools		Charter Schools		Conversion Schools		Start-Up Schools	
Service Setting	No.	%	No.	%	No.	%	No.	%
Exclusively in general education classroom	167	19.3	240	38.5*	172	20.7**	67	63.8
Exclusively in separate classroom	168	20.1	240	24.7	173	38.9**	66	4.1
Part of the time in general education classroom and part of the time in separate classroom	167	60.6	240	36.8*	173	40.4	66	32.1

SOURCES: 2002 RAND charter school and matched conventional public school surveys.

*Indicates charter school percentages that are statistically different from matched conventional public school percentages at the 5 percent level.

**Indicates conversion school percentages that are statistically different from start-up school percentages at the 5 percent level.

To determine the degree to which charter schools were homogeneous in their modes of service delivery, we looked at differences between start-up and conversion schools; these results are also displayed in Table 8.2. We found distinct differences between these two types of charter schools. Sixty-four percent of special needs students in start-up schools were mainstreamed, whereas 21 percent were mainstreamed in conversion schools, and the difference was highly statistically significant. This was counterbalanced by the fact that only 4 percent of special needs students in start-up schools were served exclusively in separate classrooms versus 39 percent in conversion schools—also a large and statistically significant difference. Finally, we found no statistically significant difference between start-up and conversion schools in the percentages of students served in pullout programs.

Differences in the size of charter schools were also associated with service delivery choices. Large charter schools mainstreamed a smaller percentage (34 percent) of their special education students than did small charter schools (61 percent), and the difference was statistically significant (see Table 8.2). However, large charter schools tended to serve larger percentages of their special education students in separate classrooms than small charter schools did—28 percent versus three percent, respectively. We found no evidence that the size of the charter school mattered in percentages of students served in pullout programs.[4]

Taken together, the findings displayed in Tables 8.1 and 8.2 paint an interesting picture of the variation in special education populations and modes of service delivery across conventional public schools, conversion schools, and start-up schools. Each type of school shows a different pattern of service delivery. Start-up schools mainstream the majority of their special needs students—a service delivery choice that may be related to constraints on finances or facilities, to a philosophy of inclusion, or to a combination of both of these reasons. Conversion schools serve a higher percentage of special needs children than do either start-up schools or conventional public

---

[4]Multivariate analyses established that the size effect disappeared when controlling for school status (start-up or conversion). Thus, the differences in service delivery by size was related to the fact that start-up schools are in general smaller than conversion schools.

schools and choose a mix of service delivery modes more evenly distributed across possible options. Conventional public schools serve the majority of their special needs students in pullout programs.

Although it is often a goal of educators to serve students with special needs in inclusive environments, it is also recognized that inclusion, in and of itself, may not create optimal learning conditions. The goal is to serve special needs students in the least restrictive environment *that best promotes their learning.* Therefore, it is not possible for us to determine whether mainstreamed students are better served than are students who participate in pullout programs or to conclude from our analyses that conventional public schools or one of the two forms of charter schools are providing a better education to their students with special needs. This might be determined only through surveys of teachers, surveys of parents, observations of classroom teaching, or achievement analyses of special education students, all of which were beyond the scope of this study.

In addition, since charter schools are schools of choice, we do not know to what extent identification rates as well as service delivery modes are a function of parental choices. For example, a parent might choose to enroll a child in a charter school precisely to remove the stigma of a special education label that was placed on the child in another school. If parents as well as schools felt, for example, that an IEP could be detrimental to a borderline child's academic and social development, then lower identification rates and the mainstreaming of identified students could go hand in hand in such schools for purely philosophical reasons.

THE USE OF SPECIAL EDUCATION AIDES

We also compared the percentage of special education aides to total staff for charter and matched conventional public schools and for the different subgroups of charter schools. Both charter and matched conventional public schools reported that about 10 percent of their total staff was composed of special education aides. The percentage of aides to total staff differed, however, between start-up schools (2 percent) and conversion schools (16 percent), and the difference was statistically significant. The percentage had no relation to the enrollment size of the school.

These percentage differences suggest that the mainstreaming of special education students in start-up schools is most likely not accompanied by the presence of special education aides in the classroom. Again, it is not possible, given these data, to judge the appropriateness of this approach. On the one hand, the mainstreamed child who does not have an aide present may avoid the stigma of being labeled as different and benefit considerably from inclusion. On the other hand, a child served in this manner may lack the support that might improve his or her ability to learn.

INCLUSION OF SPECIAL EDUCATION STUDENTS IN ASSESSMENTS

Our survey also asked principals to report the percentage of special education students who were included in the statewide STAR assessment. Evidence that schools may manipulate standardized test scores in high-stakes testing environments by increasing the identification of special needs students who can be excluded from testing has been found in other states, such as Florida (Figlio and Getzler, 2002). This phenomenon can occur when schools are allowed to exclude students in disability categories for which a diagnosis is subject to a fair amount of discretion.

But we found no evidence that schools of different types in our sample excluded different percentages of their special education students. There was no statistically significant difference in this percentage between charter and noncharter schools. In both types of schools, approximately 75 to 85 percent of special education students were included in the statewide assessment. Furthermore, the percentages were not statistically different for different types and sizes of charter schools.

From a logical standpoint, however, schools with higher identification rates than others but similar test inclusion rates for special needs students can still be suspected of gaming, since their overall test exclusion rates per 100 students will be higher. Given that conversion schools tend to have higher identification rates than other types of schools, they could perhaps be engaging in this type of gaming. This phenomenon seems unlikely, however, given that these schools serve higher percentages of severely disabled students whose diagnoses are not likely to be highly discretionary. Without a further breakdown of disability types by type of school, it is difficult to find evidence of strategic identification decisions in the face of high-stakes testing.

FUNDING AND PROVISION OF SPECIAL EDUCATION RESOURCES

The funding and provision of special education services are major issues facing the implementation of charter school policies. This section explores the different arrangements that charter schools in California have developed to fund and provide special education services.

According to state law in California, every school must belong to a SELPA. SELPAs can consist of individual schools, individual districts, groups of districts, or even whole counties.[5] SELPAs are the entities in the California education system that receive special education funding and allocate these resources among their member districts or schools.

A charter school in California can choose among three options in establishing a relationship with a SELPA. They can operate under the SELPA of their authorizing districts, much like a conventional public school. In these cases, the districts generally maintain responsibility for special education services. Charter schools can also be created as independent Local Education Agencies (LEAs), essentially school districts, and can join SELPAs as separate entities. For these schools, the SELPAs, individual districts within them, or the school itself can provide special education services. Finally, charter schools can also be established as LEAs and can create their own SELPAs, thus having primary responsibility for providing special education services. Charter schools must select one of these relationships in their charters.

As newly created entities within the education system, charter schools must establish whether legal liability with respect to special education falls on the schools or on their chartering authorities. As

[5]There are currently more than 110 SELPAs in the state.

mentioned in Chapter Four, memoranda of understanding are usually established between charter schools and their chartering authorities to clarify liability issues. Chapter Four presented data indicating that independent charter schools tended more often than dependent charter schools to bear legal liability for special education claims. If a charter school falls under a district's responsibility for special education services, the school is said to be a "legal arm" of the district for the purposes of special education and is generally considered to be a dependent charter. From surveys, chartering authorities responded that about 89 percent of their approved charter schools were legal arms of their districts. This indicates that most charter schools do not establish themselves as separate LEAs or as individual SELPAs.

The formula for the allocation of special education funds across districts and schools can differ from SELPA to SELPA. Some SELPAs provide schools with funding based on a flat percentage of ADA. Others have formulas that are calculated according to the particular special needs of the student populations being served in their schools.

In addition to receiving funding from SELPAs, schools may also contribute other school revenue to covering the cost of providing special education services. In our surveys, principals in charter and matched conventional public schools were asked what percentage of the cost of educating special education students was covered by the special education funding that their schools received. Responses revealed no significant difference between the percentages of special education costs covered by special education funds for charter and conventional public schools (about 65 to 75 percent). No significant differences arose between start-up and conversion schools or between small and large charter schools.[6] One principal in a case study school explained that the district received all special education revenues, which covered 69 percent of the funds spent on special education at the school and in exchange provided services at the school. The school provided the balance of the funds.

[6]Multivariate analysis did reveal a very small but positive and significant association between the percentage of special education costs for which funding was received and enrollment size after controlling for start-up/conversion status.

The responsibility for providing special education services can vary greatly depending on the arrangements between charter schools and their chartering authorities. Chartering authorities responded in surveys that they provide the majority of special education services in over 70 percent of the charter schools that they authorized. Chartering authorities reported that few charter schools, only about 25, provide the majority of their own special education services through school and contracted personnel. In our case studies, we found that some schools enjoyed a highly integrated and reciprocal relationship with the district. Resource specialists from the district, for example, rotated through one school. However, another school—a conversion school—complained that special education was a true bone of contention with the district. A number of case study schools contracted with outside organizations for special education services.

Findings discussed in Chapter Four indicate that chartering authorities differ in their levels of control over special education services in independent and dependent charter schools. As Table 4.5 shows, 23 percent of chartering authorities report that they have no control over special education services in independent charter schools. All chartering authorities have at least some control over special education services in dependent charter schools.

Given the wide range of liability assignments, service provision arrangements, and funding formulae possible for charter schools in California, it was not possible for us to link funding configurations to identification rates or service provision modalities. To do so would require a more detailed survey devoted to special education than was possible in this overall evaluation of charter schools.

Findings from our surveys did suggest, however, that charter schools were less likely than conventional public schools to participate in the categorical aid program for special education funding, as discussed in Chapter Five. In particular, our data also indicated that fewer start-up than conversion schools were receiving special education funding and that start-up schools are less likely to apply for categorical special education funding even when eligible. In addition, the high percentage (over 10 percent) of start-up school principals who did not know whether their schools were eligible for special education funding suggests that it is a challenge for these schools to develop the capacity that districts and SELPAs have to oversee special education.

This possibility was borne out in our case study interviews, in which several principals were critical of the lack of information available regarding application procedures for categorical aid programs. These principals explained that only recently had the state developed a comprehensive list of all categorical aid programs, and that charter schools relied primarily on local school districts and county offices of education in obtaining information about them. Thus, a more organized statewide approach to the dissemination of information on special education funding available to charter schools might benefit these schools and the students they serve.

SUMMARY

Our survey data revealed several notable differences between charter schools and matched conventional public schools and between different types of charter schools in a number of areas related to special education. These can be summarized as follows:

- We found that the percentage of students who had Individualized Education Plans was lower in charter schools than in matched conventional public schools but that the difference between them was not statistically significant unless two outlying schools that focused on special needs students and happened to be charter schools were excluded. Thus, this difference in identification rates was not particularly robust to the inclusion of outliers.
- We found strong differences in the identification of special needs students between start-up and conversion schools, with the latter having far higher percentages.
- A similar pattern emerged for the percentage of students identified with severe disabilities. Charter and matched conventional public schools showed no difference, but within the group of charter schools, these students were far more concentrated in conversion than in start-up schools.
- We found strong evidence that charter and matched conventional public schools relied on different service delivery modes

for special education. The charter schools mainstreamed far larger percentages of their special needs students, whereas the matched conventional public schools served the majority of their special needs students through pullout programs.

- Differences in service delivery patterns also emerged within the group of charter schools, with start-up schools mainstreaming larger percentages of their special needs students and conversion schools placing larger percentages of their special needs students in separate classrooms. We also found that small charter schools mainstreamed larger percentages of their IEP students than large charter schools, whereas the larger schools placed higher percentages of IEP students in separate classrooms. The differences between large and small schools disappeared, however, when controlling for school status (start-up or conversion), suggesting that the size effect was merely a result of the fact that conversion schools tended to be larger than start-up schools.
- Both charter and matched conventional public schools employed approximately the same ratio of special education aides to total staff, but start-up schools had a smaller ratio than did conversion schools.
- Both charter and matched conventional public schools included roughly the same percentage of IEP students in statewide assessments, and this percentage did not vary by type of charter school.
- Funding and service provision arrangements for special education in charter schools varied widely, and a number of schools did not take advantage of categorical aid funding streams because of a lack of information and capacity to study various options.

Chapter Nine

CONCLUSIONS AND IMPLICATIONS

Ron Zimmer and Cassandra Guarino

INTRODUCTION

This study provides the most comprehensive evaluation of California charter schools to date by examining accessibility, student achievement, governance, and operation of charter schools. Below, we provide a brief summary of the findings from our four research areas. We also note existing challenges facing charter schools and provide recommendations.

FINDINGS

Often researchers, educators, and policymakers think of charter schools as a homogenous group. In asking questions about them, they often ask what the charter school effect is. However, our analysis suggests that it is impossible to define a single charter school effect. *In fact, one of the most significant conclusions of our analysis is that there is no single charter school approach and therefore no single charter school effect.* Charter schools vary across a number of important dimensions that can affect the accessibility, student achievement, operation, and governance of the schools, as our findings below suggest:

STUDENT ACHIEVEMENT

One main objective of the legislation mandating charter schools is to "improve student learning" (EC 47601). Although this objective seems straightforward, it can have two alternative interpretations: (1) Charter schools should improve the learning of their pupils over time and (2) charter schools should outperform conventional public schools. If the objective is taken to mean that charter schools should improve the learning of their pupils over time, then our conclusions would suggest that most charter schools are meeting this objective, because both charter and conventional public schools have experienced growth in student performance in recent years. If the objective is taken to mean that charter schools must outperform conventional public schools, then the assessment leads to a different and more complex set of conclusions. In our study, we evaluated the performance of charter school students relative to conventional school students because this was deemed the question of greatest interest to policymakers. Our results suggest:

- Charter schools generally have comparable or slightly lower test scores than conventional public schools after adjusting for the ethnic and demographic characteristics of the students. *However, these effects vary across the different types of charter schools. Our evaluation suggests that, controlling for student characteristics, classroom-based conversion schools have comparable scores in certain subjects or grade levels, in other cases higher scores, and still in other cases lower scores. Classroom-based start-up schools have higher test scores than conventional public schools across grades and subjects except in elementary math, where the scores are slightly lower. Finally, nonclassroom-based conversion and start-up schools, relative to conventional public schools, have lower test scores across the board.*

Accessibility

Another major legislative objective for charter schools is to "increase the learning opportunities for all pupils, with special emphasis on expanded learning experiences for pupils who are identified as academically low achieving" (EC 47601). However, the charter law also requires that charter schools describe in their charters "the means by which the school will achieve a racial and ethnic balance among its pupils that is reflective of the general population residing within the territorial jurisdiction of the school district to which the charter petition is submitted" (EC 47605.b.5.g). Adhering to these multiple objectives can be a challenge for charter schools. In a district that has racial groups that are traditionally high-achieving, how can the charter school be both reflective of the student population of the district and target low-achieving students at the same time? Therefore, we caution our readers to bear this challenge in mind when examining the results of our accessibility analysis.

- *Access:* According to surveyed principals, access is generally similar across charter and conventional public schools. The charter school admissions process differs little from admissions processes in matched conventional public schools. Charter schools are more likely than matched conventional public schools to interview applicants, but most charter schools say they use the interview for diagnostic purposes rather than to determine eligibility for admission. Also according to the surveys, charter schools are more likely to focus their services on specific student populations.
- *Racial representativeness:* Relative to conventional public schools and controlling for the heterogeneity within school districts, charter school students are more likely to be black and less likely to be Hispanic or Asian, but no more or less likely to be white. However, the racial mix of students varies by charter school type, and start-up school students are much more likely than conventional public school students to be white and much less likely to be Hispanic or Asian whereas conversion school students are much more likely to be black and less likely to be Asian.
- *Racial integration:* In assessing the integration of students within charter and conventional public schools, for blacks, conventional public schools are somewhat more likely than charter schools to deviate from the district. For whites and Hispanics, conventional public schools are slightly less likely to deviate and for Asians, they are very slightly more likely to deviate. However, the difference between groups tends to be small.

Authorization, Governance, and Oversight

Essential elements of the charter school movement are the chartering process, governance, and oversight. The success of a charter school could very well depend on the support and flexibility the charter schools gain from their chartering authority. In our analysis, we examined these features.

- *Authorization:* The vast majority of charter schools are authorized by public school districts rather than counties or the state, and very few districts authorize more than one charter. Formal denials of charter petitions are rare.
- *Governance:* As the law intends, charter schools have greater control over decisionmaking than do regular public schools. Among charter schools, dependent charter schools are governed much more like conventional public schools than are independent charter schools.
- *Oversight:* An objective of EC 47601 is to hold charter schools "accountable for meeting measurable pupil outcomes, and provide the schools with a method to change from rule-based to performance-based accountability systems." We found that in general, chartering authorities require a low percentage of charter schools to provide accountability information such as student grades, promotion rates, and dropout rates. A higher percentage of chartering authorities require these items along with other information from dependent charter schools than from independent or undefined charter schools. Chartering authorities also revoke the charters of, or close, only a handful of schools.

Operation

An essential component of the charter school movement is to understand how charter schools are operating. In our analysis, we examined a number of operational dimensions of charter schools. In some cases, the results of our analysis have implications for charter schools' ability to be innovative as EC 47601 mandates.

- *Curriculum:* Charter schools report offering more instruction in noncore subjects such as fine arts and foreign languages than do matched conventional public schools, particularly in 4th grade.

- *Professional development:* Charter school principals report higher rates of teacher participation in informal professional development, such as mentoring and shadowing programs, than do matched conventional public school principals.
- *Parent involvement:* Charter schools differed from matched conventional public schools in the percentages offering some types of parent involvement activities, and charter schools reported higher rates of parent participation in those activities that were offered.
- *Testing:* Charter schools report less influence of STAR on instructional planning and practice than do matched conventional public schools but do not differ in reported involvement in test-preparation activities.
- *Administrative and instructional staffing:* Teachers in charter schools have less experience and are less likely to be credentialed than teachers in conventional public schools.
- *Special education:* We were unable to find definitive evidence that the proportion of special education students differed between charter and matched conventional public schools. Special education students made up a smaller proportion of students in start-up schools than in conversion schools, however. We also found that start-up schools were much more likely to mainstream their special education students—i.e., serve them in the general education classroom—than either conversion schools or matched conventional public schools. Matched conventional public schools were more likely than charter schools to rely on pullout programs to serve their special needs students.
- *Finances:* Our analysis provides evidence that charter schools, particularly start-up schools, receive fewer public resources per student than do matched conventional public schools. This is due, in part, to charter schools having significantly lower participation in categorical aid programs outside the charter school categorical block grant than matched conventional public schools. In addition, our analysis suggests that charter schools face higher facilities and special education costs than do matched conventional public schools.

CHALLENGES

Before recommendations can be made, it is important to understand the challenges facing charter schools. Throughout these chapters, we have described an array of these challenges. Here, we highlight the most pressing issues.

- *Facilities:* At the time of our study, charter schools were facing facility problems ranging from identifying and securing sites to funding. However, these issues may be addressed with new rules and regulations recently enacted by legislation.
- *Start-up costs:* In our case studies, charter schools often mentioned the difficulty of securing funds to launch the school, hire staff, and outfit the school with the furnishings and curriculum materials needed to prepare for the initial enrollment of what is often an uncertain number of pupils.
- *Categorical Aid:* Charter schools do not participate in categorical aid programs outside the block grant at the same rate as conventional public schools, which means less public funding for these schools. Additionally, these funding differences may increase in the future as the trend moves toward removing programs from the categorical aid block grant. In addition to administrative requirements, part of the reason charter schools do not participate in these categorical aid programs is that they are sometimes inconsistent with the educational philosophy of the schools. The tension between innovative research programs and funding can be strong in charter schools.
- *Regulation:* Charter schools express concerns about maintaining the autonomy and flexibility that are at the heart of the charter school concept. And yet there is a legitimate concern that some charter schools may not provide adequate education or may inappropriately use funds. These concerns have led to recent changes in auditing, monitoring, reporting, and other requirements. A critical issue is how to balance the need to hold charter schools accountable while allowing them to maintain their autonomy and not overburden them with substantial reporting requirements. There is also the issue of changes, such as the 1998 changes regarding teacher credentials, that actually curb freedoms originally granted to charter schools.

- *Racial representation:* The state mandates that charter schools be representative of their jurisdiction. This requirement is nearly impossible to meet for those charter schools found in large and diverse school districts. It is difficult for charter schools, which largely draw upon students from within their neighborhood, to attract students from other neighborhoods in proportion to the diversity of the district.
- *Special needs students:* The fact that start-up schools identify lower proportions of special needs students than do conversion or conventional public schools may stem in part from the desires of parents or school personnel to shield students from being labeled, and it may stem in part from funding constraints. The fact that start-up schools also mainstream a higher proportion of their special needs students than do conversion or conventional public schools may stem in part from a philosophy of inclusion and, again, in part from funding constraints. Start-up schools may have difficulty finding the resources to serve special needs students.
- *Student achievement:* A primary goal for policymakers is to find ways to improve the performance of nonclassroom-based charter schools so they at least score on par with conventional public schools.

RECOMMENDATIONS

Drawing on our findings, we provide policy recommendations below.

1. The legislative intent should be clearly and concisely outlined within the Educational Code to minimize misinterpretations of goals and conflicting objectives. Currently, many of the objectives are vague or create conflicts among the objectives, offering a great deal of interpretive latitude. Defining the objectives more explicitly would give chartering authorities and charter schools a greater understanding of their goals, enabling them to better develop accountability systems that are aligned with the intent of the law.
2. The state should develop a statewide student-level data system that can track the performance of individual students. Such a

system would allow the performance of schools to be more precisely evaluated.

3. The state should require that fiscal information from charter schools be collected and monitored by chartering authorities to enhance fiscal oversight. However, this needs to be done in a way that does not generate a substantial amount of additional paperwork and expense for charter schools.

4. The information collected from recommendations (2) and (3), along with information collected through other possible mechanisms, should be used by chartering authorities to identify poor performing charter schools for targeted interventions and support or possible closings.

5. Part of the reason charter schools may not have the same financial resources as conventional public schools is that they do not fully participate in categorical aid programs. According to our survey, some of these schools are "eligible but not applying"; others "don't know whether they are eligible or not." Eligible schools that do not apply for categorical aid funds may choose not to do so because of certain requirements that accompany the programs, including requirements that conflict with the schools' educational philosophy. Schools that do not know whether they are eligible obviously lack the knowledge necessary to make an informed decision. To provide the best opportunity for the long-term success of charter schools, the state should find mechanisms for providing them with equivalent funding. This may mean putting more funds into block grants as opposed to individual categorical aid programs, providing training and more accessible information to charter school principals so that they know which programs they are eligible for, and possibly providing alternative avenues by which charter schools can join together or with school districts to apply for and maintain individual programs.

6. Given the differences in special education identification rates and service delivery modes between start-up schools and conversion or conventional public schools, it is important that chartering authorities ensure that special education is adequately funded in these schools and that up-to-date resources are available to them.

7. In light of our findings on student achievement, additional research on nonclassroom-based charter schools is needed, includ-

ing more information regarding the composition of students, the nature of instruction, and the use of resources in these schools. In addition, it is important to collect information regarding the nature of oversight of these schools and to evaluate the effectiveness and implications of the funding cuts to nonclassroom-based schools required by recent legislation (SB 740). At the behest of the LAO, we will extend this current analysis by examining these issues and will provide our results in a forthcoming report.

Appendix A

RESEARCH METHODS

DATA SOURCES

Data for answering each of the research questions came from a variety of sources, as shown in Table A.1. In the table, we highlight the role each of the data sources had in the analysis.

These data are derived from both secondary and primary data sources. The secondary data include school-level, student-level, and teacher-level data provided by the California Department of Education and individual school districts. The primary data include surveys of charter schools, conventional public schools, and chartering authorities as well as case studies. The secondary data sources use common CDS (county-district-school) identification codes so that the data can be linked over time. The primary survey data also are linked to the secondary data files through these same CDS codes. The following section describes each of these data sources.

Secondary Data

Comprehensive Basic Education Data System: CBEDS contains information that CDE collects each October from school districts, schools, and certified staff on three data collection forms: the County and District Information Form (CDIF), the School Information Form (SIF), and the PAIF, respectively. The CBEDS data include staffing information (i.e., certification, full-time-equivalent, salary ranges, and teacher time allocation), school free and reduced-price lunch program participation, racial and ethnic breakdowns,

Table A.1

Data Sources

Data Source	Ch. Two: Charter School Students	Ch. Three: Student Achieve-ment	Ch. Four: Governance and Monitoring	Ch. Five: Finances and Facilities	Ch. Six: Academic Environment	Ch. Seven: Staffing	Ch. Eight: Special Education
Existing Databases							
CBEDS	X	X					
PAIF				X		X	
J-200				X			
API		X					
Statewide student-level data		X					
District student-level data		X					
Surveys							
Charter school survey	X		X	X	X	X	X
Supplemental charter school survey				X			
Conventional public school survey	X		X	X	X	X	X
Chartering authority survey			X	X	X	X	X
Case Studies							
Charter schools	X		X	X	X	X	X
Chartering authorities	X		X	X	X	X	X

language proficiency status, and other student characteristics. Our analysis includes the CBEDS data for the 1992–93 school year to the 2001–02 school year.

Professional Assignment Information Form: PAIF data are collected annually from nearly all teachers in California, starting with the 1992–93 school year. These data contain information on the qualifications, demographics, and teaching assignments for most teachers in California's public and charter schools and enable us to compare charter schools with conventional public schools and with other charter schools.

J-200: Each year, the CDE collects detailed revenue and expenditure data for each school district and county office of education in the state across a number of categories as defined by the state. School districts record this information on J-200 forms. J-200 data provide a good base for determining the type and size of revenues school districts receive as well as how school districts spend their money. Expenditures, for example, are broken into about 100 "objects of expenditures" such as teachers' salaries, textbooks, utilities, and housekeeping services. These data are easily accessible for each school district in California across several years through the CDE website.[1]

Academic Performance Index: As part of the PSAA, the API has been established to measure the academic performance and growth of schools. Each school receives an API score based on a numeric index (ranging from 200 to 1,000) that records a school's performance on standardized tests across subjects.[2] The API dataset includes the

---

[1]Ideally, we would like to have this level of detailed revenue and expenditure data for both conventional public schools and charter schools to be able to make comparisons across their finances. Such school-level data do not exist, in part, because much of the revenues and expenditures for conventional public schools are handled at the district level. To supplement the data that currently exist, we included questions on revenues and expenditures in our charter school survey that follow some of the breakdowns in the J-200 data. We will present this summary data for charter schools. In addition, we will present similar summary data from the J-200 data for school districts in California. Given the limitations of comparing district- and school-level data, we will merely present summary J-200 data to give a broader picture of school finance in California and to place the charter school data in some general context.

[2]For more information on the API, see http://www.cde.ca.gov/psaa/api/fallapi/apiinfo.pdf.

state rank of the schools, growth targets, number of students tested in aggregate and by racial/ethnic group, and student demographic characteristics. The API data are available for the school years 1999–00 through 2001–02.

Statewide Student-Level Data: CDE provided data on all California students (without a student identifier to link students over time) for the school years 1997–98 through 2001–02. These data include reading and math test scores as well as the demographic characteristics of each student. Although the data do not provide the ability to look at individual gains, they do allow an examination of gains of cohorts over time while precisely controlling for the characteristics of individual students.

District Student-Level Data: Because the state database does not allow us to link the performance of individual students over time or track the students as they move from school to school, including students moving to (from) charter schools from (to) conventional public schools, we contacted 10 major districts with a large share of charter students to gain longitudinally linked student-level data and received districtwide data from six of these districts (Chula Vista Elementary, Fresno Unified, Los Angeles Unified, Napa Valley Unified, San Diego City Unified, and West Covina Unified). These data also include reading and math test scores as well as demographic characteristics of each student and allow an examination of the gains of individual students in both charter and conventional public schools.

Primary Data

Primary data consist of three separate RAND surveys administered to all California charter schools, a matched sample of conventional public schools, and all California chartering authorities, and of case studies of a subset of charter schools and their chartering authorities. The charter school survey also included a one-page supplemental set of fiscal questions that could be sent back separately. These surveys were conducted during the spring of the 2001–02 school year.

Surveys: Separate school survey instruments were used to collect data from charter and conventional public school principals or directors. As much as possible, we tried to use consistent items across the surveys to allow for comparisons among these schools. However, in limited cases we developed unique survey items to address research questions specific to each type of school. In addition to the two school surveys, a chartering authority survey instrument was developed to collect data from administrators of local school districts, county schools districts, and the state chartering authority. To develop each of these surveys, we used the following process:

- Using the Request for Proposal (RFP) laid out by the Legislative Analyst's Office, we listed the research questions that needed to be addressed by the surveys.
- With these research questions, we examined previous research surveys and identified survey items that could be used for current analysis. In many cases, we amended the items to address our own specific needs.
- Because of the uniqueness of the current analysis, many of the RFP questions could not be addressed through the use of previous survey items. Therefore, we went through the process of developing unique survey items to address these research questions.
- Once complete drafts of the surveys were developed, we piloted each of the respective surveys with charter principals, conventional public school principals, and superintendents. Each participant provided comments, which were incorporated into a second complete draft of the surveys.
- The LAO and an advisory panel then reviewed the second draft of the survey. Their comments were incorporated into final versions of the surveys.
- RAND's Survey Research Group conducted final formatting and editing of each survey.
- We fielded the completed principal survey instruments in April of 2002 and the chartering authority survey in June of that year. For all surveys, follow-up started two weeks after the initial mailing. Follow-up ended in June 2002 for the principal survey and in September 2002 for the chartering authority survey. The survey datasets were finalized October 1, 2002.

Population Surveyed: We used the following extensive search procedure to identify the universe of charter schools. We began with a list created from merging the California charter school office publicly available data with the charter schools listed in the 2000–01 CBEDS data. Charter schools were eligible for a survey if they opened before September 15, 2001, and had a status of "operating" as of February 2002.[3] In total, 357 schools met these requirements. We then contacted the individual schools and their respective chartering authorizers to verify the data in our initial list. We made changes in our database to reflect updated information we received during these interviews, including adding any schools that were not in our original list. Twenty schools were added to our sample this way, and 25 were eliminated. Of the 25 schools that were dropped, nine had never existed, five were not charter schools (three were no longer charter schools and two were not "public charters"), two others were ineligible for our sample because they had not opened, and nine had either closed or had had their charter revoked. Thus, the final sample included 352 charter schools.

For the conventional public school surveys, we used a sample of schools selected from the 2000–01 CBEDS file. Choosing a sample of conventional public schools for comparison is complicated by the fact that charter schools serve a much different group of students than a typical conventional public school (Gill et al., 2001). Given this, we might expect that differences in governance, financing, staffing, etc., between charter schools and the overall population of conventional public schools result from differences in the students served rather than or in addition to differences related to school type. To avoid confounding differences associated with school type with differences related to students served, we used a sampling strategy that created a matched comparison group of public schools that operate with *similar* students.

Matched Sample: To create a data file of matched schools we matched charter and noncharter schools by an estimated *propensity* score (Rosenbaum and Rubin, 1983). The propensity score is the probability that a school with a given set of characteristics is a char-

[3] We were told at the time that this represented the most up-to-date list of charter schools, though it was known by personnel at CDE to be incorrect and incomplete because charter schools open and close frequently.

ter school as opposed to a conventional public school. This single value can then be used to match charter schools to noncharter schools by finding those that have similar propensity scores. As part of the matching process, we allowed a conventional public school to be matched to multiple charter schools because of budget and time constraints. Beyond computational convenience, the propensity score also has the desirable property, that the characteristics used to fit the propensity are balanced between charter schools and their matched noncharter schools.[4]

To carry out the propensity match, we used a four-step procedure:

1. We stratified charter schools into eight categories used by CDE to designated school types for all public schools. These eight categories are elementary schools, middle schools, high schools, county schools, continuation schools, juvenile hall schools, special education schools, and alternative education schools. Some charter schools had grade ranges that intersected multiple strata (e.g., kindergarten through grade 12 school intersects the elementary, middle, and high school strata). In these cases, the charter schools were included in each category and matched to a conventional public school for each category. Because of the small sample of county, continuation, juvenile hall, special education, and alternative education schools, a propensity match was not used in these cases.[5] Instead, if demographic data were available for these schools, the schools were matched based on the criteria of getting schools within 10 percent of racial characteristics of the charter schools. In many cases, demographic characteristics were not available for these schools and schools were matched to a conventional public school of the same school type within the district or the closest district. Roughly 60 charter schools were new in the 2001–02 school year and not included in the 2000–01 CBEDS. These schools could not be matched to conventional public schools. However, the unmatched charter schools were

[4]For examples of the use of propensity matches, see Fiebach et al. (1990), Connors et al. (1996), Stone et al. (1995), Lieberman et al. (1996), and Dehejia and Wahba (1999).

[5]The propensity match methodology can create good matches only with sufficient sample sizes.

included in the weighting procedures described below using demographic data from the 2001–02 school year.

2. Within grade range strata, we fit a logistic regression model to predict designation (1 = charter; 0 = conventional public) as a function of aggregate school characteristics. To guide the decision of which variables to use to do the match, we first examined the strategy used by the CDE to match schools for the API and used this as a guideline in the match. The API uses percentage mobility, percentage ethnicity, pupil socioeconomic status, percentage of teachers who are fully credentialed, percentage of teachers who are emergency credentialed, percentage of students who are English Learners, average class size per grade, and whether the school operates multitrack year-round educational programs. However, some of the variables used in the API match could be an essential part of the charter school philosophy, such as class size or year-round schools, and would reduce the operational differences observed through our surveys. Therefore, policy variables were not used in our match (e.g., average class size per grade, percentage of teachers who are fully or emergency credentialed, or whether the school operates multitrack year-round educational programs). Also, many charter schools are start-up schools with much higher mobility rates (in a case of a new school, 100 percent) and, thus, we did not include the mobility variable. In the end, we matched the charter schools using ethnicity (percentage white, black, Asian, and Hispanic), student socioeconomic status (percentage eligible for free or reduced-price lunch),[6] and percentage English Learners. Using these characteristics, predicted values for each school are created and serve as the schools' propensity scores.

3. The propensity scores for charter school i and conventional public school j are p_i and p_j. Then, the distance between these schools (d_{ij}) is estimated as the absolute value of the difference between their propensity scores, $d_{ij} = | p_i - p_j |$. We calculated the distance between each charter school and every conventional public school.

---

[6]It was later discovered that many charter schools do not participate in free or reduced-price lunch programs. Since the original propensity match included this item, the final sample had to be weighted to account for this bias.

4. We matched to each charter school the conventional public school minimum distance to it. That is, the matched conventional public school is the school that minimizes d_{ij} over all conventional public schools j.

Although the match between the two groups of schools is not perfect, it created a sample of conventional public schools with characteristics that closely match those of the charter schools. Table A.2 displays the characteristics of the matched elementary, middle, and high schools for charter schools and conventional public schools.

To create the sample of chartering authorities, we used a similar approach to the one we used to identify our sample of charter schools—we used the California charter school office list. In total, 190 possible chartering authorities were identified and contacted. Of these, 16 were not qualified to participate because they either did not actually have charter schools or their schools had closed. In addition, we were not able to identify counties or districts that were once chartering authorities but are no longer because the charter school either switched to a different chartering authorizer or closed.

Table A.2

Matched School Racial Breakdown

School Type	Schools	% White	% Black	% Hispanic	% Asian	% Other	% English Learner
Elementary	Charter	48.5	14.9	27.8	2.7	6.1	15.6
	Matched public	51.5	13.3	27.7	2.9	4.6	17.1
Middle	Charter	51.8	11.7	23.8	2.3	10.4	9.4
	Matched public	54.3	13.8	22.5	4.0	5.4	10.6
High	Charter	52.9	9.6	26.4	4.0	7.1	10.0
	Matched public	53.2	5.3	28.8	6.8	5.9	10.2

SOURCE: 2001–02 CBEDS data.

NOTE: We matched conventional public schools only to charter schools for which we had demographic information.

RESPONSE RATE

Table A.3 highlights the number surveyed for each sample, the potential respondents dropped from the sample, the number of respondents, and the percentage response rate for each sample. To improve our response rate, we provided a payment of $50 for the respondents of charter and conventional public school surveys and a $15 Barnes and Noble gift card to respondents of the chartering authority survey. We also identified nonrespondents and had extensive follow-up with these schools and chartering authorities through letters and phone calls. As highlighted in the table, our response rates were nearly 75 percent for both charter and conventional public schools, 66 percent for chartering authorities, and 56 percent for the charter supplemental survey.

Table A.3

Response Rate

Survey	Sample Size	No. of Respondents	Response Rate (%)
Charter school survey	352	257	73
Charter school supplemental survey	352	200	56
Conventional public school survey	245	184	75
Chartering authority survey	174	115	66

REWEIGHTED SAMPLE

For the analysis, the school surveys are weighted to adjust for differential response rates among and across charter and conventional public schools (Little and Rubin, 1987). The marginal distributions of demographics and school type (elementary, middle, etc.) were similar for responding and nonresponding charter schools. Elementary schools with a small percentage of black students were less likely to respond as were moderate sized schools and conversion schools. Using these characteristics we developed a logistic regression model to predict responses for each charter school. The nonresponse weight equals the inverse of the predicted probability of response from this model. The sample included only two schools with very large proportions of Asian students and both responded. Therefore, we assigned these schools nonresponse weights of 1.0.

We also weighted the responding public school sample to account for disparities between the responding public schools and the population of charter schools. We combined a subsample of charter schools with public schools into a single dataset and created an indicator variable for charter school designation. Using school characteristics, demographics, language status, and lunch status data, we fit a logistic regression model to predict charter school designation for all schools in this sample. When fitting the model, charter schools were weighted to represent the entire eligible universe. For each public school, we estimate the conditional probability that a school with its characteristics and student population is a charter school. We call this estimate p. The analysis weight for the school equals the odds of being a charter school, p/(1 – p). This weight is a propensity score weight as described in Hirano et al. (2000).

For estimating the propensity score weights for responding public schools, the analysis included only charter schools with data on student eligibility for the subsidized lunches. Many charter schools do not provide lunches for students and thus information on eligibility for free or reduced-price lunches is unavailable for their students. However, we want the weighted charter school and public school samples to be similar in terms of the proportions of these students served by the schools. Therefore we selected the subset of charter schools where the proportion of such students was not missing and was greater than zero.

When estimating propensity scores, we weighted this subsample of charter schools. Using school characteristics (grade range and conversion status) and student ethnicity data (aggregated at the school level), we developed weights to make this subset of charter schools representative of the entire sample of charter schools by modeling the probability that a charter school had data on students eligible for subsidized lunches. The weight is the inverse of this estimated probability.

The final analysis samples were all responding charter schools weighted by their nonresponse weights and all responding public schools weighted by their analysis (propensity score) weights. Table A.4 displays the characteristics of the sample after weighting.

Table A.4

Student Characteristics in the Weighted Sample

School Type	% White	% Black	% Hispanic	% Asian	% Other	% English Learner
Charter	50.1	13.5	26.8	2.8	6.8	14.8
Conventional public	47.4	11.6	30.7	3.9	6.4	17.7

SOURCE: 2001–02 CBEDS data.

CASE STUDIES

To gain insights and to enrich the description of our results, we visited a variety of charter schools and their chartering authorities in October and November 2002. Below, we describe our process of selecting the schools and the response rates.

Description of Selection Process

California charter schools are each unique in their educational philosophies and organizational structure, which makes it nearly impossible to develop a representative sample of all charter schools. Therefore, we systematically looked through extant data sources and the charter survey responses to identify major charter school categories. Then we worked with the LAO and the advisory panel to narrow the list of dimensions to three: conversion versus start-up schools, high-minority versus low-minority schools, and high-achieving versus low-achieving schools.[7] We also decided to focus only on schools that have elementary grades so that we could have systematic protocols across the schools.[8] We also included only

[7]High-minority schools are defined as having at least 50 percent black and Hispanic students and low-minority schools are defined as having less than 50 percent black and Hispanic students. High-achieving schools are defined as being in the highest 50th percentile of API scores and low-achieving schools are defined as being in the lowest 50th percentile of API scores. Establishing the definitions at the 50th percentile allows for binary classification of schools.

[8]Otherwise, separate protocols would have to be developed for high, middle, and elementary schools. Also, having a consistent protocol allows comparison across schools.

schools that responded to our survey. Using these criteria, Table A.5 illustrates the number of schools that fit into these dimensions.[9]

In selecting from schools within each of these categories, we also considered secondary factors such as geographical diversity and enrollment. Table A.6 displays the school selected for each dimension. If a school initially rejected our request to participate in the case studies, we made every attempt to replace the school with a substitute having the same dimension. However, for some dimensions we were not able to find a replacement school. Table A.6 shows three dimensions—the columns are marked with "NA"—for which the initially selected school rejected our request to participate and we could not find a substitute school.[10] In addition to these eight dimensions, we also selected four wild card schools.[11] These schools represent unique features of charter schools including state or county chartering authority, Education Management Organization status, and instructional type. These schools are listed in Table A.7. Of the four selected wild card schools, all four participated in our study. In total, we had nine schools participate in our case studies. All of the

Table A.5

Sample of Schools

	High Minority	Low Minority
	Conversion Schools	
High-achieving	6	21
Low-achieving	27	1
	Start-Up Schools	
High-achieving	17	16
Low-achieving	27	5

[9]We included only schools for which we had both data on racial breakdowns and API scores and responses to our survey. Because a school must be part of the state testing for two years to have an API score and because many charter schools are not part of the API reporting, the sample of schools was drastically reduced.

[10]One selected school was interested in participating but the principal was on emergency leave and would not return in our time frame for case study completion. In addition, only one school fit into the converted low-minority, low-achieving category and so no replacement was possible.

[11]We did not require that schools have racial breakdowns or API scores to be part of the sample, since these variables were not part of the wild card criteria.

chartering authorities associated with the case study charter schools except one participated in our case studies.

Table A.6

Core Case Study Schools

Category	School Type	% Black	% Hispanic	2001 API	Enrollment	Implementation Date
High minority/ high-achieving	Start-up	40–50	50–60	700–725	200–300	Before 1997
High minority/ high-achieving	Conversion	NA	NA	NA	NA	NA
High minority/ low-achieving	Start-up	0–10	80–90	525–550	500–600	After 1997
High minority/ low-achieving	Conversion	10–20	80–90	550–575	1,200–1,300	Before 1997
Low minority/ low-achieving	Start-up	0–10	0–10	625–650	0–100	After 1997
Low minority/ low-achieving	Conversion	NA	NA	NA	NA	NA
Low minority/ high-achieving	Start-up	NA	NA	NA	NA	NA
Low minority/ high-achieving	Conversion	0–10	20–30	825–850	700–800	Before 1997

NOTE: Values are presented as ranges to protect school identity.

Table A.7

Wild Card Case Study Schools

Category	School Type	% Black	% Hispanic	2001 API	Enrollment	Implementation Date
Wild card	Start-up	0–10	90–100	450–475	300–400	After 1997
Wild card	Start-up	40–50	10–20	NA	200–300	After 1997
Wild card	Start-up	0–10	10–20	NA	400–500	After 1997
Wild card	Start-up	0–10	0–10	NA	100–200	After 1997

NOTE: Values are presented as ranges to protect school identity.

Appendix B

CHARTER AND CONVENTIONAL PUBLIC SCHOOL COMPARISON METHODS

In Chapters Two, Four, Five, Six, Seven, and Eight, the primary aim is to analyze differences between charter schools and conventional public schools. In many cases, we also analyze the differences among different charter school types. To do these evaluations, we rely on both secondary and primary data including CBEDS, J-200, PAIF, case studies of nine charter schools and their respective chartering authorities, and survey data of charter and conventional public schools and chartering authorities. These data sources are described in more detail in Appendix A. As discussed in that appendix, charter school survey results were weighted so that the sample of charter schools reflected the population of charter schools in the state, and conventional public school results were weighted to ensure comparability with the charter school sample.

For the actual analysis, t-tests were used to assess the statistical significance of differences between group means. The t-test used linearization standard errors (Skinner, 1989) for group means as implemented in SAS Proc SURVEYREG. Linearization standard errors account for the contribution of nonconstant weights to the variability of estimates of group means.

Most of the analyses compare charter schools with conventional public schools, but in some cases we present descriptive information separately for conversion and start-up schools. We supplement the survey results with selected findings from the case studies. The case study sample is not sufficiently large or representative to permit generalization of these findings to the larger population of charter schools, but the case studies are useful for providing illustrative examples and for identifying some of the challenges faced by charter schools.

Appendix C

ACADEMIC OUTCOMES

SCHOOL-LEVEL PERFORMANCE

The statistical analysis of API scores adjusts for changes in the student composition of each school. Minority and low-SES students are known to perform poorly on academic achievement tests. Therefore, a large influx or exodus of low-achieving students would alter a school's API. The CDE excludes from the calculation of API the test score results of students in their first year at a school. CDE policy limits the potential for these first-year students to distort a school's API, but changing student composition may be an important factor for API growth if the changes continue in subsequent years.

The basic model is given by Equation (C.1):

$$API_{jt} = \theta_t + \alpha_j + \gamma_t C + x_{jt}\beta + \upsilon_{jt} \qquad \text{(C.1)}$$

where j denotes a school, t denotes a year, API is the school's index score in a given year, θ reflects an overall trend in API (not related to the individual school), α represents school-specific factors that do not change over time, γ represents possible differences in the trend in API for charter schools, C is an indicator variable that equals one if the school is a charter and zero otherwise, x is a $1 \times K$ vector of K observable factors affecting API, β is a $K \times 1$ vector of unobserved parameters, and υ is a random error term. Estimation of Equation (C.1) is difficult because the school-specific error term, α, is likely to be correlated with the observed school characteristics. For example, a school may have strong links to the neighborhood and greater involvement. These factors may mean that the API score is persistently higher for the school than would be expected from the observed characteristics of students attending the school. These estimation problems are eased by fixed-effects estimation or first-differencing of Equation (C.1). Lagging the model one period and subtracting gives

$$\Delta API_{jt} = \Delta\theta_t + \Delta\gamma_t C + \Delta x_{jt}\beta + \Delta\upsilon_{jt} \qquad (C.2)$$

The key feature of this lagging procedure is that it eliminates the school-specific error term, α.

The changing student composition of schools may be important for our analysis if charter schools are changing in different ways from conventional public schools. For example, if charters are attracting students with higher achievement potential over time (fewer minority and low-SES students), then the achievement scores of charters might outpace those of conventional public schools, because of the composition shift and not because of the performance of the charters themselves.

The API results in Tables C.1 through C.4 compare the growth in API scores for charter and conventional public schools for 1999–00, 2000–01, and 2001–02. The model adjusts API growth for changes in the background of students attending each school in each year. The statistical model estimates the change in API scores for each pair of years as a function of the change in the background characteristics of students attending the school and the charter status of the school.

In each specification, the intercept coefficient represents the average growth of a conventional public school. In each year-to-year comparison, API grows significantly for conventional public elementary and secondary schools in the state. The coefficient on charter status in Tables C.1 and C.3 shows whether the API growth for charters differed from that for conventional public schools after adjusting for the year-to-year changes in the composition of both types of schools. The charter coefficient is sometimes positive and sometimes negative, but the charter school effect is consistently insignificant across years in both elementary and secondary schools. The API evidence shows that the growth in school test scores does not differ in a statistically significant way by the charter status of a school.

Table C.1

API Annual Growth Regressions for Elementary Conventional Public Schools and Charter Schools

	1999–00	2000–01	2001–02
Charter	2.7649	–5.8517	–2.8147
	(3.7376)	(3.6977)	(2.9975)
% of students tested	–0.6883*	–0.2848	–0.1636
	(0.0876)	(0.2121)	(0.1451)
% black	–1.4252*	–0.7879*	–0.9486*
	(0.2379)	(0.2539)	(0.2409)
% American Indian	–0.4833	–0.4984	–0.4091
	(0.4704)	(0.4381)	(0.4970)
% Asian	0.1231	0.0611	–0.0529
	(0.2646)	(0.2127)	(0.2039)
% Filipino	0.8152	0.8608	0.3981
	(0.4457)	(0.4471)	(0.4198)
% Hispanic or Latino	–0.7194*	–0.4828*	–0.8095*
	(0.1770)	(0.1433)	(0.1666)
% Pacific Islander	0.2496	0.1535	–0.9798
	(0.5370)	(0.5855)	(0.5804)
% English Learner	–0.3045*	–0.4294*	–0.5591*
	(0.0978)	(0.0935)	(0.0939)
% in school lunch program	–0.2494*	–0.0403	–0.2181*
	(0.0749)	(0.0717)	(0.0738)
% first year at school	–0.1336*	–0.0727	–0.2166*
	(0.0371)	(0.0520)	(0.0523)
No lunch program at school	–4.9079	–1.2106	–6.8193
	(6.6482)	(5.3806)	(4.9859)
Constant	39.0685*	23.1350*	18.3865*
	(0.4682)	(0.4220)	(0.4048)
No. of observations	4,685	4,621	4,128
R-squared	0.34	0.32	0.38

NOTES: The results are based on CDE's API database. Standard errors are in parentheses. The regression variable for each background characteristic is the difference between the values for the current school year and the previous school year.

*Indicates coefficients that are significantly different from zero at the $\alpha = 0.05$ confidence level.

Tables C.2 and C.4 show the results for different types of charters. Start-up, conversion, and conventional public schools have very similar API growth. Similarly, charters with some nonclassroom-based instruction do no better or worse in API growth than charter schools with classroom-based instruction or conventional public schools.

Table C.2

API Annual Growth Regressions for Elementary Conventional Public Schools, Conversion Schools, and Start-Up Schools, and Whether the Charter School Offers Nonclassroom-Based Instruction

	1999–00	2000–01	2001–02
Conversion	2.2210	–4.8970	–2.2181
	(3.9986)	(3.9293)	(3.4400)
Start–up	6.1784	–13.8835	–9.3542
	(14.6342)	(14.6320)	(7.1882)
Some nonclassroom–based instruction	–10.0822	54.9830	15.3107
	(32.0215)	(33.3138)	(12.5157)
% of students tested	–0.6942*	–0.3111	–0.1453
	(0.0876)	(0.2123)	(0.1459)
% Black	–1.4257*	–0.7952*	–0.9365*
	(0.2379)	(0.2542)	(0.2413)
% American Indian	–0.4915	–0.4900	–0.4311
	(0.4705)	(0.4379)	(0.4974)
% Asian	0.1105	0.0534	–0.0425
	(0.2648)	(0.2126)	(0.2043)
% Filipino	0.8333	0.8534	0.4264
	(0.4459)	(0.4469)	(0.4207)
% Hispanic or Latino	–0.7243*	–0.4682*	–0.8030*
	(0.1770)	(0.1434)	(0.1670)
% Pacific Islander	0.2620	0.2051	–0.9955
	(0.5370)	(0.5856)	(0.5806)
% English Learner	–0.3044*	–0.4312*	–0.5601*
	(0.0978)	(0.0935)	(0.0939)
% in school lunch program	–0.2454*	–0.0399	–0.2196*
	(0.0750)	(0.0717)	(0.0739)
% first year at school	–0.1338*	–0.0758	–0.2153*
	(0.0372)	(0.0521)	(0.0523)
No lunch program at school	–4.9589	–1.8149	–7.9078
	(6.7390)	(5.3983)	(5.2143)
Constant	39.0849*	23.1165*	18.3920*
	(0.4682)	(0.4219)	(0.4050)
No. of observations	4,683	4,619	4,127
R-squared	0.34	0.32	0.38

NOTES: The results are based on CDE's API database. Standard errors are in parentheses. The regression variable for each background characteristic is the difference between the values for the current school year and the previous school year.

*Indicates coefficients that are significantly different from zero at the $\alpha = 0.05$ confidence level.

Table C.3

API Annual Growth Regressions for Secondary Conventional Public Schools and Charter Schools

	1999–00	2000–01	2001–02
Charter	–7.6683	0.0334	2.1640
	(5.9679)	(5.2354)	(4.5808)
% of students tested	–0.2814*	–0.0589	–0.2121
	(0.1275)	(0.1682)	(0.1650)
% Black	–1.4298*	–0.8109	–1.2052*
	(0.3866)	(0.4355)	(0.4344)
% American Indian	–0.9351	–0.8048	–0.5000
	(0.6730)	(0.6491)	(0.8167)
% Asian	–0.0968	–0.2176	0.2146
	(0.4158)	(0.3803)	(0.4193)
% Filipino	0.8482	0.5598	–0.9125
	(0.7423)	(0.6995)	(0.7504)
% Hispanic or Latino	–1.3833*	–1.1851*	–0.7481*
	(0.3189)	(0.3266)	(0.3059)
% Pacific Islander	–0.1680	1.1428	–1.1961
	(0.9619)	(0.9427)	(0.9664)
% English Learner	–0.2674	–0.4820*	–0.4918*
	(0.1529)	(0.1369)	(0.1618)
% in school lunch program	–0.0286	0.1466	–0.0441
	(0.0946)	(0.0984)	(0.1047)
% first year at school	0.0413	0.0255	0.0261
	(0.0473)	(0.0403)	(0.0532)
No lunch program at school	–6.4405	–5.9644	14.9186
	(6.1256)	(6.0417)	(8.1624)
Middle school	7.4231*	11.7358*	2.4064*
	(1.2068)	(1.0083)	(0.9732)
Constant	14.0374*	3.1751*	4.9533*
	(1.0592)	(0.7378)	(0.7205)
No. of observations	1,861	1,886	1,589
R-squared	0.44	0.44	0.37

NOTES: The results are based on CDE's API database. Standard errors are in parentheses. The regression variable for each background characteristic is the difference between the values for the current school year and the previous school year.

*Indicates coefficients that are significantly different from zero at the α = 0.05 confidence level.

Table C.4

API Annual Growth Regressions for Secondary Conventional Public Schools, Conversion Schools, and Start-Up Schools, and Whether the Charter School Offers Nonclassroom-Based Instruction

	1999–00	2000–01	2001–02
Conversion	–8.7029	2.7200	1.6429
	(6.0656)	(5.7072)	(5.0381)
Start–up	22.9706	–8.9481	0.5189
	(32.6277)	(31.3306)	(14.4047)
Some nonclassroom–based instruction	0.0000	25.2869	9.0088
	(0.0000)	(33.6612)	(21.2557)
% of students tested	–0.2784*	–0.0655	–0.2119
	(0.1276)	(0.1683)	(0.1652)
% Black	–1.4559*	–0.8320	–1.2108*
	(0.3876)	(0.4358)	(0.4349)
% American Indian	–0.9196	–0.8261	–0.4886
	(0.6732)	(0.6493)	(0.8178)
% Asian	–0.0874	–0.2173	0.2164
	(0.4159)	(0.3806)	(0.4209)
% Filipino	0.8509	0.5706	–0.8947
	(0.7424)	(0.6995)	(0.7521)
% Hispanic or Latino	–1.3743*	–1.1904*	–0.7518*
	(0.3190)	(0.3266)	(0.3062)
% Pacific Islander	–0.1766	1.1151	–1.1890
	(0.9620)	(0.9428)	(0.9675)
% English Learner	–0.2915	–0.4771*	–0.4914*
	(0.1550)	(0.1370)	(0.1623)
% in school lunch program	–0.0232	0.1404	–0.0425
	(0.0948)	(0.0985)	(0.1053)
% first year at school	0.0430	0.0264	0.0271
	(0.0473)	(0.0403)	(0.0534)
No lunch program at school	–6.8070	–8.3424	14.7663
	(6.1378)	(6.2562)	(8.1833)
Middle school	7.4208*	11.7871*	2.4173*
	(1.2068)	(1.0088)	(0.9744)
Constant	14.0177*	3.1675*	4.9444*
	(1.0594)	(0.7378)	(0.7213)
No. of observations	1,861	1,886	1,589
R-squared	0.44	0.44	0.37

NOTES: The results are based on CDE's API database. Standard errors are in parentheses. The regression variable for each background characteristic is the difference between the values for the current school year and the previous school year.

*Indicates coefficients that are significantly different from zero at the $\alpha = 0.05$ confidence level.

The results for student background factors in the model follow the expected patterns. Increases in the share of minority, English Learner, and low-SES students (those who participate in the free or reduced-price school lunch program) are associated with reduced growth in API for the school. Student mobility reduces API growth at the elementary school level, but mobility has no significant effect on the API growth of secondary schools.

STATEWIDE NONLONGITUDINALLY LINKED STUDENT-LEVEL DATA

CDE provided individual records for all California students who took the Stanford 9 from 1998 through 2002. The test is administered in the spring of each year at elementary and secondary schools. The analysis divided students into elementary grades (2 through 5) and secondary grades (6 through 11). The file contains 9.1 million elementary and 12.7 million secondary student-year records. About 1.5 percent of both the elementary and secondary students are enrolled in a charter over this five-year period. Although the share of charter schools is small, the file contains about 320,000 student-year records.

The file contains information on the student's English proficiency, ethnicity, parental education, eligibility for the school lunch program, and gender as well as an indication that the student has transferred to the school in the current year. These variables are used to adjust test scores for the effect of student background. The file also identifies the student's school. The file does not include a student identifier, so student performance cannot be tracked over successive years.

The statistical model for the analysis was a random effects model where a separate intercept was allowed for each school and for each grade cohort within each school. The model is based on Equation (C.3):

$$S_{ijkt} = \alpha_j + \delta_{k(j)} + \gamma C + x_{ijkt}\beta + \Delta\upsilon_{ijkt} \qquad \text{(C.3)}$$

where i, j, k, and t index individual students, schools, grades, and years, respectively; s is test score; α is an unobserved school-specific factor that does not vary over time; δ is an unobserved grade-cohort factor within each school; γ is an unobserved parameter reflecting the possible effect of charter school attendance on s; C is an indicator variable that equals one if the school is a charter school and zero otherwise, x is a $1 \times K$ vector of K observable factors affecting s, β is a $K \times 1$ vector of unobserved parameters, and υ is a random error term. The model includes a set of indicator variables for test year to allow for possible trends in the scores.

This approach corrects for the fact that charter status is not tied directly to individual students but rather to students through the schools that they attend. The grade cohort adjustment reflects the fact that many of the second-grade students at a school will be third-grade students in the next year, so there is probably some correlation between the test scores across grade cohorts at a school even after adjusting for observed student background factors.

The regression results are reported in Tables C.5 through C.8. The results for charter school status and charter type are described in Chapter Three. Low English proficiency, minority status, and participation in the free or reduced-price lunch program are inversely correlated with test scores in both reading and math at the elementary- and secondary-grade levels. Students who are new to their current school tend to score lower than students who attended the same school in the previous year. Other things equal, girls tend to score higher than boys, but the effect is insignificant for secondary-grade math.

In addition to the random effect for grade cohorts, the model also controls for the trend in achievement scores over the five-year time period. The results show that elementary school students did somewhat better in 1999 and 2000 than in 1998, but the trend has been rather flat or slightly negative since 2000. For secondary school students, the upward trend was smaller in 1999 and 2000, and it has become negative since then.

LONGITUDINALLY LINKED STUDENT-LEVEL DATA

Student-level scores were analyzed for six school districts that provided test score information with a student identifier that allowed us to track student performance over time. The results for Chula Vista Elementary, Fresno Unified, Napa Valley Unified, West Covina

Table C.5

Stanford 9 Test Regressions for Elementary Conventional Public Schools and Charter Schools

	Reading		Math	
Variable	Coefficient	Standard Error	Coefficient	Standard Error
Intercept	44.6446*	0.103	48.7307*	0.1168
Charter	0.1315	0.2082	–1.4453*	0.2264
English Learner	–10.8959*	0.0181	–7.2042*	0.0191
Ethnicity				
Black	–9.3119*	0.0271	–10.9518*	0.0288
American Indian	–4.6607*	0.0683	–4.7767*	0.0725
Asian	3.501*	0.0281	9.3518*	0.0298
Filipino	1.1189*	0.044	2.7861*	0.0466
Hispanic or Latino	–4.2393*	0.0193	–3.6057*	0.0204
Pacific Islander	–4.4771*	0.0754	–4.009*	0.0799
Other ethnicity	–2.3555*	0.0836	–1.907*	0.0886
Parental education				
Non–high school graduate	–2.5158*	0.0225	–2.0535*	0.0239
Some college	3.976*	0.0212	3.7894*	0.0225
College graduate	7.1067*	0.0235	7.0327*	0.0249
Graduate school	11.2917*	0.03	10.838*	0.0318
Decline education	–0.7346*	0.0244	–1.49*	0.0259
Education missing	–0.2298*	0.0297	–0.2726*	0.0316
School lunch program	–4.4945*	0.0204	–4.4966*	0.0217
Lunch program missing	–0.9453*	0.0291	–1.7476*	0.0309
Female	2.9643*	0.0123	0.4553*	0.013
First year at school	–3.8241*	0.017	–4.1611*	0.018
New missing	–3.2753*	0.0328	–3.381*	0.0349
Testing year				
1999	3.6135*	0.0222	3.5542*	0.0237
2000	5.407*	0.0311	5.7928*	0.0333
2001	5.1517*	0.0325	5.1454*	0.0349
2002	4.7355*	0.0345	4.9815*	0.0372

NOTE: The results are based on CDE statewide student-level data.

*Indicates coefficients that are significantly different from zero at the $\alpha = 0.05$ confidence level.

Unified, San Diego City Unified, and Los Angeles Unified are reported in Tables C.9 through C.15. Results for secondary school students are limited to San Diego and Los Angeles, because the other districts contained few (if any) secondary school students in charters. The two large urban districts also had a mix of start-up and conversion schools, so separate analyses examined how test achievement varied by charter type. Nonclassroom-based instruction was available at only one charter school in Fresno and one in San Diego, so

Table C.6

Stanford 9 Test Regressions for Secondary Conventional Public Schools and Charter Schools

	Reading		Math	
Variable	Coefficient	Standard Error	Coefficient	Standard Error
Intercept	44.4395*	0.1222	49.4443*	0.1374
Charter	–1.4594*	0.2531	–2.2585*	0.2752
English Learner	–14.6019*	0.0159	–9.5794*	0.0166
Ethnicity				
Black	–11.2297*	0.0219	–11.7061*	0.023
American Indian	–5.6383*	0.0526	–5.6541*	0.0552
Asian	2.5423*	0.0215	10.953*	0.0225
Filipino	–0.888*	0.0335	1.9182*	0.0351
Hispanic or Latino	–4.966*	0.0152	–4.7537*	0.016
Pacific Islander	–6.1852*	0.0613	–4.3319*	0.0643
Other ethnicity	–4.7052*	0.0549	–3.8133*	0.0576
Parental education				
Non–high school graduate	–0.6521*	0.019	0.0798*	0.0199
Some college	4.8375*	0.0176	4.1821*	0.0184
College graduate	6.6355*	0.018	6.3701*	0.0189
Graduate school	13.4157*	0.0229	13.1819*	0.024
Decline education	–1.4261*	0.0207	–1.7771*	0.0217
Education missing	–1.4306*	0.0271	–1.3586*	0.0285
School lunch program	–3.8896*	0.016	–3.2559*	0.0168
Lunch program missing	–1.0908*	0.0261	–1.3293*	0.0275
Female	3.0186*	0.0102	0.0021	0.0107
First year at school	–1.8028*	0.0139	–1.227*	0.015
New missing	–4.242*	0.0251	–3.7215*	0.0265
Testing year				
1999	1.476*	0.0202	0.831*	0.0216
2000	1.2207*	0.0308	0.3641*	0.0331
2001	0.5712*	0.0337	–1.0285*	0.037
2002	–0.7843*	0.0371	–3.3241*	0.0414

NOTE: The results are based on CDE statewide student-level data.

*Indicates coefficients that are significantly different from zero at the $\alpha = 0.05$ confidence level.

there is no separate examination of the effects of nonclassroom-based instruction in the analysis of the district data.

The student-level identifier is used to adjust for stable student-specific factors that may affect achievement. Some students may have greater motivation or more parental support than others. These types of unmeasured factors may persistently affect how well a student learns irrespective of whether the student attends a conventional public school or a charter school.

The statistical model adjusts for these student-specific factors by controlling for fixed student effects in the student achievement regressions. The most basic statistical model is based on Equation (C.4):

$$S_{it} = \mu_i + \gamma C_{it} + x_{it}\beta + \Delta\upsilon_{it} \tag{C.4}$$

where i and t index individual students and years, respectively; s is test score; μ is an unobserved student-specific factor that does not vary over time; γ is an unobserved parameter reflecting the possible effect of charter school attendance on s; C is an indicator variable that equals one if the school is a charter school and zero otherwise, x is a $1 \times K$ vector of K observable factors affecting s, β is a $K \times 1$ vector of unobserved parameters, and υ is a random error term. The model includes observed family background characteristics such as ethnicity and SES that are likely to affect student achievement. In addition, we suspect that some students will over- or underachieve because of unobserved factors such as parental support, student motivation, or aptitude.

The appropriate estimation of this type of model depends on the correlation between μ and x. A random effects approach assumes that unobserved factors affecting student achievement, μ, are uncorrelated with observed factors, x. This type of model would seem appropriate if we had a relatively complete set of observed factors affecting student achievement. We used an alternative fixed-effect approach that used the longitudinal nature of the data to "difference out" the μ for observations on the same individual.[1] We average Equation (C.5) for the ith level and subtract this result from Equation (C.4), so the transformed fixed-effects equation is

$$S_{it} - \overline{S}_i = \gamma(C_{it} - \overline{C}_i) + (x_{it} - \overline{x}_i)\beta + (\upsilon_{it} - \overline{\upsilon}_i) \tag{C.5}$$

where the bar above each variable is the corresponding variable mean.

---

[1] We also tested for serial correlation in the residuals in Equation (C.3). First-differencing is a preferred estimation method if there is strong positive serial correlation in panel data (Wooldridge, 2002). In this case, serial correlation was weak, so the parameters from the first-differenced model are similar to those of the fixed-effects model.

Table C.7

Stanford 9 Test Regressions for Elementary Conventional Public Schools, Conversion Schools, Start-Up Schools, and Nonclassroom-Based Schools

	Reading		Math	
Variable	Coefficient	Standard Error	Coefficient	Standard Error
Intercept	44.7114*	0.1032	48.817*	0.1166
Charter type:				
Conversion only	1.0123*	0.2354	–0.5147*	0.2546
Conversion and nonclassroom-based	–4.325*	1.6449	–9.1836*	1.843
Start–up only	0.9871	0.932	–1.4994	1.0613
Start–up and nonclassroom-based	–7.5771*	0.6995	–9.129*	0.7723
English Learner	–10.8959*	0.0181	–7.2042*	0.0191
Ethnicity				
Black	–9.3126*	0.0271	–10.9525*	0.0288
American Indian	–4.6601*	0.0683	–4.7762*	0.0725
Asian	3.5004*	0.0281	9.3513*	0.0298
Filipino	1.1181*	0.044	2.7853*	0.0466
Hispanic or Latino	–4.24*	0.0193	–3.6064*	0.0204
Pacific Islander	–4.4775*	0.0754	–4.0095*	0.0799
Other ethnicity	–2.3556*	0.0836	–1.9074*	0.0886
Parental education				
Non–high school graduate	–2.5159*	0.0225	–2.0536*	0.0239
Some college	3.9761*	0.0212	3.7898*	0.0225
College graduate	7.1071*	0.0235	7.0333*	0.0249
Graduate school	11.2919*	0.03	10.8385*	0.0318
Decline education	–0.7349*	0.0244	–1.4904*	0.0259
Education missing	–0.2304*	0.0297	–0.2724*	0.0316
School lunch program	–4.4959*	0.0204	–4.4981*	0.0217
Lunch program missing	–0.9471*	0.0291	–1.7499*	0.0309
Female	2.9643*	0.0123	0.4553*	0.013
First year at school	–3.8235*	0.017	–4.1605*	0.018
New missing	–3.2751*	0.0328	–3.3807*	0.0349
Testing year				
1999	3.6102*	0.0222	3.5501*	0.0237
2000	5.4016*	0.0311	5.7866*	0.0333
2001	5.1491*	0.0325	5.1419*	0.0349
2002	4.7334*	0.0345	4.9784*	0.0372

NOTE: The results are based on CDE statewide student-level data.

*Indicates coefficients that are significantly different from zero at the $\alpha = 0.05$ confidence level.

Table C.8

Stanford 9 Test Regressions for Secondary Conventional Public Schools, Conversion Schools, Start-Up Schools, and Nonclassroom-Based Schools

	Reading		Math	
Variable	Coefficient	Standard Error	Coefficient	Standard Error
Intercept	44.4376*	0.1227	49.4354*	0.1379
Charter type				
Conversion only	0.1084	0.3094	−1.0962*	0.335
Conversion and nonclassroom-based	−4.3659	2.3507	−8.0897*	2.6461
Start–up only	2.7535*	0.8936	2.0399*	1.0097
Start–up and nonclassroom-based	−7.2532*	0.5486	−6.8754*	0.594
English Learner	−14.6021*	0.0159	−9.5796*	0.0166
Ethnicity				
Black	−11.2302*	0.0219	−11.7065*	0.023
American Indian	−5.6388*	0.0526	−5.6546*	0.0552
Asian	2.5422*	0.0215	10.9529*	0.0225
Filipino	−0.8882*	0.0335	1.9181*	0.0351
Hispanic or Latino	−4.9662*	0.0152	−4.7538*	0.016
Pacific Islander	−6.1855*	0.0613	−4.3321*	0.0643
Other ethnicity	−4.7057*	0.0549	−3.8139*	0.0576
Parental education				
Non–high school graduate	−0.6521*	0.019	0.0798*	0.0199
Some college	4.8375*	0.0176	4.1821*	0.0184
College graduate	6.6354*	0.018	6.37*	0.0189
Graduate school	13.4157*	0.0229	13.1819*	0.024
Decline education	−1.426*	0.0207	−1.777*	0.0217
Education missing	−1.4307*	0.0271	−1.3586*	0.0285
School lunch program	−3.8901*	0.016	−3.2563*	0.0168
Lunch program missing	−1.093*	0.0261	−1.331*	0.0275
Female	3.0187*	0.0102	0.0022	0.0107
First year at school	−1.8023*	0.0139	−1.2266*	0.015
New missing	−4.2422*	0.0251	−3.7217*	0.0265
Testing year				
1999	1.4739*	0.0202	0.8296*	0.0216
2000	1.2135*	0.0308	0.3589*	0.0331
2001	0.5675*	0.0337	−1.0309*	0.037
2002	−0.7871*	0.0371	−3.3258*	0.0414

NOTE: The results are based on CDE statewide student-level data.

*Indicates coefficients that are significantly different from zero at the $\alpha = 0.05$ confidence level.

The student fixed-effect combines all student-level factors that are invariant over time and affect student achievement, so the results do not include separate parameter estimates for such student factors as ethnicity. In addition to the fixed-effects model, student-level random effects were also estimated for comparison purposes. The random-effects specification assumes that the unobserved factors affecting student performance from year to year are uncorrelated with observed student background factors.

In addition to the fixed-effects model, we estimated a random-growth model (Heckman and Hotz, 1989; Papke, 1994). The random-growth model generalizes the fixed-effects model to allow for individuals to differ not only with respect to a constant factor, μ, but also on the rate of test score growth over time. The basis for the random growth rate model is Equation (C.6):

$$S_{it} = \mu_i + \delta_i t + \gamma C_{it} + x_{it}\beta + \upsilon_{it} \quad (C.6)$$

where δ is an individual-specific growth rate. The model is now first-differenced to obtain Equation (C.7).

$$\Delta S_{it} = \delta_i + \gamma \Delta C_{it} + \Delta x_{it}\beta + \Delta \upsilon_{it} \quad (C.7)$$

The differencing eliminates the μ, and δ becomes the intercept of the differenced equation.[2] Equation (C.6) is estimated by fixed effects to obtain estimates of γ and β. The available student background variables do not vary over time, so the x vector consists of a test year variable to detect any trend in scores.

The results for the fixed-effects and random-growth model were similar. The differencing method used in the random-growth model requires that student records be included in the analysis only when successive test score records are available. This inherently eliminated all test scores for the 1997–98 school year, because the STAR test was not administered in 1996–98. Similarly, we lose the first-year record for students entering a school district or starting elementary school. These data requirements meant that the random-growth

---

[2]The growth term simplifies because $\delta_i t - \delta_i(t-1) = \delta_i$.

model was estimated for a much smaller sample than the fixed-effects model.

We also estimated a random-effects model based on Equation (C.4). In each case, the estimated student-specific error term was significantly correlated with student background variables in the model and therefore produces unreliable estimates of the effect of attending a charter school. This indicates that the parameter estimates from the random-effects model are inconsistent because of omitted variables. This violation of the random-effects assumptions suggested that the fixed-effects or the random-growth specification was more appropriate for this model.

Table C.9

Charter School Status Regressions for Fixed-Effects Model on Pooled Student Data from Districts

	Elementary		Secondary	
	Reading	Math	Reading	Math
Charter	–0.0848	–0.6776*	0.2767*	–0.3816*
	(0.0882)	(0.1068)	(0.0921)	(0.1021)
Trend	1.6107*		0.0323*	0.7389*
	(0.0080)		(0.0070)	(0.0078)
Constant	36.7761*	46.3624*	38.7003*	41.6877*
	(0.0251)	(0.0093)	(0.0224)	(0.0247)
No. of observations	1,554,666	1,598,639	1,351,000	1,360,492

SOURCE: Pooled district student-level data.

NOTE: Standard errors are in parentheses.

*Indicates coefficients that are significantly different from zero at the $\alpha = 0.05$ confidence level.

Table C.10

Charter School Status Regressions for Random-Effects Model on Pooled Student Data from Districts

	Elementary		Secondary	
	Reading	Math	Reading	Math
Charter	–0.2148	–1.6440*	0.3392*	–0.1959
	(0.1589)	(0.1912)	(0.1714)	(0.1885)
Constant	1.6033*	1.7558*	0.2832*	0.5099*
	(0.0135)	(0.0163)	(0.0138)	(0.0152)
No. of observations	816,364	854,899	749,413	757,760

SOURCE: Pooled district student-level data.

NOTE: Standard errors are in parentheses.

*Indicates coefficients that are significantly different from zero at the $\alpha = 0.05$ confidence level.

Table C.11

Charter School Status Regressions for Elementary Reading in Fixed-Effects Model, by District

	Chula Vista Elementary	Fresno Unified	Los Angeles Unified	Napa Unified	San Diego City Unified	West Covina Unified
Charter	–2.2091*	–3.2806*	0.0986	–1.4964*	0.8842*	0.0821
	(0.3620)	(0.4950)	(0.1767)	(0.5710)	(0.1107)	(0.6378)
Trend	2.0921*	0.5280*	2.1432*	1.8898*	0.6437*	0.5784*
	(0.0436)	(0.0309)	(0.0102)	(0.0833)	(0.0153)	(0.0928)
Constant	39.3724*	37.0271*	32.6859*	45.0836*	45.9710*	45.9933*
	(0.1495)	(0.0975)	(0.0338)	(0.2389)	(0.0410)	(0.2923)
No. of observations	59,033	111,418	1,010,480	186,60	340,142	14,933

SOURCE: Pooled district student-level data.

NOTE: Standard errors are in parentheses.

*Indicates coefficients that are significantly different from zero at the α = 0.05 confidence level.

Table C.12

Charter School Status Regressions for Elementary Math in Fixed-Effects Model, by District

	Chula Vista Elementary	Fresno Unified	Los Angeles Unified	Napa Unified	San Diego City Unified	West Covina Unified
Charter	–4.6918*	–2.7988*	0.0378	–2.0256*	–0.9183*	–2.5363*
	(0.4432)	(0.5906)	(0.2131)	(0.6865)	(0.1271)	(0.8073)
Trend	2.7504*	0.7265*	1.6458*	2.4029*	0.7368*	0.9831*
	(0.0535)	(0.0371)	(0.0123)	(0.1011)	(0.0175)	(0.1181)
Constant	43.8262*	40.7171*	39.3367*	46.9619*	49.7142*	51.0503*
	(0.1829)	(0.1167)	(0.0403)	(0.2901)	(0.0469)	(0.3705)
No. of observations	60,546	115,428	1,042,681	19,277	345,530	15,177

SOURCE: Pooled district student-level data.

NOTE: Standard errors are in parentheses.

*Indicates coefficients that are significantly different from zero at the α = 0.05 confidence level.

Table C.13

Charter School Status Regressions for Elementary Reading in Random-Growth Model, by District

	Chula Vista Elementary	Fresno Unified	Los Angeles Unified	Napa Unified	San Diego City Unified	West Covina Unified
Charter	–2.2210*	–4.7630*	–0.5996	–1.4095	0.4074*	–0.8603
	(0.6951)	(0.8256)	(0.3431)	(1.1582)	(0.1950)	(1.2049)
Constant	1.9864*	0.4223*	2.0794*	1.6899*	0.6598*	0.5280*
	(0.0715)	(0.0530)	(0.0169)	(0.1339)	(0.0276)	(0.1553)
No. of observations	29,124	58,068	518,864	9,279	193,893	7,136

SOURCE: Pooled district student-level data.

NOTE: Standard errors are in parentheses.

*Indicates coefficients that are significantly different from zero at the $\alpha = 0.05$ confidence level.

Table C.14

Charter Status Regressions for Elementary Math in Random-Growth Model, by District

	Chula Vista Elementary	Fresno Unified	Los Angeles Unified	Napa Unified	San Diego City Unified	West Covina Unified
Charter	–5.3567*	–4.3705*	–0.2647	–0.3453	–1.5402*	–5.5058*
	(0.8411)	(0.9542)	(0.4159)	(1.3970)	(0.2267)	(1.5665)
Constant	2.8765*	1.0714*	2.1573*	2.4676*	0.6743*	1.4516*
	(0.0885)	(0.0632)	(0.0205)	(0.1697)	(0.0321)	(0.2026)
No. of observations	30,385	61,810	546,711	9,763	198,865	7,365

SOURCE: Pooled district student-level data.

NOTE: Standard errors are in parentheses.

*Indicates coefficients that are significantly different from zero at the $\alpha = 0.05$ confidence level.

Table C.15

Charter School Type Regressions for Fixed-Effects Model in Los Angeles Unified and San Diego City Unified Districts

	Los Angeles Unified		San Diego City Unified	
	Reading	Math	Reading	Math
Conversion	0.2592	0.5829*	2.1835*	0.0295
	(0.1928)	(0.2329)	(0.1343)	(0.1535)
Start-up	–0.3479	–1.5017	–1.7147*	–2.8661*
	(0.6649)	(0.8036)	(0.1881)	(0.2179)
Trend	2.1451*	1.6480*	0.6671*	0.7538*
	(0.0103)	(0.0123)	(0.0153)	(0.0176)
Constant	32.7023*	39.3530*	45.9198*	49.6777*
	(0.0338)	(0.0404)	(0.0411)	(0.0470)
No. of observations	1,007,807	1,039,922	340,142	345,530

SOURCE: Pooled district student-level data.

NOTE: Standard errors are in parentheses.

*Indicates coefficients that are significantly different from zero at the $\alpha = 0.05$ confidence level.

The results for the fixed-effects and random-growth model are reported below. Separate models were estimated for reading and math scores at the elementary and secondary school levels. The first set of tables are for test scores pooled across districts. The results from the pooled fixed-effects model in Table C.9 were used to construct Figure 3.5, but the results from the random-growth model in Table C.10 were similar.

Tables C.11 through C.15 are the separate results for the Chula Vista Elementary, Fresno Unified, Los Angeles Unified, Napa Unified, San Diego City Unified, and West Covina Unified districts. Elementary school results are reported for all six districts. The secondary school analysis was restricted to Los Angeles and San Diego, since there were few charter secondary school enrollments in the other four districts.

Appendix D

SURVEYS ADMINISTERED FOR THE STUDY

PUBLIC SCHOOL SURVEY

1-5/

FORM: 8-10/ PUB

Completion of the questionnaire is voluntary. All responses to this survey will be strictly confidential. Individual respondents never will be identified by name or any other manner that could allow another researcher, government official, or member of the public to infer their identity.

BATCH ☐☐☐☐ 11-14/

If you would like to receive a $50 honorarium for completing this survey, please PRINT your name, school name, school mailing address, and school district in the space below. Remove this tear-off sheet from the survey and place it in the "confidential" envelope and enclose it in the LARGE RAND business reply envelope with your completed survey. No postage is needed.

PLEASE PRINT:

Today's Date: ______________________

Name ____

School ____

School Address: ____________________________________

City ________________ State ______ Zip code ________________

School District______________________________________

THANK YOU FOR PARTICIPATING!
WE WILL MAIL YOU A CHECK FOR $50 AS SOON AS WE RECEIVE THIS FORM.

RAND, 1700 Main Street, Santa Monica, CA 90407

1. In this school, approximately what percentage of all students are instructed (excluding routine homework and extended student illness)...

a. ...exclusively or primarily at a school site? [ ][ ][ ] % 15-17/

b. ...more or less equally at private home(s) and at a school site? [ ][ ][ ] % 18-20/

c. ...exclusively or primarily at private home(s)? [ ][ ][ ] % 21-23/

d. Other? (Please Describe:______________________________) [ ][ ][ ] % 24-26/

TOTAL [1][0][0] % 27-28/

2. Are you the principal of this school?

☐ Yes 29/
☐ No, please specify your title______________________________ 30-31/

3. What grades are offered in this school? *(Check all that apply)*

☐ Prekindergarten	☐ 2nd	☐ 5th	☐ 8th	☐ 11th
☐ Kindergarten	☐ 3rd	☐ 6th	☐ 9th	☐ 12th
☐ 1st	☐ 4th	☐ 7th	☐ 10th	☐ Ungraded

4. How many instructional days are offered by this school? (If you are a multi-track school, please specify the number of instructional days per track.)

[ ][ ][ ] 53-55/

Total Instructional Days Per Year

5. For the school year 2001-02, did this school have more students than it could accommodate?

☐ Yes → If 'Yes,' how many students? [ ][ ][ ] 56/

☐ No Students 57-59/

6. During the school year 2001-02, approximately what percentage of this school's students came from the local attendance area?

[ ][ ][ ] % 60-62/

Percentage

☐ *Don't Know* 63/

7. Do any students in the local attendance area attend a charter school?

☐ Yes 64/

☐ No → **Go to Question 9**

☐ Don't Know → **Go to Question 9**

8. Please indicate if you agree or disagree with the following statements

Mark (X) one box per line

a. <u>This school</u> or the district has restructured compensation to teachers in response to the introduction of charter schools.	☐ Agree	☐ Disagree	☐ Don't Know	65/
b. <u>This school</u> or the district has restructured hiring/firing/discipline policies of teachers in response to the introduction of charter schools.	☐ Agree	☐ Disagree	☐ Don't Know	66/
c. <u>This school</u> or the district has changed the curriculum in response to the introduction of charter schools.	☐ Agree	☐ Disagree	☐ Don't Know	67/
d. <u>This school</u> or the district has changed instructional practices in response to the introduction of charter schools.	☐ Agree	☐ Disagree	☐ Don't Know	68/
e. <u>This school</u> or the district has changed professional development in response to the introduction of charter schools.	☐ Agree	☐ Disagree	☐ Don't Know	69/

9. Characterize the effect that the introduction of charter schools has had on <u>this school</u> in the following categories:

	Very Positive	Some-what Positive	No Effect	Some-what Negative	Very Negative	
a. Financial security	☐	☐	☐	☐	☐	70/
b. Ability to acquire necessary resources from the district or state	☐	☐	☐	☐	☐	71/
c. Teacher recruitment/retention	☐	☐	☐	☐	☐	72/
d. Ability to attract and retain students	☐	☐	☐	☐	☐	73/
e. Ability to educate students	☐	☐	☐	☐	☐	74/
f. Parental satisfaction	☐	☐	☐	☐	☐	75/

CARD 02 **ID** 6-7/ 1-5/

10. a. Did this school start providing instruction in the last five years? 8/

- ☐ Yes
- ☐ No → **Go to Question 11**

b. When did the school start providing instruction as a public school? 9-12/

☐☐ / ☐☐

Month Year

11. a. Does this school seek to focus its services on a specific population of students? 13/

- ☐ Yes
- ☐ No → **Go to Question 12**

b. Please specify the categories of students the school focuses its services

Check all that apply

a. ☐ Students with disabilities 14/

b. ☐ Low-income students 15/

c. ☐ Students of a specific racial/ethnic minority group 16/

d. ☐ Limited English Proficient students 17/

e. ☐ Students with academic problems 18/

f. ☐ Students with discipline problems 19/

g. ☐ Students with special aptitudes, skills, or talents 20/

(Please describe________________________________) 21-22/

12. Does this school's admissions process include any of the following elements?

Mark (X) one box per line

	Not used	Used for diagnostic purposes only	Used to determine eligibility for admission	
a. Admission test or standardized achievement test	☐	☐	☐	23/
b. Academic record	☐	☐	☐	24/
c. Special student aptitudes, skills, or talents	☐	☐	☐	25/
d. Personal interview	☐	☐	☐	26/
e. Recommendations	☐	☐	☐	27/

13. How much control does this school have over the following decisions and policies? / **How important is your current level of control to the operation of the school?**

	No Control 1	2	3	Full Control 4	Not Important 1	2	3	Very Important 4	N/A	
a. Student disciplinary policies	☐	☐	☐	☐	☐	☐	☐	☐	☐	28-29/
b. Student assessment policies (except state mandated tests)	☐	☐	☐	☐	☐	☐	☐	☐	☐	30-31/
c. Staff salaries and benefits	☐	☐	☐	☐	☐	☐	☐	☐	☐	32-33/
d. Budgetary expenses other than salaries and benefits	☐	☐	☐	☐	☐	☐	☐	☐	☐	34-35/
e. Curriculum	☐	☐	☐	☐	☐	☐	☐	☐	☐	36-37/
f. Staff hiring, discipline, and dismissal	☐	☐	☐	☐	☐	☐	☐	☐	☐	38-39/

14. Around the first of October, approximately how many full time equivalent (FTE) staff worked in each of the following categories in this school?

	(Enter 0 if none) **Full-time equivalent**	
a. Teachers	☐☐☐	40-42/
b. Teacher aides or paraprofessionals	☐☐☐	43-45/
c. Special education aides	☐☐☐	46-48/
d. Total staff (including a, b, c, and other staff)	☐☐☐	49-51/

15. Are the following criteria important in considering applicants for teaching positions in <u>this school</u>?

Mark (X) one box per line

	Not Important 1	2	3	Very Important 4	
a. Full standard state credential for field to be taught	☐	☐	☐	☐	52/
b. At least emergency permit or endorsement for field to be taught	☐	☐	☐	☐	53/
c. College major in field to be taught	☐	☐	☐	☐	54/
d. Passage of a CBEST test of basic skills	☐	☐	☐	☐	55/
e. Passage of the PRAXIS or SSAT test of subject knowledge or extensive college work in the subject area to be taught	☐	☐	☐	☐	56/
f. Non-educational skills or real world experience	☐	☐	☐	☐	57/

16. For the school year 2001-2002, how many of the following were <u>newly</u> hired in <u>this school</u>?

a. Full-time teachers	☐☐☐☐	Teachers	58-61/
b. Part-time teachers	☐☐☐☐	Teachers	62-65/
c. Teacher aides or paraprofessionals	☐☐☐☐	Teachers	66-69/

17. Does <u>this school</u> have a written agreement with a teacher's union or organization for the purpose of collective bargaining or meet-and-confer decisions?

☐ Yes 70/
☐ No

18. How many contracted days does a full-time teacher work per year?

☐☐☐ Days Per Year 71-73/

19. How often do teachers voluntarily work more than the required number of hours in <u>this school</u>:

Please check one 74/

☐ Rarely or Never
☐ Sometimes
☐ Often

CARD 03 6-7/

ID 1-5/

20. Does this school currently use any pay incentives such as cash bonuses, salary increases or different steps on the salary schedule to...

	Regularly	Occasionally	Never	
a. ...reward teachers who have attained National Board for Professional Teaching Standards certification?	☐	☐	☐	8/
b. ...reward teachers from Public School Accountability Act (PSAA)?	☐	☐	☐	9/
c. ...reward excellence in teaching (excluding PSAA)?	☐	☐	☐	10/
d. ...reward completion of in-service professional development?	☐	☐	☐	11/
e. ...reward lead teachers?	☐	☐	☐	12/
f. ...recruit or retain teachers to teach in fields of shortage?	☐	☐	☐	13/

21. Approximately what percent of teachers in this school participated in each of the following types of professional development activities at least once during the past year?

	0-25%	26-50%	51-75%	76-100%	
a. Workshops or conferences	☐	☐	☐	☐	14/
b. Courses for college credit	☐	☐	☐	☐	15/
c. Teacher study groups, collaboratives, or networks	☐	☐	☐	☐	16/
d. Mentoring, shadowing, peer observation or coaching programs	☐	☐	☐	☐	17/

22. Does this school provide teachers with time for professional development during regular contract hours?

☐ Yes 18/

☐ No → **Go to Question 24**

23. Are the following used to provide teachers in this school with time for professional development during regular contract hours?

a. Substitute teachers to cover teachers' classes	☐ Yes	☐ No	19/
b. Early dismissal or late start for students	☐ Yes	☐ No	20/
c. Professional days built in during the school year	☐ Yes	☐ No	21/
d. Professional days built in before or after the school year	☐ Yes	☐ No	22/
e. Common planning time for teachers	☐ Yes	☐ No	23/
f. Reduced teacher work loads (less time in the classroom with students or less time on assigned non-instructional duties)	☐ Yes	☐ No	24/

24. Are the following means of facilitating parent participation in place at this school?
("Parents" includes parents or other family members or guardians.)

	If 'YES,' mark what proportion of parents participated:	Yes	No	Few	Less than Half	About Half	More than Half	Most	
a.	Open house or back-to-school night	☐	☐	☐	☐	☐	☐	☐	25-26/
b.	Regularly scheduled schoolwide parent-teacher conferences	☐	☐	☐	☐	☐	☐	☐	27-28/
c.	Special subject-area events (e.g. science fair, concert)	☐	☐	☐	☐	☐	☐	☐	29-30/
d.	Parent education workshops or courses	☐	☐	☐	☐	☐	☐	☐	31-32/
e.	Written contract between school and parent	☐	☐	☐	☐	☐	☐	☐	33-34/
f.	Parents as volunteers in the school	☐	☐	☐	☐	☐	☐	☐	35-36/
g.	Parents involved in instructional issues	☐	☐	☐	☐	☐	☐	☐	37-38/
h.	Parents involved in governance	☐	☐	☐	☐	☐	☐	☐	39-40/
i.	Parents involved in budget decisions	☐	☐	☐	☐	☐	☐	☐	41-42/

25. Has this school implemented the following?

a.	Block scheduling	☐ Yes	☐ No	43/
b.	Before-school or after-school enrichment programs	☐ Yes	☐ No	44/
c.	Academic intersessions or summer school activities for students needing extra assistance to meet academic expectations	☐ Yes	☐ No	45/
d.	Academic intersessions or summer school activities for students seeking academic advancement or acceleration	☐ Yes	☐ No	46/

26. Does this school have a bilingual program? 47/

☐ Yes
☐ No

For schools with 4th grade students

27. In a typical week, how many hours of instruction does the *typical fourth-grade* student receive in...

Mark (X) one box per line

	None	1-2 hours per week	3-4 hours per week	5-6 hours per week	7 or more hours per week	
a. English/language arts	☐	☐	☐	☐	☐	48/
b. Mathematics	☐	☐	☐	☐	☐	49/
c. Computer Skills	☐	☐	☐	☐	☐	50/
d. Social Studies	☐	☐	☐	☐	☐	51/
e. Sciences	☐	☐	☐	☐	☐	52/
f. Foreign Language	☐	☐	☐	☐	☐	53/
g. Fine or Performing Arts	☐	☐	☐	☐	☐	54/
h. Physical Education	☐	☐	☐	☐	☐	55/

For schools with 7th grade students

28. In a typical week, how many hours of instruction does the *typical seventh-grade* student receive in...

Mark (X) one box per line

	None	1-2 hours per week	3-4 hours per week	5-6 hours per week	7 or more hours per week	
a. English/language arts	☐	☐	☐	☐	☐	56/
b. Mathematics	☐	☐	☐	☐	☐	57/
c. Computer Skills	☐	☐	☐	☐	☐	58/
d. Social Studies	☐	☐	☐	☐	☐	59/
e. Sciences	☐	☐	☐	☐	☐	60/
f. Foreign Language	☐	☐	☐	☐	☐	61/
g. Fine or Performing Arts	☐	☐	☐	☐	☐	62/
h. Physical Education	☐	☐	☐	☐	☐	63/

CARD 04 6-7/

ID 1-5/

For schools with 12th grade students → ***(Complete questions 29 and 30)***

29. For high school graduates of the class of 2002, how many years of instruction are required in each of the following areas?

How Many Years

(For example 1 . 5 Years)

a.	English/Language Arts	☐ . ☐ Years	8-10/
b.	Mathematics	☐ . ☐ Years	11-13/
c.	Computer Science	☐ . ☐ Years	14-16/
d.	Social Sciences, Social Studies (e.g., history, geography, economics)	☐ . ☐ Years	17-19/
e.	Physical or Biological Sciences	☐ . ☐ Years	20-22/
f.	Foreign Languages	☐ . ☐ Years	23-25/
g.	Fine or Performing Arts	☐ . ☐ Years	26-28/
h.	Physical Education	☐ . ☐ Years	29-31/
i.	Other (Please Specify:________________________)	☐ . ☐ Years	32-34 35-36

For schools with 12th grade students

30. How many Advanced Placement (AP) courses does this school offer?
(Please count a course as one course if it is offered more than one time in a school year)

☐☐☐ AP courses 37-39/

31. How many computers are used for instructional purposes in this school?
(Enter 0 if none)

☐☐☐☐ Computers 40-43/

32. Are STAR (Standardized Testing and Reporting) data used for any of the following purposes in this school?

a.	To realign the curriculum	☐ Yes	☐ No	44/
b.	To assign students to supplemental instruction, practice, or tutoring	☐ Yes	☐ No	45/
c.	To determine next year's instructional focus	☐ Yes	☐ No	46/
d.	To allocate resources	☐ Yes	☐ No	47/
e.	To identify problems with teaching	☐ Yes	☐ No	48/
f.	To shape the content of professional development	☐ Yes	☐ No	49/

33. Please indicate if this school is taking each of the following actions this year:

a.	Holding staff meetings that focus on the STAR testing program	☐ Yes	☐ No	50/
b.	Developing a school plan for improving performance on the STAR tests	☐ Yes	☐ No	51/
c.	Implementing test-preparation activities for STAR	☐ Yes	☐ No	52/

34. Is this school eligible to participate and does it participate in the following state and/or federal aid programs?

Mark (X) one box per line

		Currently Receiving Funding	Application Pending	Ineligible to Apply	Eligible but Not Applying	Don't Know Whether Eligible or Not	
a.	K-3 class size reduction	☐	☐	☐	☐	☐	53/
b.	Pupil transportation	☐	☐	☐	☐	☐	54/
c.	Public Schools Accountability Act	☐	☐	☐	☐	☐	55/
d.	Special education funding	☐	☐	☐	☐	☐	56/
e.	Title 1 funding	☐	☐	☐	☐	☐	57/
f.	Staff development buyout days	☐	☐	☐	☐	☐	58/
g.	Child nutrition programs (national school lunch program, special milk program)	☐	☐	☐	☐	☐	59/
h.	Supplemental instruction program	☐	☐	☐	☐	☐	60/
i.	Desegregation program	☐	☐	☐	☐	☐	61/
j.	Beginning teacher support program	☐	☐	☐	☐	☐	62/

35. For the school year 2001-02, how much private funding did this school receive?

$ ☐ , ☐☐☐ , ☐☐☐ . 00 63-69/

36. In the 2001-02 school year, how many students enrolled in this school have an Individual Education Plan (IEP) because they have disabilities or are special education students?

(Enter 0 if none)

☐☐☐ Number of IEP Students → **If 'Zero,' please skip to Question 41** 70-72/

37. How many of these students have severe disabilities (e.g., severe autism, deaf-blindness, severe development delay, severe emotional disturbance, severe hearing impairment or deafness, severe mental retardation, multiple disabilities, severe orthopedic impairment, traumatic brain injury, or severe visual impairments or blindness)?

(Enter 0 if none)

☐☐☐ Number of Students with Severe Disabilities 73-75/

CARD 05 6-7/

ID 1-5/

38. How many special education students are currently being served in each of the following instructional settings or services in this school?

a. Exclusively in general education classrooms ☐☐☐☐ 8-11

b. Exclusively in separate classrooms (i.e., in self-contained special classrooms or departmentalized special education classes) ☐☐☐☐ 12-15/

c. Part of the time in general education classrooms and part of the time in separate classrooms (i.e., pull-out programs) ☐☐☐☐ 16-19/

39. Approximately what percentage of this school's special education students are included in statewide assessment (SAT 9)?

☐☐☐ % 20-22/

Percentage

40. Approximately what percentage of the cost of educating special education students are covered by the funding this school receives for special education students?

☐☐☐ % 23-25/

Percentage

41. Does this school have a program that supports gifted and talented students?

☐ Yes 26/

☐ No → **Go to question 43**

42. How does this school identify its gifted and talented population?

☐ STAR 9 (Standardized Tests) 27/

☐ Individually Administered IQ Tests 28/

☐ Group Administered IQ Tests 29/

☐ RAVEN Matrices 30/

☐ Other 31/

(Please Specify: ______________________________) 32-33/

43. How many students in this school were disciplined in the following ways this year?

a. Suspended in school	☐☐☐☐	34-37/
b. Suspended out of school	☐☐☐☐	38-41/
c. Expelled	☐☐☐☐ Students	42-45/

44. Please indicate the approximate percentage of students for whom these issues are a problem in this school.

	Percent of students	
a. Student tardiness	☐☐☐ %	46-48/
b. Student absenteeism	☐☐☐ %	49-51/
c. Students cutting class	☐☐☐ %	52-54/
d. Physical conflicts with other students	☐☐☐ %	55-57/
e. Student pregnancy	☐☐☐ %	58-60/
f. Student use of alcohol	☐☐☐ %	61-63/
g. Student drug use	☐☐☐ %	64-66/
h. Student disrespect for teachers	☐☐☐ %	67-69/
i. Students dropping out	☐☐☐ %	70-72/
j. Poor student health	☐☐☐ %	73-75/

45. Please answer the following questions:

a. How long have you been principal of this school?	☐☐ Years	76-77/
b. How many total years of school administration experience do you have?	☐☐ Years	78-79/
c. How many total years of classroom teaching experience, if any, do you have?	☐☐ Years	80-81/

CARD 06 6-7/

ID 1-5/

46. What was your most recent occupation before becoming principal of <u>this school</u>? 8/

a. ☐ Principal of another public school
b. ☐ Principal of a private school
c. ☐ Assistant Principal at <u>this school</u>
d. ☐ Assistant Principal at another public school
e. ☐ Assistant Principal at a private school
f. ☐ Other school administrative position at a public school
g. ☐ Other school administrative position at a private school
h. ☐ Teacher at <u>this school</u>
i. ☐ Teacher at another school
j. ☐ Other occupation within the field of education
k. ☐ Other occupation outside the field of education

47. What is your highest degree?

Please check one 9/

a. ☐ Less than a Bachelor's Degree
b. ☐ Bachelor's Degree
c. ☐ Master's Degree
d. ☐ Doctorate Degree

48. Do you have....

a. ...a full teaching credential? ☐ Yes ☐ No 10/
b. ...an administrative credential? ☐ Yes ☐ No 11/

49. a. Do you also teach in <u>this school</u>?

☐ Yes 12/
☐ No → **Go to Question 50** 13-14/

b. If so, for how many hours per week? ☐☐ Hours Per Week

50. Are you Male or Female? 15/

☐ Male
☐ Female

51. What is your race/ethnicity?

Mark (X) only one box

a. ☐ American Indian or Alaska Native (Aleut, Alaska Indian, Yupik, Inupiat) 16

b. ☐ Asian or Pacific Islander (Japanese, Chinese, Filipino, Korean, Asian Indian, Vietnamese, Hawaiian, Guamanian, Samoan, other Asian)

c. ☐ Black, not Hispanic

d. ☐ White, not Hispanic

e. ☐ Hispanic

52. Please specify a range of your current gross annual salary in <u>this school</u>?

Mark (X) only one box 17/

a. ☐ Less than $50,000

b. ☐ $50,001 to $65,000

c. ☐ $65,001 to $80,000

d. ☐ $80,001 to $95,000

e. ☐ $95,001 to $110,000

f. ☐ $110,001 to $125,000

g. ☐ $125,001 to $140,000

h. ☐ Over $140,000

53. How much time, on average, do you work for <u>this school</u>?

a. Hours per week during regular school year ☐☐ Hours Per Week 18-19/

b. Hours per week during summer ☐☐ Hours Per Week 20-21/

54. How many contracted days do you work per year?

☐☐☐ Days Per Year 22-24/

THANK YOU FOR COMPLETING THE SURVEY!

Please return the survey in the enclosed self-addressed, stamped envelope to:

RAND
Attn: David Coleman, SRG-1
1700 Main Street
Santa Monica, CA 90407

CHARTER SCHOOL SURVEY

1-5/

FORM: 8-10/ CH2

Completion of the questionnaire is voluntary. All responses to this survey will be strictly confidential. Individual respondents never will be identified by name or any other manner that could allow another researcher, government official, or member of the public to infer their identity.

BATCH 11-14/

If you would like to receive a $50 honorarium for completing this survey, please PRINT your name, school name, school mailing address, and chartering authority in the space below. Remove this tear-off sheet from the survey and place it in the "confidential" envelope and enclose it in the LARGE RAND business reply envelope with your completed survey. No postage is needed.

PLEASE PRINT:

Today's Date: ______________________

Name ____

School ____

School Address: ____________________________________

City ________________ State ______ Zip code ______________

Chartering Authority __________________________________

THANK YOU FOR PARTICIPATING!
WE WILL MAIL YOU A CHECK FOR $50 AS SOON AS WE RECEIVE THIS FORM.

RAND, 1700 Main Street, Santa Monica, CA 90407

BEFORE STARTING THE SURVEY, PLEASE COMPLETE THE FOLLOWING QUESTIONS:

A. Is this school a public charter school?

☐ Yes, Continue... 15/
☐ No → If 'NO,' please **STOP** the survey and return it to RAND in the envelope provided.

B. Has your charter been revoked or withdrawn, or have you suspended operation?

☐ Yes → If 'YES,' please **STOP** the survey and return it to RAND in the envelope provided.
☐ No, Continue... 16/

C. What is the state's chartering number for this school?

☐☐☐ 17-19/

D. How many instructional sites are included in this charter number?

a. School sites ☐☐☐ 20-22/

b. Instructional sites in private homes ☐☐☐ 23-25/

c. Other types of instructional sites ☐☐☐ 26-28/

d. None (Enter 0) ☐ 29/

E. How many instructional sites are you reporting for in this survey?

a. School sites ☐☐☐ 30-32/

b. Instructional sites in private homes ☐☐☐ 33-35/

c. Other types of instructional sites ☐☐☐ 36-38/

F. How many students are enrolled in the site(s) you are reporting for in this survey?

☐☐☐☐☐ 39-43/

FOR THE REST OF THE SURVEY QUESTIONS, "this school" REFERS TO THE SITE(S) AND NUMBER OF STUDENTS YOU SPECIFIED ABOVE.

1. In this school, approximately what percentage of all students are instructed (excluding routine homework and extended student illness)**...**

a. ...exclusively or primarily at a school site? ☐☐☐ % 44-46/

b. ...more or less equally at private home(s) and at a school site? ☐☐☐ % 47-49/

c. ...exclusively or primarily at private home(s)? ☐☐☐ % 50-52/

d. Other? (Please Describe:________________________) ☐☐☐ % 53-55/

TOTAL 1 0 0 % 56-57/

2. Are you the principal/director of this school?

☐ Yes 58/
☐ No, please specify your title________________________ 59-60/

3. What grades are offered in this school? *(Check all that apply)*

☐ Prekindergarten	☐ 2nd	☐ 5th	☐ 8th	☐ 11th
☐ Kindergarten	☐ 3rd	☐ 6th	☐ 9th	☐ 12th
☐ 1st	☐ 4th	☐ 7th	☐ 10th	☐ Ungraded

CARD 02 6-7/
ID 1-5/

4. How many instructional days are offered by this school? (If you are a multi-track school, please specify the number of instructional days per track.)

☐☐☐ 8-10/
Total Instructional Days Per Year

5. For the school year 2001-02, did this school have more students apply than it could accommodate?

☐ Yes → If 'Yes,' how many students? ☐☐☐ 11/
☐ No Students 12-14/

6. During the school year 2001-02, approximately what percentage of this school's students came from the local attendance area?

☐☐☐ % 15-17/
Percentage
☐ *Don't Know* 18/

7. **a. Is this school a not-for-profit school?**

☐ Yes 19/
☐ No

b. Is this school part of an Education Management Organization (EMO)?

☐ Yes, please name the organization: ______________________ 20/
☐ No 21-22/

8. Is this school facility or parts of the facility...

a.	...leased from a commercial source?	☐ Yes	☐ No	23/
b.	...provided by a district, free or at a nominal cost?	☐ Yes	☐ No	24/
c.	...leased at, or near, market price from a district?	☐ Yes	☐ No	25/
d.	...privately rented or owned?	☐ Yes	☐ No	26/
e.	...donated by sponsors other than a district?	☐ Yes	☐ No	27/
f.	...obtained through another arrangement?	☐ Yes	☐ No	28/

If "Yes," Describe______________________ 29-30/

____

9. **a. When was this school's current charter granted?**

☐☐ / ☐☐ 31-34/
Month Year

b. Who granted this charter to the school? 35/

☐ The local school district (Please specify:______________________) 36-37
☐ A school district other than the local school district 38-39/
(Please specify:______________________)
☐ County Office of Education
☐ State Board of Education

c. Was your application initially rejected by a local school district?

☐ Yes 40/
☐ No

d. Is this charter school a newly created school or was it a pre-existing public school?

☐ A newly created school (start-up school) 41/
☐ A pre-existing public school

10. When did this school start providing instruction as a public charter school? 42-45/

☐☐ / ☐☐
Month Year

11. a. Does this school seek to focus its services on a specific population of students? 46/

- ☐ Yes
- ☐ No → **If 'NO,' go to Question 12**

b. Please specify the categories of students the school focuses its services
(*Check all that apply*)

- a. ☐ Students with disabilities 47/
- b. ☐ Low-income students 48/
- c. ☐ Students of a specific racial/ethnic minority group 49/
- d. ☐ Limited English Proficient students 50/
- e. ☐ Students with academic problems 51/
- f. ☐ Students with discipline problems 52/
- g. ☐ Students with special aptitudes, skills, or talents 53/
  (Please describe________________________________) 54-55/

12. Does this school's admissions process include any of the following elements?

Mark (X) one box per line

	Not used	Used for diagnostic purposes only	Used to determine eligibility for admission	
a. Admission test or standardized achievement test	☐	☐	☐	56/
b. Academic record	☐	☐	☐	57/
c. Special student aptitudes, skills, or talents	☐	☐	☐	58/
d. Personal interview	☐	☐	☐	59/
e. Recommendations	☐	☐	☐	60/

13. How much control does this school have over the following decisions and policies? / **How important is your current level of control to the operation of the school?**

	No Control 1	2	3	Full Control 4	Not Important 1	2	3	Very Important 4	N/A	
a. Student disciplinary policies	☐	☐	☐	☐	☐	☐	☐	☐	☐	61-62/
b. Student assessment policies (except state mandated tests)	☐	☐	☐	☐	☐	☐	☐	☐	☐	63-64/
c. Staff salaries and benefits	☐	☐	☐	☐	☐	☐	☐	☐	☐	65-66/
d. Budgetary expenses other than salaries and benefits	☐	☐	☐	☐	☐	☐	☐	☐	☐	67-68/
e. Curriculum	☐	☐	☐	☐	☐	☐	☐	☐	☐	69-70/
f. Staff hiring, discipline, and dismissal	☐	☐	☐	☐	☐	☐	☐	☐	☐	71-72/

14. Does this school have a Memorandum of Understanding with a chartering authority?

☐ Yes 73/
☐ No

15. Around the first of October, approximately how many full-time equivalent (FTE) staff worked in each of the following categories in this school?

	(Enter 0 if none) Full-time equivalent	
a. Teachers	☐☐☐	74-76
b. Teacher aides or paraprofessionals	☐☐☐	77-79/
c. Special education aides	☐☐☐	80-82/
d. Total staff (including a, b, c, and other staff)	☐☐☐	83-85/

16. Who employs the teachers at this school?
Please check one

☐ District 86/
☐ Educational Management Organization
☐ School
☐ Other (Please Specify: ______________________________) 87-88/

CARD 03 6-7/

ID 1-5/

17. Are the following criteria important in considering applicants for teaching positions in <u>this school</u>?

Mark (X) one box per line

	1 Not Important	2	3	4 Very Important	
a. Full standard state credential for field to be taught	☐	☐	☐	☐	8/
b. At least emergency permit or endorsement for field to be taught	☐	☐	☐	☐	9/
c. College major in field to be taught	☐	☐	☐	☐	10/
d. Passage of a CBEST test of basic skills	☐	☐	☐	☐	11/
e. Passage of the PRAXIS or SSAT test of subject knowledge or extensive college work in the subject area to be taught	☐	☐	☐	☐	12/
f. Non-educational skills or real world experience	☐	☐	☐	☐	13/

18. For the school year 2001-02, how many of the following were <u>newly</u> hired in <u>this school</u>?

a. Full-time teachers ☐☐☐☐ Teachers 14-17/

b. Part-time teachers ☐☐☐☐ Teachers 18-21/

c. Teacher aides or paraprofessionals ☐☐☐☐ Teachers 22-25/

19. Does <u>this school</u> have a written agreement with a teacher's union or organization for the purpose of collective bargaining or meet-and-confer decisions?

☐ Yes 26/

☐ No

20. How many contracted days does a full-time teacher work per year?

☐☐☐ Days Per Year 27-29/

21. How often do teachers voluntarily work more than the required number of hours in <u>this school</u>:

Please check one

☐ Rarely or Never

☐ Sometimes 30/

☐ Often

22. Is there a salary schedule (i.e., a fixed salary based on years of experience and education) for teachers at <u>this school</u>?

☐ Yes 31/
☐ No

23. Does <u>this school</u> currently use any pay incentives such as cash bonuses, salary increases or different steps on the salary schedule to...

	Regularly	Occasionally	Never	
a. ...reward teachers who have attained National Board for Professional Teaching Standards certification?	☐	☐	☐	32/
b. ...reward teachers from Public School Accountability Act (PSAA)?	☐	☐	☐	33/
c. ...reward excellence in teaching (excluding PSAA)?	☐	☐	☐	34/
d. ...reward completion of in-service professional development?	☐	☐	☐	35/
e. ...reward lead teachers?	☐	☐	☐	36/
f. ...recruit or retain teachers to teach in fields of shortage?	☐	☐	☐	37/

24. Approximately what percent of teachers in <u>this school</u> participated in each of the following types of professional development activities at least once during the past year?

	0-25%	26-50%	51-75%	76-100%	
a. Workshops or conferences	☐	☐	☐	☐	38/
b. Courses for college credit	☐	☐	☐	☐	39/
c. Teacher study groups, collaboratives, or networks	☐	☐	☐	☐	40/
d. Mentoring, shadowing, peer observation or coaching programs	☐	☐	☐	☐	41/

25. Does <u>this school</u> provide teachers with time for professional development during regular contract hours?

☐ Yes 42/
☐ No → **Go to Question 27**

26. Are the following used to provide teachers in <u>this school</u> with time for professional development during regular contract hours?

a. Substitute teachers to cover teachers' classes	☐ Yes	☐ No	43/
b. Early dismissal or late start for students	☐ Yes	☐ No	44/
c. Professional days built in during the school year	☐ Yes	☐ No	45/
d. Professional days built in before or after the school year	☐ Yes	☐ No	46/
e. Common planning time for teachers	☐ Yes	☐ No	47/
f. Reduced teacher work loads (less time in the classroom with students or less time on assigned non-instructional duties)	☐ Yes	☐ No	48/

27. Are the following means of facilitating parent participation in place at this school?
("Parents" includes parents or other family members and guardians.)

If 'YES,' mark what proportion of parents participated:	Yes	No	Few	Less than Half	About Half	More than Half	Most	
a. Open house or back-to-school night	☐	☐	☐	☐	☐	☐	☐	49-50/
b. Regularly scheduled schoolwide parent-teacher conferences	☐	☐	☐	☐	☐	☐	☐	51-52/
c. Special subject-area events (e.g. science fair, concert)	☐	☐	☐	☐	☐	☐	☐	53-54/
d. Parent education workshops or courses	☐	☐	☐	☐	☐	☐	☐	55-56/
e. Written contract between school and parent	☐	☐	☐	☐	☐	☐	☐	57-58/
f. Parents as volunteers in the school	☐	☐	☐	☐	☐	☐	☐	59-60/
g. Parents involved in instructional issues	☐	☐	☐	☐	☐	☐	☐	61-62/
h. Parents involved in governance	☐	☐	☐	☐	☐	☐	☐	63-64/
i. Parents involved in budget decisions	☐	☐	☐	☐	☐	☐	☐	65-66/

28. Are parents or family members required to participate or volunteer at this school?

☐ Yes → If 'YES,' how many hours are required per year? ☐☐☐ Hours per year 67/

☐ No 68-70/

29. Does this school offer the following?

a. A curriculum that focuses on an ethno-centric or cultural theme	☐ Yes	☐ No	71/
b. A bilingual program	☐ Yes	☐ No	72/

30. Has this school implemented the following?

a. Block scheduling	☐ Yes	☐ No	73/
b. Before-school or after-school enrichment programs	☐ Yes	☐ No	74/
c. Academic intersessions or summer school activities for students needing extra assistance to meet academic expectations	☐ Yes	☐ No	75/
d. Academic intersessions or summer school activities for students seeking academic advancement or acceleration	☐ Yes	☐ No	76/

CARD 04 6-7/

ID 1-5/

For schools with 4th grade students

31. In a typical week, how many hours of instruction does the *typical fourth-grade* student receive in...

Mark (X) one box per line

	None	1-2 hours per week	3-4 hours per week	5-6 hours per week	7 or more hours per week	
a. English/language arts	☐	☐	☐	☐	☐	8/
b. Mathematics	☐	☐	☐	☐	☐	9/
c. Computer Skills	☐	☐	☐	☐	☐	10/
d. Social Studies	☐	☐	☐	☐	☐	11/
e. Sciences	☐	☐	☐	☐	☐	12/
f. Foreign Language	☐	☐	☐	☐	☐	13/
g. Fine or Performing Arts	☐	☐	☐	☐	☐	14/
h. Physical Education	☐	☐	☐	☐	☐	15/

For schools with 7th grade students

32. In a typical week, how many hours of instruction does the *typical seventh-grade* student receive in...

Mark (X) one box per line

	None	1-2 hours per week	3-4 hours per week	5-6 hours per week	7 or more hours per week	
a. English/language arts	☐	☐	☐	☐	☐	16/
b. Mathematics	☐	☐	☐	☐	☐	17/
c. Computer Skills	☐	☐	☐	☐	☐	18/
d. Social Studies	☐	☐	☐	☐	☐	19/
e. Sciences	☐	☐	☐	☐	☐	20/
f. Foreign Language	☐	☐	☐	☐	☐	21/
g. Fine or Performing Arts	☐	☐	☐	☐	☐	22/
h. Physical Education	☐	☐	☐	☐	☐	23/

For schools with 12th grade students → ***(Complete questions 33 and 34)***

33. For high school graduates of the class of 2002, how many years of instruction are required in each of the following areas?

How Many Years

(For example 1 . 5 *Years)*

a.	English/Language Arts	☐ . ☐ Years	24-26/
b.	Mathematics	☐ . ☐ Years	27-29/
c.	Computer Science	☐ . ☐ Years	30-32/
d.	Social Sciences, Social Studies (e.g., history, geography, economics)	☐ . ☐ Years	33-35/
e.	Physical or Biological Sciences	☐ . ☐ Years	36-38/
f.	Foreign Languages	☐ . ☐ Years	39-41/
g.	Fine or Performing Arts	☐ . ☐ Years	42-44/
h.	Physical Education	☐ . ☐ Years	45-47/
i.	Other (Please Specify:______________________________)	☐ . ☐ Years	48-50/ 51-52/

For schools with 12th grade students

34. How many Advanced Placement (AP) courses does this school offer?
(Please count a course as one course if it is offered more than one time in a school year)

☐☐ AP courses 53-54/

35. How many computers are used for instructional purposes in this school?
(Enter 0 if none)

☐☐☐☐ Computers 55-58/

36. Are STAR (Standardized Testing and Reporting) data used for any of the following purposes in this school?

a.	To realign the curriculum	☐ Yes	☐ No	59/
b.	To assign students to supplemental instruction, practice, or tutoring	☐ Yes	☐ No	60/
c.	To determine next year's instructional focus	☐ Yes	☐ No	61/
d.	To allocate resources	☐ Yes	☐ No	62/
e.	To identify problems with teaching	☐ Yes	☐ No	63/
f.	To shape the content of professional development	☐ Yes	☐ No	64/

37. Please indicate if <u>this school</u> is taking each of the following actions this year:

a.	Holding staff meetings that focus on the STAR testing program	☐ Yes	☐ No	65/
b.	Developing a school plan for improving performance on the STAR tests	☐ Yes	☐ No	66/
c.	Implementing test-preparation activities for STAR	☐ Yes	☐ No	67/

38. What type of funding does this charter school receive?
Please check one

☐ Block grant, locally funded 68/

☐ Block grant, direct-funded

☐ Not in the Block Grant, funded through the district revenue limit

39. For the school year 2001-02, is <u>this school</u> eligible to participate and does it participate in the following state and/or federal aid programs?

Mark (X) one box per line

		Currently Receiving Funding	Application Pending	Ineligible to Apply	Eligible but Not Applying	Don't Know Whether Eligible or Not	
a.	K-3 class size reduction	☐	☐	☐	☐	☐	69/
b.	Pupil transportation	☐	☐	☐	☐	☐	70/
c.	Public Schools Accountability Act	☐	☐	☐	☐	☐	71/
d.	Special education funding	☐	☐	☐	☐	☐	72/
e.	Title 1 funding	☐	☐	☐	☐	☐	73/
f.	Staff development buyout days	☐	☐	☐	☐	☐	74/
g.	Child nutrition programs (national school lunch program, special milk program)	☐	☐	☐	☐	☐	75/
h.	Supplemental instruction program	☐	☐	☐	☐	☐	76/
i.	Desegregation program	☐	☐	☐	☐	☐	77/
j.	Beginning teacher support program	☐	☐	☐	☐	☐	78/

CARD 05 ID 6-7/ 1-5/

40. Does the sponsoring agency provide any of the following goods and services?

a.	Payroll	☐ Yes	☐ No	8/
b.	Bookkeeping	☐ Yes	☐ No	9/
c.	Budget preparation	☐ Yes	☐ No	10/
d.	Assistance in meeting federal or state regulations	☐ Yes	☐ No	11/
e.	Administrative support to apply for and maintain categorical funding	☐ Yes	☐ No	12/

41. To what extent do you agree or disagree with the following statements regarding this charter school's finances?

Mark (X) one box per line

	Strongly Agree	Agree	Uncertain	Disagree	Strongly Disagree	
a. The charter school block grant funding model satisfies the legislative requirement to be simple.	☐	☐	☐	☐	☐	13/
b. The charter school block grant funding model provides at least as much operational funding as would be available to a similar public school serving a similar pupil population.	☐	☐	☐	☐	☐	14/
c. Our school is struggling with financing capital expenditures.	☐	☐	☐	☐	☐	15/
d. It is difficult for our school to obtain or fund liability insurance.	☐	☐	☐	☐	☐	16/
e. Our school has the expertise to handle payroll, bookkeeping and budget preparations.	☐	☐	☐	☐	☐	17/
f. Our school has given up pursuing certain categorical funds because they are too complex.	☐	☐	☐	☐	☐	18/
g. Adequate oversight is provided of the charter school funds.	☐	☐	☐	☐	☐	19/

42. For the school year 2001-02, how much private funding did this school receive?

$ ☐ , ☐☐☐ , ☐☐☐ . 00 20-26/

43. In the 2001-02 school year, how many students enrolled in this school have an Individual Education Plan (IEP) because they have disabilities or are special education students?

(Enter 0 if none)

☐☐☐ Number of IEP Students → **If 'Zero,' please skip to Question 48** 27-29/

44. How many of these students have severe disabilities (e.g., severe autism, deaf-blindness, severe development delay, severe emotional disturbance, severe hearing impairment or deafness, severe mental retardation, multiple disabilities, severe orthopedic impairment, traumatic brain injury, or severe visual impairments or blindness)?

(Enter 0 if none)

☐☐☐ Number of Students with Severe Disabilities 30-32/

45. How many special education students are currently being served in each of the following instructional settings or services in <u>this school</u>?

a. Exclusively in general education classrooms ☐☐☐☐ 33-36/

b. Exclusively in separate classrooms (i.e., in self-contained special classrooms or departmentalized special education classes) ☐☐☐☐ 37-40/

c. Part of the time in general education classrooms and part of the time in separate classrooms (i.e., pull-out programs) ☐☐☐☐ 41-44/

46. Approximately what percentage of <u>this school's</u> special education students are included in statewide assessment (SAT 9)**?**

☐☐☐ % 45-47/

Percentage

47. What percentage of the cost of educating special education students are covered by the funding <u>this school</u> receives for special education students?

☐☐☐ % 48-50/

Percentage

48. Does <u>this school</u> have a program that supports gifted and talented students?

☐ Yes 51/

☐ No → **Go to question 50**

49. How does <u>this school</u> identify its gifted and talented population?

☐ STAR 9 (Standardized Tests) 52/

☐ Individually Administered IQ Tests 53/

☐ Group Administered IQ Tests 54/

☐ RAVEN Matrices 55/

☐ Other 56/

(Please Specify: ______________________________) 57-58/

CARD 06 6-7/

ID 1-5/

50. How many students in this school were disciplined in the following ways this year?

		Students	
a.	Suspended in school	☐☐☐☐	8-11/
b.	Suspended out of school	☐☐☐☐	12-15/
c.	Expelled	☐☐☐☐	16-19/

51. Please indicate the approximate percentage of students for whom these issues are a problem in this school.

		Percent of students	
a.	Student tardiness	☐☐☐ %	20-22/
b.	Student absenteeism	☐☐☐ %	23-25/
c.	Students cutting class	☐☐☐ %	26-28/
d.	Physical conflicts with other students	☐☐☐ %	29-31/
e.	Student pregnancy	☐☐☐ %	32-34/
f.	Student use of alcohol	☐☐☐ %	35-37/
g.	Student drug use	☐☐☐ %	38-40/
h.	Student disrespect for teachers	☐☐☐ %	41-43/
i.	Students dropping out	☐☐☐ %	44-46/
j.	Poor student health	☐☐☐ %	47-49/

52. Please answer the following questions:

a.	How long have you been principal of this school?	☐☐ Years	50-51/
b.	How many total years of school administration experience do you have?	☐☐ Years	52-53/
c.	How many total years of classroom teaching experience, if any, do you have?	☐☐ Years	54-55/

53. What was your most recent occupation before becoming principal of <u>this school</u>? 56/

a. ☐ Principal/Director of another public school

b. ☐ Principal/Director of a private school

c. ☐ Assistant Principal at <u>this school</u>

d. ☐ Assistant Principal at another public school

e. ☐ Assistant Principal at a private school

f. ☐ Other school administrative position at a public school

g. ☐ Other school administrative position at a private school

h. ☐ Teacher at <u>this school</u>

i. ☐ Teacher at another school

j. ☐ Other occupation within the field of education

k. ☐ Other occupation outside the field of education

54. What is your highest degree?

Please check one 57/

a. ☐ Less than a Bachelor's Degree

b. ☐ Bachelor's Degree

c. ☐ Master's Degree

d. ☐ Doctorate Degree

55. Do you have....

a. ...a full teaching credential? ☐ Yes ☐ No 58/

b. ...an administrative credential? ☐ Yes ☐ No 59/

56. a. Do you also teach in <u>this school</u>?

☐ Yes 60/

☐ No → **Go to Question 57** 61-62/

b. If so, for how many hours per week? ☐☐ Hours Per Week

57. Are you Male or Female? 63/

☐ Male

☐ Female

58. What is your race/ethnicity?

Mark (X) only one box

a. ☐ American Indian or Alaska Native (Aleut, Alaska Indian, Yupik, Inupiat) 64/

b. ☐ Asian or Pacific Islander (Japanese, Chinese, Filipino, Korean, Asian Indian, Vietnamese, Hawaiian, Guamanian, Samoan, other Asian)

c. ☐ Black, not Hispanic

d. ☐ White, not Hispanic

e. ☐ Hispanic

59. Please specify a range of your current gross annual salary in <u>this school</u>?

Mark (X) only one box 65/

a. ☐ Less than $50,000

b. ☐ $50,001 to $65,000

c. ☐ $65,001 to $80,000

d. ☐ $80,001 to $95,000

e. ☐ $95,001 to $110,000

f. ☐ $110,001 to $125,000

g. ☐ $125,001 to $140,000

h. ☐ Over $140,000

60. How much time, on average, do you work for <u>this school</u>?

a. Hours per week during regular school year ☐☐ Hours Per Week 66-67/

b. Hours per week during summer ☐☐ Hours Per Week 68-69/

61. How many contracted days do you work per year?

☐☐☐ Days Per Year 70-72/

THANK YOU FOR COMPLETING THE SURVEY!

Please return the survey in the enclosed self-addressed, stamped envelope to:

RAND
Attn: David Coleman, SRG-1
1700 Main Street
Santa Monica, CA 90407

Charter School Supplemental Survey

Instructions: Please fill out this survey and mail it back in the enclosed business reply envelope or fax it to David Coleman at 310-260-8009.

1. What is the range and average of full-time teachers' yearly base salaries at this school?

a. Lowest/per year $ [ ][ ][ ] , [ ][ ][ ] . 0 0

b. Highest/per year $ [ ][ ][ ] , [ ][ ][ ] . 0 0

c. Average salary/per year $ [ ][ ][ ] , [ ][ ][ ] . 0 0

2. For the school year 2001-02, what was this school's...

a. Total revenues? $ [ ][ ][ ] , [ ][ ][ ] , [ ][ ][ ] . 0 0

b. Total expenditures? $ [ ][ ][ ] , [ ][ ][ ] , [ ][ ][ ] . 0 0

3. What was this school's total revenue during the 2001-02 school year, if applicable, from the following sources?

Total Revenue ($)

a. State revenue limit/charter school general purpose entitlement $ [ ][ ] , [ ][ ][ ] , [ ][ ][ ] . 0 0

b. Charter school categorical block grant $ [ ][ ] , [ ][ ][ ] , [ ][ ][ ] . 0 0

c. Special education $ [ ][ ] , [ ][ ][ ] , [ ][ ][ ] . 0 0

d. Title 1 $ [ ][ ] , [ ][ ][ ] , [ ][ ][ ] . 0 0

4. For the 2001-02 school year, what were this school's expenditures on each of the following?

a. Teacher salaries and benefits $ [ ][ ][ ] , [ ][ ][ ] , [ ][ ][ ] . 0 0

b. Other staff salaries and benefits $ [ ][ ][ ] , [ ][ ][ ] , [ ][ ][ ] . 0 0

5. What percentage, if any, of total revenues generated by this school is retained by your sponsoring agency for oversight, contracting and encroachment?

(Enter 0 if none)

a. [ ][ ][ ] . [ ] % Oversight
Percent of total revenues

b. [ ][ ][ ] . [ ] % Contracting
Percent of total revenues

c. [ ][ ][ ] . [ ] % Encroachment
Percent of total revenues

Your name:____________________ School Name:________________________

Title/position:____________________ Daytime Phone Number:__________________

THANK YOU FOR COMPLETING THE SURVEY!

RAND
1700 Main Street
Santa Monica, CA 90401

CHARTERING AUTHORITY SURVEY

BARCODE 1-5/

FORM: 8-10/ AUT

We will use the information you give us for research purposes only. We will protect the confidentiality of this information, and will not disclose your identity or information that identifies you to anyone outside of the research project, except as required by law. We will not identify you in any reports we write. We will destroy all information that identifies you at the end of the study.

BATCH ☐☐☐☐ 11-14/

RAND
1700 Main Street
Santa Monica CA 90407

We expect to release the results of RAND's study in July 2003. If you would like to receive a copy of the results of this survey, please PRINT your name and mailing address in the space below. Remove this tear-off sheet from the survey, place it in the "survey results" envelope and enclose it in the LARGE RAND business reply envelope with your completed survey. No postage is needed.

PLEASE PRINT:

Today's Date: ____________________

Name: ____

Address: ____

City: ____________________ State: __________ Zip code: __________

Chartering Authority Name: ______________________________

THANK YOU FOR PARTICIPATING!

RAND
1700 Main Street
Santa Monica CA 90407

1. What is your position at this chartering authority?

Position: ______________________________ 15-16/

2. How many petitions for charter schools have been submitted to this chartering authority since 1992? *(Please count applicants that submitted more than one petition for a particular school only once.)*

☐☐ # of petitions 17-18/

3. Of the number of petitions submitted, how many are currently:

a. Approved, operating, and still valid ☐☐ 19-20/

b. Approved, but not yet operating ☐☐ 21-22/

c. Approved, but later revoked ☐☐ 23-24/

d. Approved, but later closed ☐☐ 25-26/

e. Pending ☐☐ 27-28/

f. Denied ☐☐ 29-30/

g. Not valid because they were withdrawn prior to approval ☐☐ 31-32/

h. Other (Please specify:______________________________) ☐☐ 33-34/

35-36/

TOTAL NUMBER OF PETITIONS SUBMITTED SINCE 1992 ☐☐ 37-38/

(Should equal # of petitions in Question 2)

4. If any petitions were denied, as stated in Question 3f, how many were denied for each of the following reasons? *(Please double count if a petition was denied for more than one reason)*

Number of petitions denied

a. Unsound educational programs ☐☐ 39-40/

b. Demonstrably unlikely to succeed ☐☐ 41-42/

c. Inadequate number of required signatures ☐☐ 43-44/

d. Did not contain reasonably comprehensive descriptions of the required 15 elements (A-O elements) ☐☐ 45-46/

e. Did not contain an affirmation of each of the four conditions described in Educational Code 47605(d) ☐☐ 47-48/

f. Other (Please specify:______________________________) ☐☐ 49-50/

51-52/

5. Does this chartering authority have a set of written guidelines or a scoring rubric for use in determining whether to approve charter petitions?

☐ Yes 53/

☐ No

6. Does this chartering authority provide its charter schools with any of the following goods and services?

	Yes	No	If "Yes," how many charter schools?	
a. Payroll	☐	☐	☐☐	54-56/
b. Bookkeeping	☐	☐	☐☐	57-59/
c. Budget preparation	☐	☐	☐☐	60-62/
d. Assistance in meeting federal or state regulations	☐	☐	☐☐	63-65/
e. Administrative support to apply for and maintain categorical funding	☐	☐	☐☐	66-68/

7. a. Does this chartering authority currently pay for any charter school facility costs?

☐ Yes 69/

☐ No → **If "No," go to Question 8**

b. How does this chartering authority pay for charter school facility costs?

Check all that apply

1.	General fund revenues	☐	70/
2.	School bonds	☐	71/
3.	Grant applications	☐	72/
4.	Parcel tax	☐	73/
5.	Other (Please describe:____________) 75-76/	☐	74/

8. Does this chartering authority currently provide space within existing non-charter school facilities for instructional use by charter schools?

☐ Yes 77/

☐ No

9. To what extent do you agree or disagree with the following statements regarding charter school finances?

Mark (X) one box per line

	Strongly Agree	Agree	Uncertain	Disagree	Strongly Disagree	
a. The charter school block-grant-funding model satisfies the legislative requirement to be simple.	☐	☐	☐	☐	☐	78/
b. The charter school block-grant-funding model provides at least as much operational funding as would be available to a similar school district serving a similar pupil population.	☐	☐	☐	☐	☐	79/
c. This chartering authority is struggling with financing charter school capital expenditures.	☐	☐	☐	☐	☐	80/
d. Our charter schools place a financial burden on this chartering authority.	☐	☐	☐	☐	☐	81/
e. Most of our charter schools have the expertise to handle payroll, bookkeeping, and budget preparations.	☐	☐	☐	☐	☐	82/
f. Most of our charter schools have given up pursuing certain categorical funds because they are too complex.	☐	☐	☐	☐	☐	83/
g. We are able to provide adequate oversight for our charter schools' funds.	☐	☐	☐	☐	☐	84/

10. a. How many charter schools under this chartering authority are included in this chartering authority's responsibility as an LEA for special education (i.e., how many are legal arms of the chartering authority for special education purposes)?

☐☐ *Number of charter schools* 8-9/

(If none, go to Question 11)

b. For how many of these do you directly provide the majority of their special education services?

☐☐ *Number of charter schools* 10-11/

c. How many of these provide the majority of their own special education services through school and contracted personnel? Please list the names of these charter schools.

☐☐ *Number of charter schools* 12-13/

School Name:

School 1:____________________ 14-16/

School 2:____________________ 17-19/

School 3:____________________ 20-22/

11. a. Does this chartering authority charge any of the schools under its authority (charter or non-charter) on a per ADA basis for the excess costs of special education?

☐ Yes 23/

☐ No → **If "No," go to question 11c.**

b. If so, what is the current charge per ADA?

$ ☐ , ☐☐☐ Charge per ADA 24-27/

c. If not, do you use some other method for distributing costs among the schools? Please explain:

____________________ 28-29/

____

____

12. If any of the charter schools under this chartering authority are independent LEAs or SELPAs for special education purposes, please list their names.

If none, check this box ☐ and go to Question 13 30/

School Name:

School 1:____________________ 31-33/

School 2:____________________ 34-36/

School 3:____________________ 37-39/

13. Which of the following statements characterize the professional development offered to teachers by this chartering authority?

Check all that apply

a.	Some professional development programs are offered ONLY to non-charter school teachers. Charter school teachers are NOT PERMITTED to participate.	☐	*40/*
b.	Some professional development programs are offered ONLY to charter school teachers. Non-charter school teachers are NOT PERMITTED to participate.	☐	*41/*
c.	Some professional development programs are mandatory for both non-charter and charter school teachers.	☐	*42/*
d.	Some professional development programs are mandatory for non-charter school teachers but optional for charter school teachers.	☐	*43/*
e.	Some professional development programs are mandatory for charter school teachers but optional for non-charter school teachers.	☐	*44/*

14. Who pays for charter school teachers' participation in professional development?

Check all that apply

a. ☐ Charter School *45/*

b. ☐ Chartering Authority *46/*

c. ☐ Teacher *47/*

d. ☐ Other (Please specify:______________________________) *48/*

49-50/

15. a. In total, how many staff members do you have assigned to charter school oversight, including coordination and assistance?

1. Full-time staff assigned full time to charter school oversight ☐☐ *51-52/*
2. Full-time staff assigned part time to charter school oversight ☐☐ *53-54/*
3. Part-time staff assigned to charter school oversight ☐☐ *55-56/*

b. Do any of the staff members responsible for oversight...

1. ...also teach at one or more of your charter schools?	☐ Yes	☐ No	*57/*
2. ...also serve as principal or administrator of one or more of your charter schools?	☐ Yes	☐ No	*58/*
3. ...have expertise in special education?	☐ Yes	☐ No	*59/*

16. What situations have prompted this chartering authority to take the following types of actions toward charter schools?

SITUATIONS	Increased support or resources	Increased supervision of school	Investigation of school	Revocation of charter	Other disciplinary action	
	ACTIONS TAKEN FOR EACH SITUATION *Check all that apply on each line*					
a. Complaints received from parents	☐	☐	☐	☐	☐	*60-64/*
b. Declining enrollment	☐	☐	☐	☐	☐	*65-69/*
c. Financial irregularities	☐	☐	☐	☐	☐	*70-74/*
d. Credit or unit irregularities	☐	☐	☐	☐	☐	*75-79/*
e. Low test scores	☐	☐	☐	☐	☐	*80-84/*
f. Student disciplinary incidents	☐	☐	☐	☐	☐	*85-89/*
g. High dropout rates	☐	☐	☐	☐	☐	*90-94/*
h. Complaints from teachers	☐	☐	☐	☐	☐	*95-99/*
i. Complaints from teacher unions	☐	☐	☐	☐	☐	*100-104/*
j. Failure to comply with terms of the charter	☐	☐	☐	☐	☐	*105-109/*
k. Failure to comply with state or federal laws	☐	☐	☐	☐	☐	*110-114/*

17. a. Are you a County or State Office of Education?

☐ Yes 8/

☐ No → **If "No," go to Question 18**

b. Is the district or districts where your charter schools are located providing:

...facilities for the school(s)? ☐ Yes ☐ No 9/

...other resources for the school(s)? ☐ Yes ☐ No 10/

Please skip questions 18 and 19 if you are a County or State Office of Education.

18. a. Have you authorized any charter schools that do not operate within your local attendance boundaries?

☐ Yes (Please answer "yes" if you have chartered a charter school that has at least one site outside your local attendance boundaries.) 11/

☐ No → **If "No," go to Question 19**

b. If so, how many charter schools?

☐☐ *Number of charter schools* 12-13/

c. Of these charter schools, is the district where your charter schools are located providing:

...facilities for the school(s)? ☐ Yes ☐ No 14/

...other resources for the school(s)? ☐ Yes ☐ No 15/

Please skip question 19 if you are a County or State Office of Education.

19. a. Are there any charter schools within your local attendance boundaries that were authorized by an outside chartering authority?

☐ Yes (Please answer "yes" if a multi-site charter school has at least one site within your district and is not authorized by this chartering authority.) 16/

☐ No → **If "No," go to Question 20**

b. How many charter schools?

☐☐ *Number of charter schools* 17-18/

c. Of these charter schools, are you providing:

...facilities for the school(s)? ☐ Yes ☐ No 19/

...other resources for the school(s)? ☐ Yes ☐ No 20/

20. a. Does this chartering authority have a definition of independent and dependent charter schools?

☐ Yes 21/

☐ No → **If "No," go to Question 21**

b. Please provide your definitions of independent and dependent charter schools below:

Dependent Charter School: ______________________________ 22-23/

____

____

Independent Charter School: ______________________________ 24-25/

____

____

21. Please list the schools that are currently chartered by this chartering authority:

Check all that apply

School Name	Charter School Number	Independent	Dependent (Please leave blank if you do not define charter schools as independent and dependent)	Multi-site	Run by an EMO	Exclusively Site-based	Exclusively Homebased/ Independent Study	Combination Site-based and Home-based/ Independent Study
1. ______	☐☐☐	☐	☐	☐	☐	☐	☐	☐
2. ______	☐☐☐	☐	☐	☐	☐	☐	☐	☐
3. ______	☐☐☐	☐	☐	☐	☐	☐	☐	☐
4. ______	☐☐☐	☐	☐	☐	☐	☐	☐	☐
5. ______	☐☐☐	☐	☐	☐	☐	☐	☐	☐
6. ______	☐☐☐	☐	☐	☐	☐	☐	☐	☐
7. ______	☐☐☐	☐	☐	☐	☐	☐	☐	☐
8. ______	☐☐☐	☐	☐	☐	☐	☐	☐	☐

For Questions 22 through 28, answers may differ depending on whether charter schools are considered "dependent" or "independent." Therefore, please answer the questions in the left-hand response columns for your "independent" charter schools and in the right-hand response columns for your "dependent" charter schools. If you do not define charters as independent or dependent, place your answers in the left-hand response columns. If you have both types of charters under your authority, please answer both sets of response columns.

For example: If you are answering the following question for schools that are not defined as either independent or dependent, you will fill your answers on the left hand column for questions, as shown in sample below.

Which of the following types of information does this chartering authority require of charter schools?

	Independent or Undefined Charter Schools					Dependent Charter Schools				
	Require charter schools to submit?	How important is each of the following in enabling you to oversee your charter schools? Not Important 1	2	3	Very Important 4	Require charter Schools to submit?	How important is each of the following in enabling you to oversee your charter schools? Not Important 1	2	3	Very Important 4
a. School calendar and schedule ...	☒ →	☐	☐	☒	☐	☐ →	☐	☐	☐	☐
b. Curriculum information	☐ →	☐	☐	☐	☐	☐ →	☐	☐	☐	☐
c. Parent satisfaction survey	☐ →	☐	☐	☐	☐	☐ →	☐	☐	☐	☐
d. Portfolios of student work	☒ →	☐	☐	☐	☒	☐ →	☐	☐	☐	☐
e. School attendance data	☒ →	☐	☐	☐	☒	☐ →	☐	☐	☐	☐

Please continue on next page →

22. Which of the following types of information does this chartering authority require of each type of charter school?

	Independent or Undefined Charter Schools					Dependent Charter Schools				
	Require charter schools to submit?	If required, how important is this information in enabling you to oversee your charter schools? Not Important 1	2	3	Very Important 4	Require charter schools to submit?	If required, how important is this information in enabling you to oversee your charter schools? Not Important 1	2	3	Very Important 4
a. School calendar and schedule...	☐→	☐	☐	☐	☐	☐→	☐	☐	☐	☐
b. Curriculum information	☐→	☐	☐	☐	☐	☐→	☐	☐	☐	☐
c. Parent satisfaction survey.........	☐→	☐	☐	☐	☐	☐→	☐	☐	☐	☐
d. Graduation / promotion rates ...	☐→	☐	☐	☐	☐	☐→	☐	☐	☐	☐
e. Student attendance data..........	☐→	☐	☐	☐	☐	☐→	☐	☐	☐	☐
f. Student admission data	☐→	☐	☐	☐	☐	☐→	☐	☐	☐	☐
g. Standardized achievement test data	☐→	☐	☐	☐	☐	☐→	☐	☐	☐	☐
h. Student demographic information	☐→	☐	☐	☐	☐	☐→	☐	☐	☐	☐
i. Student grades........................	☐→	☐	☐	☐	☐	☐→	☐	☐	☐	☐
j. Portfolios of student work	☐→	☐	☐	☐	☐	☐→	☐	☐	☐	☐
k. Number of dropouts.................	☐→	☐	☐	☐	☐	☐→	☐	☐	☐	☐
l. Student discipline information...	☐→	☐	☐	☐	☐	☐→	☐	☐	☐	☐
m. Number of transfers	☐→	☐	☐	☐	☐	☐→	☐	☐	☐	☐
n. Financial reports or budgets	☐→	☐	☐	☐	☐	☐→	☐	☐	☐	☐
o. Evidence of liability insurance...	☐→	☐	☐	☐	☐	☐→	☐	☐	☐	☐
p. Evidence of adequacy/safety of facilities.................................	☐→	☐	☐	☐	☐	☐→	☐	☐	☐	☐
q. Evidence of teacher credentialing..........................	☐→	☐	☐	☐	☐	☐→	☐	☐	☐	☐

23. How many times per year, if any, does this chartering authority use the following methods to monitor each type of charter school?

	Independent or Undefined Charter Schools			Dependent Charter Schools			
	Converted charter schools	Site-based start-up charter schools	Homebased or Independent Study charter schools	Converted charter schools	Site-based start-up charter schools	Homebased or Independent Study charter schools	
	How many times per year? (enter "0" if none)	How many times per year? (enter "0" if none)	How many times per year? (enter "0" if none)	How many times per year? (enter "0" if none)	How many times per year? (enter "0" if none)	How many times per year? (enter "0" if none)	
a. Scheduled visits to school?	☐☐	☐☐	☐☐	☐☐	☐☐	☐☐	*8-19/*
b. Unscheduled visits to school?	☐☐	☐☐	☐☐	☐☐	☐☐	☐☐	*20-31/*
c. Financial audit?	☐☐	☐☐	☐☐	☐☐	☐☐	☐☐	*32-43/*

24. What is the typical schedule for evaluating each type of charter school that operates under this chartering authority to see if it is meeting the educational goals set forth in its charter?

	Independent or Undefined Charter Schools					Dependent Charter Schools					
	NA	More than once a year	Once a year	Less than once a year	Never	NA	More than once a year	Once a year	Less than once a year	Never	
	Mark (X) one box per line					*Mark (X) one box per line*					
a. Converted charter schools	☐	☐	☐	☐	☐	☐	☐	☐	☐	☐	*44-45/*
b. Start-up charter schools (excluding Homebased or Independent Study charter schools)	☐	☐	☐	☐	☐	☐	☐	☐	☐	☐	*46-47/*
c. Homebased or Independent Study charter schools	☐	☐	☐	☐	☐	☐	☐	☐	☐	☐	*48-49/*

25. Does this chartering authority exercise a different degree of control (i.e., decision-making authority) over the following types of ongoing operations in its charter schools than in its non-charter schools?

	Independent or Undefined Charter Schools				Dependent Charter Schools				
	No control	Less control	Same level of control	More control	No control	Less control	Same level of control	More control	
	Mark (X) one box per line				*Mark (X) one box per line*				
a. Student disciplinary policies	☐	☐	☐	☐	☐	☐	☐	☐	*50-51/*
b. Student assessment policies except state-mandated tests	☐	☐	☐	☐	☐	☐	☐	☐	*52-53/*
c. Staff salaries and benefits	☐	☐	☐	☐	☐	☐	☐	☐	*54-55/*
d. Budgetary expenses, other than salaries and benefits	☐	☐	☐	☐	☐	☐	☐	☐	*56-57/*
e. Curriculum	☐	☐	☐	☐	☐	☐	☐	☐	*58-59/*
f. Staff hiring, discipline, and dismissal	☐	☐	☐	☐	☐	☐	☐	☐	*60-61/*
g. Special education	☐	☐	☐	☐	☐	☐	☐	☐	*62-63/*
h. Professional development	☐	☐	☐	☐	☐	☐	☐	☐	*64-65/*

26. According to the charter, memorandum of understanding, or other written policies, who is generally legally liable in each of the following areas?

	Independent or Undefined Charter Schools					Dependent Charter Schools					
	Charter school	Chartering authority	Both	Not specified in writing	Don't know	Charter school	Chartering authority	Both	Not specified in writing	Don't know	
	Mark (X) one box per line					*Mark (X) one box per line*					
a. Financial obligations	☐	☐	☐	☐	☐	☐	☐	☐	☐	☐	*66-67/*
b. Health and safety issues	☐	☐	☐	☐	☐	☐	☐	☐	☐	☐	*68-69/*
c. Special education and disability-related claims	☐	☐	☐	☐	☐	☐	☐	☐	☐	☐	*70-71/*
d. Harassment claims	☐	☐	☐	☐	☐	☐	☐	☐	☐	☐	*72-73/*
e. Civil rights issues	☐	☐	☐	☐	☐	☐	☐	☐	☐	☐	*74-75/*
f. Other education-related claims	☐	☐	☐	☐	☐	☐	☐	☐	☐	☐	*76-77/*
g. Other employment-related claims	☐	☐	☐	☐	☐	☐	☐	☐	☐	☐	*78-79/*

27. Are any charters school teachers under this chartering authority subject to collective bargaining contracts?

Independent or Undefined Charter Schools	Dependent Charter Schools	
☐ Yes ☐ No	☐ Yes ☐ No	*80-81/*

28. Does this chartering authority...

Independent or Undefined Charter Schools *check all that apply*		Dependent Charter Schools *check all that apply*		
a. ...require charter schools to follow a district's hiring policies regarding qualifications for teachers?	☐	a. ...require charter schools to follow a district's hiring policies regarding qualifications for teachers?	☐	*82-83/*
b. ...require charter schools to follow a district's procedures for firing teachers?	☐	b. ...require charter schools to follow a district's procedures for firing teachers?	☐	*84-85/*
c. ...interview teachers who apply to work in charter schools?	☐	c. ...interview teachers who apply to work in charter schools?	☐	*86-87/*
d. ...help place teachers in charter schools?	☐	d. ...help place teachers in charter schools?	☐	*88-89/*
e. ...review and approve the hiring of each charter school teacher?	☐	e. ...review and approve the hiring of each charter school teacher?	☐	*90-91/*
f. ...retain the right to dismiss teachers in charter schools?	☐	f. ...retain the right to dismiss teachers in charter schools?	☐	*92-93/*
g. ...permit teachers to transfer between charter and non-charter schools?	☐	g. ...permit teachers to transfer between charter and non-charter schools?	☐	*94-95/*

29. Please add any additional comments regarding your experience as a chartering authority:

____ 96-97/

____

____

____

____

____

____

98/

THANK YOU FOR COMPLETING THE SURVEY!

Please place your completed survey in the RAND postage-paid envelope and send to:

RAND
Attn: David Coleman, Mail Stop – SRG-1
1700 Main Street
Santa Monica CA 90407

BIBLIOGRAPHY

Ahearn, E. M., C. M. Lange, L. M. Rhim, and M. J. McLaughlin, *Project Search: Special Education as Requirement in Charter Schools* (final report of a research study: Cross-state analysis of findings and summaries of state case studies), Alexandria, VA: National Association of State Directors of Special Education, 2001.

Anderson, L., N. Adelman, K. Finnigan, L. Cotton, M. B. Donnelly, and T. Price, *A Decade of Public Charter Schools: Evaluation of the Public Charter Schools Program: 2000–2001 Evaluation Report*, Washington, D.C.: U.S. Department of Education, 2002.

Ascher, C., R. Jacobowitz, and Y. McBride, *Standards-Based Reform and the Charter School Movement in 1998–99: An Analysis of Four States* (final report to the Edna McConnell Clark Foundation), New York: Institute for Education and Social Policy, 1999.

Becker, H. J., K. Nakagawa, and R. G. Corwin, "Parent Involvement Contracts in California's Charter Schools: Strategy for Educational Improvement or Method of Exclusion?" *Teachers College Record*, Vol. 98, 1997, pp. 511–536.

Bettinger, E. P, "The Effect of Charter Schools on Charter Students and Public Schools," unpublished paper, Cleveland, OH: Case Western Reserve University, November 2002.

Bierlein, L. A., "The Charter School Movement," in D. Ravitch and J.P. Viteritti, eds., *New York Schools for a New Century*, New Haven, CT: Yale University Press, 1997, pp. 37–60.

Brunner, E., and J. Sonstelie, "Coping with Serrano: Voluntary Contributions to California's Local Public Schools," paper presented at the 89th Annual Conference on Taxation, National Tax Association, October 1997.

Bryk, A. S., V. E. Lee, and J. B. Smith, "High School Organization and Its Effects on Teachers and Students," in W. H. Clune and J. F. Witte, eds., *Choice and Control in American Education,* Vol. 1, London: Falmer Press, 1990, pp. 135–226.

California Department of Education, "Charter School Funding Model Pursuant to Chapter 78, Statutes of 1999," 1999, available at www.cde.ca.gov/charter/funding/csfundmodel.html.

California Department of Education, "Update of Charter School Law and Funding Model," February 11, 2000, available at www.cde.ca.gov/charter/funding/advfmltr_2-00.html.

California Department of Education, "Charter School Block Grant Estimated Funding Rates," August 2001, available at www.cde.ca.gov/charter/funding/0102csestfundrates.html.

California Department of Education, "Charter School Description of Programs," January 12, 2002, available at www.cde.ca.gov/charter/funding/descrip_list.html.

California State Auditor, *California's Charter Schools: Oversight at All Levels Could Be Stronger to Ensure Charter Schools' Accountability* 2002-104, Sacramento, CA: Bureau of State Audits, 2002.

Center for Applied Research and Educational Improvement, *Minnesota Charter Schools Evaluation: Final Report,* Minneapolis, MN: University of Minnesota, 1998.

Center for Education Reform, "Charter School Highlights and Statistics," 2003, available at http://www.edreform.com.

Charter School Development Center, "New Legislative Restrictions and Opportunities," *Charter School Currents,* Sacramento, CA: CSU Institute for Education Reform, California State University, Fall 2001.

Charter School Development Center, "State Budget: Mixed Results for Charter Schools as Governor Davis Vetoes Charter Block Grant Funds," *Charter School Currents*, Sacramento, CA: CSU Institute for Education Reform, California State University, Fall 2002.

Connors, A. F., T. Speroff, N. V. Dawson, C. Thomas, F. E. Harrell, D. Wagner, N. Desbiens, L. Goldman, A. W. Wu, R. M. Califf, W. J. Fulkerson, H. Vidaillet, S. Broste, P. Bellamy, J. Lynn, and W. Knaus, "The Effectiveness of Right Heart Catheterization in the Initial Care of Critically Ill Patients," *The Journal of the American Medical Association*, Vol. 276, No. 11, 1996, pp. 889–897.

Corwin, R. G., and J. Flaherty, *Freedom and Innovation in California's Charter Schools,* Los Alamitos, CA: Southwest Regional Laboratory, 1995.

Cullen, J. B., B. A. Jacob, and S. D. Levitt, "The Impact of School Choice on Student Outcomes: An Analysis of the Chicago Public Schools," Cambridge, MA: National Bureau of Economic Research Working Paper No. 7888, 2000.

Danner, J., and J. C. Bowman, *The Promise and Perils of Charter School Reform,* Nashville, TN: Tennessee Institute for Public Policy, 2002.

Darling-Hammond, L., B. Berry, and A. Thoreson, "Does Teacher Certification Matter? Evaluating the Evidence," *Educational Evaluation and Policy Analysis,* Vol. 23, No. 1, 2001, pp. 57–77.

Dehejia, J. H., and S. Wahba, "Causal Effects in Nonexperimental Studies: Reevaluating the Evaluation of Training Programs," *Journal of the American Statistical Association*, Vol. 98, No. 448, 1999, pp. 1053–1062.

Dianda, M. R., and R. G. Corwin, "Vision and Reality: A First-Year Look at California's Charter Schools," Los Alamitos, CA: Southwest Regional Laboratory, 1994.

Fiebach, N. H., E. F. Cook, T. H. Lee, D. A. Brand, G. W. Rouan, M. Weisberg, and L. Goldman, "Outcomes in Patients with Myocardial Infarction Who Are Initially Admitted to Stepdown Units: Data from the Multicenter Chest Pain Study," *American Journal of Medicine,* Vol. 89, 1990, pp. 15–20.

Figlio, D. N., and L. S. Getzler, "Accountability, Ability and Disability: Gaming the System," Cambridge, MA: National Bureau of Economic Research Working Paper 9307, 2002.

Finn, C. E., B. V. Manno, and G. Vanourek, *Charter Schools in Action.* Princeton, NJ: Princeton University Press, 2000.

Fisk, E., and H. Ladd, *When Schools Compete: A Cautionary Tale,* Washington, D.C.: Brookings Institution, 2000.

Garet, M. S., A. C. Porter, L. Desimone, B. F. Birman, and K. S. Yoon, "What Makes Professional Development Effective? Results from a National Sample of Teachers," *American Educational Research Journal,* Vol. 38, 2001, pp. 915–946.

Gates, S. M., J. S. Ringel, L. Santibañez, K. E. Ross, and C. H. Chung, *Who Is Leading Our Schools? An Overview of School Administrators and Their Careers,* Santa Monica, CA: RAND, MR-1679-EDU, 2003.

Gill, B. P., M. P. Timpane, K. E. Ross, and D. J. Brewer, *Rhetoric Versus Reality: What We Know and What We Need to Know About Vouchers and Charter Schools,* Santa Monica, CA: RAND, 2001.

Goldhaber, D., and D. Brewer, "Does Teacher Certification Matter? High School Teacher Certification Status and Student Achievement," *Educational Evaluation and Policy Analysis,* Vol. 22, No. 2, 2000, pp. 129–145.

Goldhaber, D., and D. Brewer, "Evaluating the Evidence on Teacher Certification: A Rejoinder," *Educational Evaluation and Policy Analysis,* Vol. 23, No. 1, 2001, pp. 79–86.

Gronberg, T. J., and D. W. Jansen, "Navigating Newly Chartered Waters: An Analysis of Texas Charter School Performance," San Antonio and Austin, TX: Texas Public Policy Foundation, 2001, available at http://www.tppf.org.

Hanusheck, E. A., J. F. Kain, and S. G. Revkin, "The Impact of Charter Schools on Academic Achievement," unpublished paper, December 2002.

Hart, G. K., and S. Burr, "The Story of California's Charter School Legislation," *Phi Delta Kappan,* Vol. 78, No. 1, 1996, pp. 37–40.

Hassel, Bryan C., *The Charter School Challenge: Avoiding the Pitfalls, Fulfilling the Promise,* Washington, D.C.: Brookings Institution, 1999.

Heckman, J. J., and V. J. Hotz, "Choosing Among Alternative Nonexperimental Methods for Estimating the Impact of Social Programs: The Case of Manpower Training," *Journal of the American Statistical Association,* Vol. 84, No. 408, 1989, pp. 862–875.

Hirano, K., G. Imbens, and G. Ridder, *Efficient Estimation of Average Treatment Effects Using the Estimated Propensity Score,* National Bureau of Economic Research Technical Report, Working Paper 251, 2000.

Horn, J., and G. Miron, *Evaluation of the Michigan Public School Academy Initiative: Final Report,* Kalamazoo, MI: The Evaluation Center, Western Michigan University, 1999.

Hoxby, C. M., *School Choice and School Productivity (Or Could School Choice Be a Tide That Lifts All Boats?*), Cambridge, MA: National Bureau of Economic Research Working Paper 8873, 2002.

Hoxby, C. M., ed., *The Economics of School Choice,* University of Chicago Press for the National Bureau of Economic Research, 2003.

Hsieh, C. T., and M. Urquiola, "When Schools Compete, How Do They Compete? An Assessment of Chile's Nationwide School Voucher Program," 2002.

Izu, J. A., L. Carlos, K. Yamashiro, L. Picus, N. Tushnet, and P. Wohlstetter, *The Findings and Implications of Increased Flexibility and Accountability: An Evaluation of Charter Schools in Los Angeles Unified School District,* Los Alamitos, CA: WestEd, 1998.

Koehler, P., et al., *Creating Excellence for All Students: Transforming Education in Los Angeles,* San Francisco, CA: WestEd, 2003.

Lacireno-Paquet, N., T. T. Holyoke, M. Moser, and J. R. Henig, "Creaming Versus Cropping: Charter School Enrollment Practices in Response to Market Incentives," *Educational Evaluation and Policy Analysis*, Vol. 24, No. 2, 2002, pp. 145–158.

Lieberman, E., J. M. Lang, A. Cohen, R. D'Agostino, Jr., S. Datta, and F. D. Frigoletto, "Association of Epidural Analgesia with Caesareans in Nulliparous Women," *Obstetrics and Gynecology*, Vol. 88, 1996, pp. 993–1000.

Little Hoover Commission, *The Charter Movement: Education Reform School by School*, Sacramento, CA, 1996.

Little, R.J.A., and D. B. Rubin, *Statistical Analysis with Missing Data*, New York: Wiley, 1987.

Looney, M., *Charter School Closures: The Opportunity for Accountability*, Washington, D.C.: The Center for Education Reform, 2002.

McCullagh, P., and J. A. Nelder, *Generalized Linear Models*, 2nd edition, London: Chapman and Hall, Chapter 3, 1986, p. 55.

Miron, G., and C. Nelson, *Autonomy in Exchange for Accountability: An Initial Study of Pennsylvania Charter Schools*, The Evaluation Center: Western Michigan University, October 2000.

Miron, G., and C. Nelson, *What's Public About Charter Schools?* Thousand Oaks, CA: Corwin Press, Inc., 2002.

Miron, G., N. C. Nelson, and J. Risley, *Strengthening Pennsylvania's Charter School Reform: Finding from the Statewide Evaluation and Discussion of Relevant Policy Issues*, The Evaluation Center: Western Michigan University, 2002.

Nathan, J., *Charter Schools: Creating Hope and Opportunity for American Education*, San Francisco, CA: Jossey-Bass, 1996.

Nathan, J., "Controversy: Charters and Choice," *The American Prospect*, Vol. 9, November–December 1998, available at www.prospect.org.

National Education Association, *Rankings and Estimates*, Washington, D.C., 2002.

Papke, L. E., "Tax Policy and Urban Development: Evidence from the Indiana Enterprise Zone Program," *Journal of Public Economics,* Vol. 54, 1994, pp. 37–49.

Powell, J., J. Blackorby, J. Marsh, K. Finnegan, and L. Anderson, *Evaluation of Charter School Effectiveness,* Menlo Park, CA: SRI International, 1997.

Rogosa, D., "Interpretive Notes for the Academic Performance Index," Stanford University, 2000, available at www.cde.ca.gov/psaa/api/fallapi/apnotes.pdf.

Rosenbaum, P., and D. B. Rubin, "The Central Role of the Propensity Score in Observational Studies for Causal Effects," *Biometrika,* Vol. 70, 1983, pp. 41–55.

Rothstein, R., "Charter Conundrum," *American Prospect,* Vol. 39, 1998, pp. 46–60, available at www.prospect.org.

RPP International, *The State of Charter Schools: National Study of Charter Schools Third-Year Report,* Washington, D.C.: U.S. Department of Education, 1999.

RPP International, *The State of Charter Schools: National Study of Charter Schools Fourth-Year Report,* Washington, D.C.: Office of Educational Research and Improvement, U.S. Department of Education, 2000.

Rouse, C. E., "Private School Vouchers and Student Achievement: An Evaluation of the Milwaukee Parental Choice Program," *Quarterly Journal of Economics,* Vol. 113, No. 2, 1998a, pp. 553–602.

Rouse, C. E., "Schools and Student Achievement: More Evidence from the Milwaukee Parental Choice Program," *Economic Policy Review,* Vol. 4, No. 1, 1998b, pp. 61–76.

School Services of California, "Evaluating New and Renewal Charter School Proposals," presentation by Paul Goldfinger and Robert J. Henry, March 2001.

Skinner, C. J., "Introduction to Part A," in C. J. Skinner, D. Holt, and T.M.F. Smith, eds., *Analysis of Complex Surveys*, New York: Wiley, 1989, pp. 23–57.

Solomon, L., K. Park, and D. Garcia, "Does Charter School Attendance Improve Test Scores? The Arizona Results," Phoenix, AZ: Goldwater Institute Center for Market Based Education, 1999.

Stecher, Brian M., and George W. Bohrnstedt, *Class Size Reduction in California: The 1998–99 Evaluation Findings,* Santa Monica, CA: RAND, 2000.

Stone, R. A., S. Obrosky, D. E. Singer, W. N. Kapoor, and M. J. Fine, "Propensity Score Adjustment for Pretreatment Differences Between Hospitalized and Ambulatory Patients with Community-Acquired Pneumonia," *Medical Care,* Vol. 33, 1995, pp. AS56–AS66.

Sugarman, S. D., "Charter School Funding Issues," *Education Policy Analysis Archives,* Vol. 10, No. 34, 2002.

U.S. Department of Education, Office of the Under Secretary, Planning and Evaluation Service, Elementary and Secondary Education Division, *Evaluation of the Public Charter Schools Program: Year One Evaluation Report,* Washington, D.C., 2000.

Vergari, S., "Charter Schools: A Primer on the Issues," *Education and Urban Society,* Vol. 31, No. 4, 1999, pp. 389–405.

Wells, A. S., L. Artiles, S. Carnochan, C. W. Cooper, C. Grutzik, J. J. Holme, A. Lopez, J. Scott, J. Slayton, and A. Vasudeva, *Beyond the Rhetoric of Charter School Reform: A Study of Ten California School Districts,* Los Angeles, CA: University of California, 1998.

Wohlstetter, P. W., N. C. Griffin, and D. Chau, "Charter Schools in California: A Bruising Campaign for Public School Choice," in S. Vergari, ed., *The Charter School Landscape: Politics, Policies, and Prospects,* Pittsburgh, PA: University of Pittsburgh Press, 2002, pp. 32–53.

Wooldridge, Jeffrey, *Econometric Analysis of Cross Section and Panel Data,* Cambridge, MA: MIT Press, 2002.

Zimmer, R., C. Krop, T. Kaganoff, K. Ross, and D. Brewer, *Private Giving to Public Schools and Districts in Los Angeles County: A Pilot Study,* Santa Monica, CA: RAND, MR-1429-EDU, 2001.